LIVING IN
FRANCE

LIVING IN FRANCE

Philip Holland

ROBERT HALE · LONDON

© *Philip Holland 1983, 1985, 1987, 1989, 1990*
First published in Great Britain 1983
Second edition 1985
Reprinted with revisions 1986
Third edition 1987
Reprinted three times 1988
Reprinted 1989
Fourth edition 1989
Reprinted four times 1989
Reprinted 1990
Fifth edition 1990

Robert Hale Limited
Clerkenwell House
Clerkenwell Green
London EC1R OHT

British Library Cataloguing in Publication Data
Holland, Philip
Living in France: the essential guide for
property purchasers and residents – 5th ed.
1. France – Visitor's guides
I. Title
914.4′04838

ISBN 0-7090-4139-9

Photoset by Rowland Phototypesetting Limited
Bury St Edmunds, Suffolk
Printed in Great Britain by
St Edmundsbury Press Limited
Bury St Edmunds, Suffolk
Bound by Woolnough Bookbinding Limited

Contents

Living in France

Illustrations

PICTURE CREDITS

J. Allan Cash: 1. Thomas A. Wilkie: 3, 15. Photobank:
4–7, 13–14. French National Tourist Office: 8–12, 17–19.
Loïc-Jahan: 16.

MAPS

Preface

It is hoped that this book will be of practical help to those who live or intend to live in France, whether on a permanent or part-time basis. The information which it gives has been chosen and the advice and warnings are offered as a result of personal experience. Its first edition, which appeared in 1983, was prompted by seeing so many people needlessly floundering for lack of understanding of how to set about doing things in France. That it is now in its fifth edition perhaps justifies me in thinking that I may have been of help to my readers.

Much has changed in France even in the last five years and the magic date of 1992 is chanted in that country as much as in other Common Market countries as a mysterious event which is intended to flatten frontiers and weld together all the peoples of Western Europe. My feeling is that the French consider it primarily from the viewpoint of what advantage it will bring to France. In that they are not alone, for one of the very few things which seems truly common to the citizens of all Common Market countries is the intention that one's own country should extract from the EEC more than it is necessary to inject into it.

It is worth remembering that the vast majority of those whose mother tongue is English, does *not* belong to the European Community. Over the years, much has been done to simplify the procedures which apply to nationals of one EEC country visiting, living or working in another. This does not make life in France for those who come from countries outside the Community more difficult; it may, however, mean more paper work and less understanding of how things are done at home than in the case of those who come to France from an EEC country.

Since 1981, France has lived through a doctrinaire Socialist government, a period of cohabitation, when it had a left-wing President and a right-wing government. Currently it has a socialist government which seems to be kept in power either by the temporary lack of ill-will of its Conservative opponents or the opponents' inability to speak with one voice. The truth is that no matter what government is in power, the French are dissatisfied with it and the voter who today was responsible for returning one government to power will tomorrow, as a matter of principle, complain loudly about it.

I have, in the 4th edition, rewritten and split into two the chapter in previous editions on Insurance, Health and Pensions because I have found that many people have particular problems with French insurance and with French Securité Sociale. I have done all I can to ensure that each new edition contains information which is up-to-date but it is inevitable that there is a time-lag before a new edition actually appears, and it must not be assumed that all the facts remain correct throughout its life. It is worthwhile checking to see if there have been alterations. My aim has been to put up sign-posts, where necessary, pointing to which expert to consult. 'Every man his own doctor or his own lawyer', is often a rapid and expensive way to the grave or to ruin. Please do not listen to kind friends who tell you how they managed to get by on their own. Their needs are not necessarily yours and, in any event, you will only hear of their successes.

At one time I was unable to reach any conclusion why in France it seemed to be so difficult to obtain the kind of all-embracing assistance from a professional adviser which one takes for granted in the UK, the States and many other countries. I have now decided that this can only be because the average Frenchman considers that he knows enough not to need this help since where there is a serious need for this kind of professional advice, there would be plenty of advisers anxious to earn a living. It may well be that the average Frenchman does know enough of his own system, but the non-Frenchman cannot, and he must not assume that mere silence indicates that some serious assistance is, in fact, not necessary. In addition, therefore, to not listening to friends, remember to follow the sign-posts erected in this book and actively to seek help from the right quarter.

It pays handsomely to acquire more than a smattering of French. It is not only flattering to the French but a courtesy on your part. It is also one of the ways to avoid that cold stare of incomprehension which can only too often clothe the French shop assistant's face. It would be foolish to expect sympathy of the Italian or Spanish kind when you massacre the French tongue but plaudits are frequent for those who make a real effort to master the language.

The French have reason to be proud of many of their institutions although they are suitably concerned about the shortcomings of some. The system suffers a little from the fact that every Frenchman is 50% revolutionary (1989 was the bicentenary of the French Revolution during which year this percentage undoubtedly increased) and 50% dyed-in-the-wool conservative. Incidentally, this is *not* reflected in the French flag. The red of the *tricolore* is not the colour of blood; the flag links the white of the Kings of France with the red and blue of Paris and symbolizes the unity of King and people. An earnest yearning for change and improvement goes hand in hand with a respect for old values and tradition.

The first edition of this book was written with the British reader in mind and comparisons were exclusively between France and the United Kingdom. However, there are many visitors to France who are not British but whose mother tongue, or most frequently used second language, is English. In subsequent editions, I therefore attempted to widen the comparisons by the only practical method available – by deleting many specific references to the United Kingdom. To have multiplied the references to the countries of all of those who might read this book would have given me immense pleasure – but not, I think, its readers. It is for this reason that I have included in the Appendices information which may be of use to readers of nationalities other than British.

Since the appearance of the fourth edition, France has finally done away with Exchange Control, although from a practical point of view, it had ceased to bother the foreigner much during the last twelve or eighteen months of its life. Even so, the French resident is not wholly unfettered in his financial transactions. The Tax authorities have been given the power specifically to require the disclosure of assets held abroad by the French resident.

A far more practical relaxation is that of the application to many foreigners owning holiday homes in France of the rule which previously applied only to French citizens living abroad. As a result, the vast majority of foreigners will be exempt from Capital Gains Tax on the sale of their houses and flats. It is very difficult to know whether the Parliamentary question put to the Finance Minister which elicited the joyful answer was a 'leg pull' or not, but it is worth quoting in part: 'The capital gain realized on the sale of a principal private residence is exonerated from tax. Such residence can . . . be that (in France) of a Frenchman who is (nevertheless) resident abroad. Now, foreigners wishing to take advantage of that relief are becoming naturalized French and thus avoiding the imposition of French Capital Gains Tax . . . What amendments does the Minister intend to make to avoid such fraud in the future?' I have often suggested in the past how, with propriety, French Capital Gains Tax could be avoided (not evaded), but it never occurred to me to suggest that my interlocutor take on French citizenship, nor I am sure did it occur to anyone else to make such a suggestion. However, readers are now substantially free from the apparent need to forsake their country in order to avoid the payment of Capital Gains Tax in France when they sell their holiday homes there.

The last year has also seen an increase in the extension of the areas in France where the British (but not those of other nationalities) have bought property. May I give a word of warning? Provided that a buyer in such parts is certain that he likes the climate, finds the locals easy to get on with and can journey between France and England as quickly as he was told he could, he may have every good reason to desert those parts of France where traditionally his compatriots have always bought. Long acquaintance with non-French buyers in those traditional areas has given the Estate Agents and *notaires* at least some idea of their special problems. The British come cold to other areas, but the French are, not unnaturally, warm to receive them. Whether the buyer has been introduced to French property by agents in the UK or France, he must insist on having his own Notary, *not* one who is the choice of the seller's agents but of a suitable local adviser who is knowledgeable in both French and English law and practice, without whose advice he should do and sign nothing.

As always, I am grateful to those who have been kind enough to say that they found this book to have been of help to them, although I feel that the Swedish reader who bought two copies because he found its chapter on French tax invaluable was perhaps being over-effusive. In particular, I owe a special debt of gratitude to the Manager, Assistant Manager and staff of National Westminster Bank S.A. in Nice and to Me. Chantal Pasqualini and Me. Guy Rousseau, Notaires Associés of Nice. I am also grateful to those who provide a steady stream of suggestions designed (usually with success) to invite me to include, exclude or clarify; supported, I am bound to say, by the amazing continued patience of my publishers.

April 1990

CHAPTER 1

La Douce France

When Eleanor of Aquitaine, having had her marriage to Louis VII of France annulled, married Henry Plantagenet in 1152, she brought as her dowry the whole of south-western France. When her husband became Henry II of England two years later, he also inherited the dukedom of Normandy and the *comté* of Anjou. Those whose schooldays are now far behind them may forget that the accession of Henry II marks the beginning of the struggle for power between England and France which was to last for centuries. Linked dynastically and by blood ties, it was not until the turn of the twentieth century that the *Entente Cordiale* was revived by Edward VII. Although this friendship has been cemented by two World Wars, the French and the British still tend to regard each other somewhat warily across the Channel.

Many other countries have strong ties with France. The present Queen of Denmark has married a Frenchman. Sweden's Royal Family is descended from a Frenchman and even before the Bernadotte family came on the scene, the Swede Axel von Fersen was sufficiently pro-French to make the arrangements for the flight of the French Royal Family to Varennes.

Frenchmen were among the first to colonize the New World and were there a hundred years before the arrival of the Mayflower. To this day, the inhabitants of the Province of Quebec and of the State of Maine are the direct descendants of these settlers and many of the place names commemorate the early explorers from France, such as Verrazano, Champlain and La Salle. Today, the links between Quebec, and Canada in general, with France are closer emotionally than those of the United States with the United Kingdom. The French have never really lost Canada.

Benjamin Franklin, the first ambassador of a free United States of America, was the darling of Paris and every French person not only knows his name but what he did to cement the ties of friendship between France and America. And there cannot be any full-blooded American who doesn't cherish the name of Lafayette. An aristocrat, he was, however, responsible for the modern colours of France, combining the red and blue of Paris with the white of the Bourbons. It is interesting that a country as republican as France has kept these colours and incorporated them into its national flag.

Because of the vast difference in temperament and way of life, the majority of British have for many years looked upon France as the quintessence of 'Abroad'. Indeed, probably more of them visit France than any other country, even if they are only *en route* for Spain, Portugal or Italy. It is clear that once the Channel Tunnel is built, the flow will increase and it will, one hopes, become equal in both directions which it is not today.

It is worth remembering that, although in England the average child is taught that much of France once belonged to the English Crown, in France children learn that William the Conqueror was the man who brought England to her knees. It is not, however, so much the triumph over Harold that stirs the French child's breast as the idea of the civilizing effect that that victory had on the vanquished Anglo-Saxons. Indeed, much is made of France's civilizing influence throughout the centuries on the rest of the world.

France is the largest country in Western Europe, with an area of a little under 213,000 square miles. Its overseas *départements*, such as Guadeloupe, Martinique and St Pierre-et-Miquelon, which are one-time colonial territories (some of which were colonized as early as 1635), all send deputies and/ or senators to Paris and have a direct say in the French Government.

Metropolitan France (which includes Corsica) is divided into ninety-six *départements* which are loosely equivalent to

British counties. In a standard textbook on the Political and Administrative Institutions in France published before the local government decentralization measures of the mid-eighties came into force the following may be read, printed in heavy type. "All comes from the capital; all goes back to the capital; a solid hierarchy is established and administrative regulations are identical over all the national territory." No neater summing-up of the total dependence of the whole country, from hamlet to city, on Paris, could be found. Indeed, towns and other communities were literally under the legal guardianship of the *département*, itself ruled over by a *préfet*, appointed from Paris. In theory, at least, the honoured title of *préfet*, whose functions were codified by Napoleon in order to ensure that the whole country was ruled from Paris, has disappeared and is replaced by that of '*commissaire de la République*'. It seemed improbable that, in a country which frequently resorted to a monetary system which had been out of date for nearly twenty years, the *préfet* would not be called by his old title for many years to come and indeed this is precisely what has occurred. Certainly, whatever he eventually comes to be called in future generations, his offices will always remain, in the mind of every Frenchman, if not in fact, in the *préfecture*.

As to currency, even now, a considerable proportion of the population will break into old francs at the drop of a hat and this is particularly noticeable where the price of what is being discussed is high, such as property, and one can resort to millions. It can be confusing to the foreigner, but a look of total disbelief on your part will usually produce the price quoted divided by a hundred. Even children born long after the change to the current franc took place, often resort to the old usage and the media frequently uses 'centimes' alone to ensure that there is no confusion between the old and the current franc.

Since early in 1982, the *département* and the *région*, which is a larger local government administrative area made up of a number of *départements*, are now both governed solely by representatives of the local electorate, whilst Corsica, which has for long agitated for independence, has attained a considerable degree of "home rule". But even the then recent Socialist government had not felt itself able to cut completely the links which bind local to central government. "If," said the Circular to the new *Commissaires de la République*, "the law has now confided to the locally elected representatives of the *départements* and the *régions* the executive power, it has also reaffirmed the unity of the representation of the State. These two principles are, in any event, complementary. If local communities are to act with any degree of efficiency, there can be only one spokesman capable of speaking for the State in every circumstance and of taking, with those communities, concerted action."

It is quite unnecessary that you should understand the history or philosophy behind these progressive measures. You will still be directed to the *préfecture* or *sous-préfecture*, and in many districts houses will continue to be numbered according to the number of metres from that building – or from the *mairie*, if that is all the local community can boast. However, this modernization of the French local government system is an excellent example of the red of the revolution and the blue of the conservative which mingle in the political heart of every Frenchman.

Since time immemorial, France has also been divided into approximately twenty historical provinces with an indeterminate number of complex and illogical sub-divisions. Thus, for instance, Guyenne, which, with its northern neighbour Gascony, makes up the largest official province in France, includes in its area Quercy, Agenais, the Landes, Condomois, Bazadois and many more. True Provence covers only the *départements* of Alpes Maritimes, Basses Alpes or Alpes de Haute Provence, Var, Vaucluse, Bouches du Rhône and part of the Gard. For tourist and indeed for other purposes, it is often stretched to cover a great deal more. History, food, wine, people, accents and much else besides tend to be described by reference to the provinces and their sub-divisions rather than by reference to *départements* or to towns. A good deal of confusion can be avoided if the newcomer to France acquaints himself with these names and the areas they represent. Maps showing the *départements* and provinces appear overleaf.

Like that of any other great nation in Europe, France's history has been one of changing frontiers – the last was after the Second World War when her borders with Italy were slightly altered – frequent wars with her neighbours and constant endeavour to unify the country. The latter was really only finally achieved during the last hundred years. Before this, people outside Paris gave scant heed to what was happening even in a neighbouring province, and quite large areas spoke languages other than French. Indeed, this diversity of tongues persisted until the First World War, and even today in many areas local *patois* is regularly spoken.

France's main colonial expansion in North Africa and the Far East took place in the nineteenth century. In 1963 she had to re-integrate a vast influx of French colonials from Algeria ('*piednoirs*') and establish profitable occupations for them in France to compensate for the loss of capital and income left in Algeria. The name comes from the high black boots worn in the last century by the Alsatians who constituted the majority of settlers and the name does not refer, as many non-French are prone to believe, to their having burnt their feet black in the desert! A notable witness to the policies adopted to this end is the French Golden Delicious apple, which has flooded the EEC fruit market. The manner in which the French have coped with the dissolution of their Empire is totally different from the British, but signs of a colonial past are very apparent in most towns. Among others are the Vietnamese restaurants which replace Chinese and the North African – mostly Moroccan, who are considered to be the best cooks in the Maghreb – which take the place of Indian Curry Houses.

The French are not racist but have a marked tendency to be impartially xenophobic, unless it is in their interests to be otherwise. For the newcomer, the best way to counteract this is to pay them the compliment of behaving in as French a way as possible.

The *departements* of France

Provincial

Ain	01	Loire (Haute)	43
Aisne	02	Loire-Atlantique	44
Allier	03	Loiret	45
Alpes de-Haute-Provence	04	Lot	46
Alpes (Hautes)	05	Lot et Garonne	47
Alpes-Maritimes	06	Lozère	48
Ardèche	07	Maine-et-Loire	49
Ardennes	08	Manche	50
Ariège	09	Mahne	51
Aube	10	Marne (Haute)	52
Aude	11	Mayenne	53
Aveyron	12	Meurthe-et-Moselle	54
Belfort	90	Meuse	55
Bouches-du-Rhône	13	Morbihan	56
Calvados	14	Moselle	57
Cantal	15	Nièvre	58
Charente	16	Nord	59
Charente-Maritime	17	Oise	60
Cher	18	Orne	61
Corrèze	19	Pas-de-Calais	62
Corse du Sud	2A	Puy-de-Dôme	63
Corse (Haute)	2B	Pyrénées-Atlantiques	64
Côte d'Or	21	Pyrénées (Hautes)	65
Côtes du Nord	22	Pyrénées Orientales	66
Creuse	23	Rhin (Sas)	67
Dordogne	24	Rhin (Haute)	68
Doubs	25	Rhône	69
Drôme	26	Saône (Haute)	70
Eure	27	Saône-et-Loire	71
Eure-et-Loir	28	Sarthe	72
Finistère	29	Savoie	73
Gard	30	Savoie (Haute)	74
Garonne (Haute)	31	Seine Maritime	76
Gers	32	Sèvres (Deux)	79
Gironde	33	Somme	80
Hérault	34	Tarn	81
Ille-et-Vilaine	35	Tarn-et-Garonne	82
Indre	36	Var	83
Indre et Loire	37	Vaucluse	84
Isère	38	Vendée	85
Jura	39	Vienne	86
Landes	40	Vienne (Haute)	87
Loir-et-Cher	41	Vosges	88
Loire	42	Yonne	89

Paris area

Essonne	91	Seine Saint Denis	33
Hauts-de-Seine	92	Val-de-Marne	94
Paris (Ville de)	75	Val-d'Oise	95
Seine-et-Marne	77	Yvelines	98

The provinces of France

The economic and social structure of any European country cannot adequately be covered in less than a hundred pages. Suffice it to say that France is no longer primarily an agricultural country although she has the best wine in the world, has a highly regarded dairy industry (from a gastronomic rather than an efficiency viewpoint) and produces a greater variety of fruit than possibly any other European country. But it must also be remembered that she has the largest iron-ore deposits in Europe and an enviable amount of bauxite, to say nothing of coal and natural gas. France also has the most powerful hydro-electric power plant in Europe at Donzère-Mondragon on the Rhône. French cars and aircraft are found the world over. She also exports a considerable amount of chemicals, iron and steel, glass, textiles and perfumery products, has a rapidly expanding nuclear power industry and is among the world's leaders in computers.

It is, however, often said that France's greatest export is her culture. The Alliance Française has vast sums to spend abroad disseminating French literature, theatre, films and art. Through the many French Institutes found all over the world, anyone who cares to take the trouble can learn French and French literature and acquire a great deal of information about France in all its aspects at minimal cost. This preoccupation with Culture and a pride in 'Le Patrimoine' (the French Heritage) is noticeable throughout the whole of France. Exhibitions, lectures, concerts, opera and ballet are not confined to Paris and the larger towns, but this very sincerely felt pride in things French finds generous expression throughout the country.

When, some years ago, France voted in her first, for a long time, Socialist President and Government it was hoped that such radical change would improve the unemployment position. M. Mitterand tried to apply Keynesian economics and increase public spending (and jobs). The President nationalized many large banks, insurance companies and industrial concerns. In the event, unemployment became worse in common with the rest of Europe. The French turned round and voted in a new right-wing Government which has quickly put into reverse all nationalization plans. Alas, the unemployment figures have hardly budged. The French continue to complain – about everything. Some of their complaints are listened to and acted upon. The Government was fearful that the student riots at the end of 1986 would become a blueprint of those of 1968 and quickly shelved ideas about changing the university curriculum and fee structure. Now the French have what is virtually a coalition government, which seems to be producing very little of excitement at home, but is throwing its weight around in anticipation of what is promised for 1992.

France has a solid middle class, which is constantly replenished by ambitious, well-educated and energetic young people, anxious to get on in their jobs, either in the higher echelons of the Civil Service or, better still, in an international corporation, which will give them thirteen or fourteen months' pay a year, a company car and private health insurance. Owning the apartment you live in, a *résidence secondaire* and holidays abroad are all desirable goals. Nevertheless, for all that France is a welfare state, there is considerable hardship, if not poverty. As in the rest of Europe, there are plenty of not very well housed poor and the number of HLM (*habitations à loyer modéré*) flats available is inadequate, particularly in Paris and the industrial areas. France also has considerable problems with its North African immigrants who are the backbone of the building trade.

It is pointless to make general comparisons with other countries, since the basic requirements of the Frenchman and his counterpart elsewhere are very different. He will hardly ever economize on food, which in quality and quantity is far more important to the French than anything else. The run-of-the-mill French housewife is less 'house proud' than the British, Dutch and Scandinavian housewife. Standing on one's own rights but waging a continual battle against Authority is a national pastime in France. On the other hand, the average Frenchman is considerably more patriotic than most – or at least is ostensibly so – and easily indulges in visible demonstrations in support of *La Gloire* and *La Patrie*.

The French attitude towards foreigners varies from one

part of France to another. In the south, which has had a tourist industry for over 150 years, the tourist and particularly the foreign tourist is an important part of the local economy. The British were among the first to come to the French Riviera, and it should be remembered that an Englishman, Lord Brougham, founded Cannes as a resort in 1838. Indeed, so ubiquitous were the British in the 1830s and 1840s that Alexandre Dumas *père* recounts that for the Niçois all foreigners, irrespective of age, sex or dress, came from a strange town shrouded in fog called London. When asking one day of an hotelier who the new arrivals were, he received the reply: 'Some English people, but I don't know whether they are French or German!' Things have improved greatly since then, and despite their firm belief that French is obviously the best and most beautiful language in the world, efforts to speak foreign languages, and above all English, are not lacking. However, they still find it difficult to believe that anyone can be well educated if they do not speak adequate French, and anyone who intends living permanently in France will miss much of the many good things which France has to offer if some effort to speak the language is not made. This effort is appreciated. In general terms the French believe that French is best, and that statement encompasses everything from architecture to zoos.

After a long battle against the increasing use of 'franglais' which in some of its forms varies from the ludicrous to the abominable, the Academie Française seems temporarily to have lost heart. At the same time, the French appear to have accepted that their language is no longer that of diplomacy or even widely spoken and have admitted that English is now the language most readily understood in most parts of the world. They have buckled to, and English is now the principal foreign language taught in schools – and not without success.

Nevertheless, they are from time to time capable of curious excesses of chauvinism. To mark the beginning of the last decade of the twentieth century, the French have appointed a Minister for Rock to make good the failure to reap the commercial benefits of this type of noise which on almost all the local French radio stations accompanies what passes for English or American. The Minister admits that French sounds very odd when used for Rock. He is right and since, whatever else may be said about it, French is a beautiful language to hear if it is well spoken, it is devoutly to be hoped that the Minister fails in his task.

Notwithstanding that it is possible to eat very badly (and very expensively at the same time) in France and that the television is full of advertisements for convenience foods, it is also true that the French are much more serious about food than most of their neighbours.

The French are great eaters-out and, except in Paris, early eaters-out. Anyone who has decided to live in France should follow his French neighbour to his restaurant and eschew the more obvious places catering to its tourists' tastes. The most excellent meals can be eaten at prices considerably below those in many European countries. You are well advised to listen to the recommendations of the owner or chef and never fail to try local food. It is worth remembering that restaurants other than four-star which provide a *menu conseillé* are obliged to display it both inside and outside. This, at its cheapest, represents good, if at times somewhat unimaginative, value for money. There are many, many restaurants where these menus vary in price from 55–100 francs for four or five courses. Prices in restaurants almost always include service and VAT, which is charged on food in France. Peak holiday time is perhaps not the best time to judge the smaller restaurants, and certainly, as elsewhere, motorway fast food is no guide whatsoever to the secrets of French cooking.

Compared with many countries, wine is cheap, if you stick to a local variety or the owner's *vin de la maison* (see chapter 21). To drink Bordeaux in Burgundy, Alsace in the Bordelais or Chablis in Provence can be an expensive and disappointing experience, except in the very best restaurants, where it will be expensive in any event. There is much pleasure to be had in seeking out one's favourite local wine. *Marchands de vin*, who can be very helpful, and hypermarkets and the larger supermarkets can supply all the local and non-local wines you mày wish to try, and there are enough to satisfy the most exigent oenophile. The price of champagne in restaurants is horrific.

Although the average Frenchman is today rather more hospitable to foreigners than he was in the past, it is still unlikely that you will be invited to many French houses. Having had a Frenchman and his wife to dine, he is much more likely to repay this hospitality by taking you to a restaurant. This is for a variety of complex social reasons, which are incomprehensible to anyone who has not lived in France for at least four or five years. Basically, it boils down to his being ashamed of his home, usually without reason, and his intense desire constantly to be shown in a good, and expensive light. It is a very Latin weakness and obtains more in the south, where the Mediterranean way of life is carried on out of doors.

The French character is different and complex. Sometimes it delights. Sometimes it puzzles. On occasion, it can provide surprises. Moreover, France is a vast country, so that local conditions, topography and climate play a far greater part than they do in e.g. Great Britain. The draw to foreigners lies in France's unique combination of people, history, geography, architecture and the variety of her countryside and climate. Most of the time the French really do try to live up to their motto '*Liberté, Egalité, Fraternité*,' if not always to the letter, at least in spirit.

CHAPTER 2

Leaving for France

It is somewhat ill-advised to leave a country where you have been living for years without considering the effect it will have on your affairs. The most important people to consult are naturally your accountant and lawyer, who, it is hoped, will base their advice to you on information and advice given to them by an expert in France who has a thorough and up to date practical knowledge of the legal and tax systems both in your own country and in France or can obtain those through the right contacts.

Even if you are leaving your home country for good, you may consider not necessarily taking all your assets with you. Assuming there are no controls on what you may take out of your country, you will still need advice on whether from a tax and death duty point of view, you will do better to take all your assets out of your country and where then to put them. This really needs skilled advice and it can be dangerous to defer the final decision until you have become established in France. You will also possibly find that if you wish to leave assets in your country, you can invest them in a way which is free of tax and of death duties in that country. In this connection, consider very carefully the French law relating to Wills and inheritance in Chapter 10.

There is always plenty of scope for advice on how to minimize income tax and death duties. The one rule you must always follow is that you plan in advance and do not leave the taking of advice until the cost of unscrambling your affairs is prohibitive. It is axiomatic that it costs far less to get the right advice first, than to put right the traps you have fallen into for lack of advice or an abundance of poor advice. It really is a question of teamwork between advisers.

It is sometimes possible to achieve a tax saving by buying property in the name of a company, but very careful advice is needed. Certain non-French companies owning property in France are caught by special rules, which can have punitive results for the unwary. On the whole, the *société civile immobilière*, which is a kind of French limited partnership, is seldom suitable vehicle for buying property in France, although it is far more likely to be suggested by a Notary than is the use of a non-French company.

For those used to a legal system which recognizes trusts, it is essential to appreciate that French law does not recognize them. This is the situation until such time as France ratifies a recent Convention on the recognition of trusts (on which the Finance Minister who doubtless sees their use as an excellent method of tax avoidance). Under a system which recognizes trusts, things can be unscrambled comparatively simply and cheaply, but not so in France. Property belongs to the person in whose name it is registered, whether he is the real owner or only a nominee. It can be very irritating to see your property, which was held for the best of reasons by a trustee, go to his family on his death and for you to have to 'buy' it back from them at a cost of at least 10% of its value.

It is absolutely essential to get your accountant to advise you on the rules about residence for tax purposes in your country and what tax liabilities you may incur if you do not follow such rules. You will not be condemned to the life of a tax-exile pop star, most of whose problems on this score exist in the mind of the sensational Press only, but it is ridiculous to be liable for tax in a country you are about to leave only for lack of advice.

No two people's affairs are alike, and there are so many individual circumstances which affect each case that it would be dangerous to quote examples. Any examples comparing the tax liabilities which can arise in your home country and in France during your life or on your death can only be given by your accountant working in close co-operation with a

French counterpart. Nor is it desirable to attempt to explain any of the many tax-saving schemes which are available in the right circumstances. Tax avoidance, as opposed to tax evasion, is no more illegal in France than in other countries though the philosophy is slightly different.

You must get careful advice about ceasing to be resident for tax purposes in your own country. In certain countries the formalities can be comparatively simple. In the UK, for example, when you approach the Revenue with a view to establishing your non-residence for tax purposes, you will be asked to complete a form showing, among other things, your UK income, which, when you have signed it, should be handed to the French tax authorities for their countersignature and returned by them to the UK. It has, it must be admitted, on occasions taken many months for this form to filter back to the Inspector of Foreign Dividends who, if called on, will himself intercede with the French Revenue. In theory, this passage of the form through the hands of the French fiscal authorities will result in your getting into the French tax system but sometimes it does not. The *raison d'être* behind this procedure is that the UK Revenue assumes that if you claim you are not resident in the UK, it is reasonable to suppose that you have become resident elsewhere and what better indication of this than that you submit yourself to another country's tax system. On the other hand, the Danes, for example, seem not satisfied with mere submission to a foreign tax system but usually need to see that you have actually paid French tax before granting non-residence status. Hence, they are very likely to ask you for a French tax receipt before giving you non-residence status in Denmark. It would appear that the French tax authorities automatically 'leak' information to the tax authorities of Belgium and Denmark about property purchases in France by citizens of those countries. This may be the case with all Common Market countries. It is difficult to guess what, if any, effect 1992 will have on this. On the whole, the fiscal authorities of most countries are selfish enough to bend their efforts to extracting tax from their own citizens and are not vastly interested in helping their neighbours to do likewise in their own countries.

It is also worth giving a thought to (without becoming obsessed by) the currency in which you keep your assets and, indeed, your income. Do not rush to change all your capital into French francs or indeed into any other particular currency. This is something which does require expert advice, and even when expert, is about as certain as your favourite racing tipster's advice on who will win the Grand National. Nevertheless, it is advice which should be obtained and is best obtained from a suitable bank in France (see Chapter 13). This is because you will no longer be thinking in terms of other currencies in relation to your native country but in relation to French francs, and there is no reason why your bank manager in the country you are leaving should be expected to have the 'feel' of financial conditions in France.

Do not be too hasty to close your bank account at home. It is likely that you will go back from time to time or wish to buy things there and have them sent to France. Books for example are very expensive in France and few books in English other than those published in the UK are available (see page 239 for the names and addresses of some English bookshops in France). There is nothing more irritating than to see bank charges for currency exchanges, and some of these at least can be avoided if you keep an account open in your home country in its currency. You can of course keep any currency other than francs in a French bank account, but if you come from a country where the Eurocheque system is in force, a cheque book coupled with a Eurocheque cheque card is by far the fastest and simplest way of obtaining money during banking hours throughout Western Europe. Certain credit cards e.g. Visa, American Express, Access and Mastercharge will also produce cash. However, if you have a bank account in a Common Market country, you can apply to your manager for the issue to you of Eurocheques. These can be used in France either to obtain cash of up to 1250 francs per day from any bank which exhibits the Eurocheque sign or for the payment of purchases in many shops up to the current limit of 1,250 francs per cheque. Some shops make a charge when you use a Eurocard because they say that their banks charge them – this is totally contrary to the Eurocheque Convention, but it is no use arguing. Cheque cards, for reasons explained elsewhere, do not exist in France but are said to be in the pipeline though it is not known when they will come into use. If you keep an account in your home country, impress on your manager there that when you give instructions for the transfer of cash from your account that he carries them out literally to the letter.

If it is your intention to reside permanently in France, you are required to obtain a *visa de longue durée* which will lead to the issue to you of a *carte de séjour*. This application, which costs a nominal amount and includes children of the family under sixteen, must be made to one of the French Consulates-General in your country of residence, which is not necessarily your home country. A list of these in a number of countries appears in Appendix A. The application cannot be made directly to any authority in France. The application must be supported by evidence from your bank of your financial situation, to make certain you do not become a burden on the French state, certain other simple information and a medical certificate. Currently it takes about seven to twelve weeks to process the application. You are entitled to stay three months in France without any visa, and this stay can be prolonged by application to the local *préfecture*, but this is not the way to go about getting a *visa de longue durée*. On taking up permanent residence you go to your local *préfecture* and on the basis of your visa apply for a *carte de séjour*. This will be issued to you, initially for a period of one year, and costs nothing. At the end of the first year the *carte de séjour* will need renewing, and you will be required to produce a certificate from your bank in France to show that you have sufficient cash available to maintain yourself in France and pay a smallish fee. The new *carte de séjour* will be valid for three years. At the end of this period the process is repeated, and a *carte de séjour* for ten years is issued.

However, though the rules about obtaining a *carte de séjour* are precisely as mentioned above, the Ministry of the Interior

An example of a *"bon bourgeois"* block of flats in fashionable Paris near the Bois de Boulogne

One of the modern luxury blocks high above Villefranche on the Côte d'Azur

A game of *boules* at La Chapelle St. Martin en Plaine, near Blois

Cafés in the Old Town, St. Malo

confirms that, in the case of Common Market citizens, the Préfet of each Département has discretion to grant *cartes de séjour* by direct application to the *Préfecture* without previously obtaining a *visa de longue durée*. The Alpes-Maritimes and the Var among the Départements adopt this procedure or as one of the local officials somewhat cryptically says 'We do not apply the law'. Short of questioning every *Préfecture* in France, it is not possible to know which do and which do not 'apply the law'. Enquiries to French Consulates in Common Market countries will certainly result in insistence on the *visa de longue durée* procedure. It seems sensible, therefore, before becoming involved in this procedure that (unless you have some special reason for wanting to obtain a *visa de longue durée* – to prove, for example, before you actually leave your own country your intention of ceasing to reside there) you enquire of the *Préfecture* in the area where you are thinking of settling to see what procedure is adopted there.

As a national of a Common Market country, if you wish to set up business in France, you can obtain the necessary *carte de commerce* subject only to the same conditions as are required of French nationals. If you want to carry on a profession such as doctor, dentist or accountant, you will have to make your own peace with the appropriate French professional bodies notwithstanding EEC rules on this subject, and you will need special advice and considerable persistence. If you are not a national of a Common Market country, you do not have the automatic privilege of working in France and you should make enquiries at one of the French Consulates in your own country.

Remember that in France the rule is that you should always carry your 'papers' with you. It may be difficult to get used to doing this, especially for men, who in the warmer parts of the country find themselves deprived of all their usual pockets. You will not be incarcerated for lack of 'papers', nor will you be subject to sudden checks, but you will be asked for them if stopped by the police for a traffic offence or in similar circumstances. In any case a *carte de séjour* is a very simple form of identification, and if only as a matter of courtesy to the country in which you are living, it should always be carried. In fact, for the French, it is not obligatory to have an identity card, but to be the proud non-possessor of a card gives rise to such suspicion (and practical problems) that there can be very few French people who do not have one.

In general terms you are allowed to bring into France to furnish either your new permanent home or your holiday flat or villa all its contents free of import duty and TVA subject to certain not very onerous conditions. The Customs authorities are very reasonable, and if you bring in brand-new curtains or similar items where they realize that your old ones will not fit your new home, they are unlikely to charge you provided you do not abuse this indulgence.

The procedure is simple, but if it is not followed, you will encounter wholly unnecessary difficulties and delays when your furniture arrives in France. You will also be involved in the quite unnecessary outlay of a deposit of about a quarter of the duty and TVA (for which you are not liable) and which will only be refunded to you when the process of clearing customs has been completed.

The rules differ slightly depending on whether you are a Common Market citizen or not and whether you are taking up permanent residence in France or merely furnishing a holiday home.

Common Market citizens

Residents of the Channel Islands, British citizens though they maybe, are not EEC citizens and do not benefit from the following rules.

1. Permanent Residence.
You may import all your personal belongings (with certain exceptions, which since they just might apply to you should be checked) including happily up to fifty bottles of wine which the French call 'the end of your cellar' provided that they show evident signs of your use and they were bought all

taxes paid in your country of origin. You may bring all such goods into France at one time, or over a period, but the last transfer must be within twelve months of establishing residence in France. Strictly speaking, you are not allowed to dispose of these goods for twelve months after their importation.

You should date and sign an inventory in French in duplicate with values for each item and provide evidence that you previously had a residence out of France and that you have acquired a residence in France. The former requirement can cause problems in countries where the local town hall does not provide certificates of residence but local French Consulates will advise. Proof of a new home in France can be by a copy of the lease or by a certificate from a *Notaire* confirming the purchase of a property. With these documents in its hands, the company which transports your goods should have no problems.

2. Holiday Home.

Here you are limited to furniture and household equipment, which are clearly not new and such as are reasonably needed to furnish a holiday home. You must be the owner of your home in France or have a lease of at least one year. Again, you may not dispose of these goods for a period of twelve months and, in addition, you should not sell, let or lend your holiday home within a similar period.

The formalities in this case are slightly more complex. You must make a request for free entry of the goods in triplicate to the Regional Director of Customs in the area where your holiday home is situated. French Consulates should be able to provide the forms and the appropriate address. An inventory with values should accompany the forms with proof of ownership of or lease of your home in France and evidence of your principal place of residence out of France (see above). In due course, you will receive authorization from French Customs and a stamped copy of your inventory. These documents are all that your transporter will need but they can take a little time to obtain.

Non-Common Market citizens

1. Permanent Residence.
Basically the same procedures as for Common Market citizens
are involved but you must have owned the goods in question
for at least six months and you must have lived permanently
out of France for a year before their importation.

2. Holiday Home.
The formalities are similar to those for Common Market
citizens but there are stricter limitations. You must have
owned the goods for at least six months and either be the
owner of your holiday home by purchase or hold it under a
lease of at least two years. You may not sell, lease or lend
your home for a period of two years after importation of the
goods. In this case, only Import Duty is waived. French TVA
will be payable.

Whatever is the country of your origin, there are special
arrangements for newly married couples taking up residence
in France. You may bring in the contents of your bottom
drawer (the rules curiously say even if they are new!) and
normal wedding presents up to a fairly small amount – smaller
for non-Common Market citizens than for those from the
Common Market – varying according to the value in francs
of the Common Market Ecu. Such goods can only be imported
free during a two month period before or within four months
after the wedding, though the French heart will probably be
willing to stretch things a little if you do not abuse its sentimental tendencies. You need, of course, proof of your marriage
or evidence of your intended marriage (which in certain
countries where marriages can take place at short notice might
be difficult) and a detailed signed inventory in duplicate with
values. You may be asked to complete a form at the place of
entry of the goods into France and possibly provide a guarantee for TVA and duty if the goods arrive before your marriage,
presumably in case the marriage is called off.

There are special arrangements for goods you inherit and
for students taking up residence in France to study. The

formalities are not complex, but you should enquire at a French Consulate in your own country or, if you are already in France, at the local Customs office.

If your house or flat is owned through the medium of a company of which you are the effective owner and you, as will presumably be the case, have the unlimited free use of it, the above rules will apply as though the company was or was not an EEC citizen depending on your citizenship. What then is needed, in addition to the documents referred to above, is a formal letter from the company confirming that you have such use for a period of more than two years. On the whole, make the letter look as official as possible. For technical reasons the period of ten years is an excellent one.

Special rules applying to the import of cars will be found in Chapter 11 on Cars and Driving.

It may seem that this procedure has been detailed at rather great length. This has been done deliberately because the French Customs authorities have let it be known that they are 'fed to the teeth' with the procedure not being adhered to by certain carriers and are threatening to become as deliberately unhelpful to those who do not try to conform as they are kind and helpful to those who make the effort. Choose, therefore, with the greatest care the firm you use to transport your belongings and make certain that they are up-to-date in their knowledge of the rules. Many are, but quite a number are not. Do not trust any firm which says that it can by-pass the formalities including making it appear that goods are imported from an EEC country, when in fact they are not. It may well be that at certain ports of entry Customs surveillance may be lax but that is not the same as dodging the rules and the French Customs Service is very efficient.

The cost of transportation obviously varies from country to country and from company to company, but it is fairly true to say that non-French Northern Europe firms are usually cheaper than French, and certainly insurance rates are lower. The bill on a move to the Côte d'Azur of the contents of a two or three-roomed flat can be considerable. Thought, therefore, should be given to the desirability of furnishing a flat from the French end. If you are coming from a Common Market country, you will probably not be charged the equivalent of TVA in your country, but the French will charge you 18.6% on the cost of the journey, so the whole question of the cost of transporting furniture needs considerable thought. A typical example – the cost of a move from London to Nice can be around £2,500 exclusive of TVA.

You should have no difficulty in finding doctors who speak English in Paris or in the larger towns in France (see Appendix E). If you require a continuous supply of any drug or pills, it is worth finding out before you leave your home country through your doctor or an international pharmacy whether they are available in France and if so under what brand name. You must not expect French chemists to be familiar with a non-French brand name or to accept a foreign prescription. There are few drugs which do not have their equivalent in France, but you may occasionally find that certain anti-coagulants and heart pills are difficult to find in a form exactly corresponding to your country's Pharmacopoeia. In such circumstances the answer is to get your own doctor to give you a more or less permanent prescription and to import them personally to France, preferably in their original sealed package and clearly marked for Customs as to their nature. You cannot get a French chemist to do this for you since it must be done on a personal basis. No import duty or TVA is payable on such importations. Chapter 16 deals with how to join the French National Health system (*Securité Sociale*) and with pensions.

There is no quarantine for animals brought into France. All that is currently required to bring an ordinary domestic pet into the country is a recent certificate that it is free from disease, is not less than three months old and has had a rabies inoculation within the last thirty days. This certificate can usually be obtained from your local vet and, in the case of UK nationals, where special rules about rabies apply, from the Ministry of Agriculture, Animal Health Division, Export Section, Hook Rise, Tolworth, Surbiton, Surrey. It is, however, advisable to check with your nearest French Consulate that this type of certificate is still all that is required before arriving at the frontier with the family cat, dog, or hamster. Current regulations require all dogs in France to be tattooed and to have an annual anti-rabies injection. The certificate proving this injection must show the tattoo number. This is because rabies inoculations are quite expensive and the French in the past have been inclined to make one inoculation and one certificate do for as many dogs as they have! Remember that you will not be able to take any animal to the UK, even for the shortest visit, as the UK regulations, in an effort to keep rabies out of the country, are draconian.

The BBC broadcasts the Overseas Service on medium wave for reception in northern Europe but this can usually be received, at least during the hours of darkness, all over France. Short wave transmissions from the BBC and most countries can be received without much difficulty anywhere in France day and night, though mountains seem not to help. Hence it is hardly worth bringing a radio which will not get short wave frequencies but it is worth buying such a set out of France, where prices are usually considerably lower. In certain parts of France, private stations provide programmes in English, and some relay BBC Overseas Service received by satellite. The Cote d'Azur is well served in this way by Radio Monte Carlo which broadcasts this service all night long, by Radio 104 which has a number of BBC news programmes throughout the day and by a station just over the border in Italy which provides a 24-hour programme. French radio which is available from a vast number of national and local stations is a good way of learning the language. It is not worth bringing a TV set unless it is either dual standard or the country in which you have been using it uses the SECAM system. Conversion of any other set to the French system is a prohibitive expense and without this you will never be able to pick up any channel with sound and picture synchronized. Appendix D contains information about the overseas services broadcast by a number of countries and these services are the best way of keeping in touch with 'home' news and also information about satellite TV programmes which can be seen in France. On the other hand, one of the best ways of learning French is to watch television. Both black and white and colour sets can be hired at not unreasonable prices. Licences are required for TV sets, details of which will also be found in Appendix D.

Finally, the citizens of many countries may vote in their own countries' elections even if they have been resident in France for some time. Local Consuls have the necessary information and probably the right forms for completion.

CHAPTER 3

Where to Live

Before deciding where to live in France, a great deal of heart-searching must be done. It is important to know as clearly as possible just what you want out of life. If retiring to France, then a total change of lifestyle can be contemplated, but no one should cut himself off from the company of his fellow men simply to 'get away from it all'. Within a short time he can become very lonely indeed. Someone who has spent forty years in the country with gardening as his main hobby is not going to be happy in a small flat with an even smaller balcony. If his previous garden proved too much work, then a smaller one in France could be just the right change. On the other hand, someone who has spent all his life in a large industrial town will find the French countryside (or any countryside for that matter) very quiet, and somewhere like Beaulieu or Villefranche between Nice and Monte Carlo may well suit his ideas of change and getting away from it all – but not all the time. If you are a person who is used to popping out to shop at the last minute and likes the luxury of plenty of restaurants, cinemas and other entertainments on your doorstep, do not plump for a dear little house in the middle of a vineyard. You will spend a great deal of time in your car getting to and from the bright lights.

A place which has proved ideal for Easter and summer holidays for many years may become intolerable in autumn and winter when all the happy holiday-makers have left and rain and wind are the daily fare. The advice is: always visit your future home town in winter and/or out of season before purchasing, unless you are very sure. Even safer, try to see it in all seasons. As in many countries, spring is beautiful all over France, but summer can often be too hot, and winter too cold or windy or wet, and presumably the object of leaving your own country is not to worsen your lot.

If you intend to travel around a lot then perhaps a flat is better than a house or villa since there is always a *concierge* to keep an eye on it for you and pass on telephone and electricity bills, which if they moulder in the letter box will ensure that on arrival you are without light or heat or any means of communication. On the other hand with a villa you have usually no charges except those you have personally incurred, and if you are lucky, a kind neighbour may watch over your property for you – but you cannot count on that. Pros and cons such as these must be weighed very carefully before buying.

The approximate number of nationals of various countries holding Residence Permits in France are:

Australia 1,200
Canada 4,900
Denmark 2,700
Eire 2,500
Netherlands 16,000
New Zealand 330
Sweden 4,400
United Kingdom 43,500
United States 23,200

It is, however, impossible to know how many more own homes in France but do not live there on a permanent basis and therefore do not need *permis de séjour*. It is probable that of all foreigners with homes in France, some eighty per cent are currently to be found in the south of France, though there is a small but well-established British colony in the north-west and there has for very many years been a British colony in the area from Bordeaux to the Spanish border. The Dordogne area has also of recent years become popular with foreigners.

Figures for the Côte d'Azur area are interesting. The Tourist Authority for that area estimates that in a typical year nearly 4,500,000 non-French visitors visit the region; this includes those who have 'holiday homes'. Of these, a little over

500,000 are British, 158,000 are American, 540,000 are Dutch and about 350,000 are of other nationalities whose mother tongue was English or for whom English is their second language, e.g. Scandinavians, Canadians, Australians and New Zealanders. It is also interesting to know that, to within a few francs, the visitors of these nationalities spent per day almost exactly the same amount, with the exception of the Americans who used to spend double that amount but now, to the distress of the tourist trade, have succumbed to the waning dollar.

The greatest influx of non-French buyers has been along the coastal strip from Marseille to Menton and in the *départements* of the Var and Alpes Maritimes inland to a depth of approximately fifteen to twenty miles. It looks as though this pattern may now change with the building of the Channel Tunnel. There is now a much more active British market in the sale of property in the north-west of France and it must be admitted that in general terms prices are lower there than in the south, which is certainly more expensive than that other area which is so attractive to the British and the Dutch – the Dordogne. All must depend on what the buyer is looking for. Certainly there will be very little difference in the weather on any day in Kent and the Pas de Calais but it may be more exciting to be able regularly to spend the weekend in a French rather than in an English cottage. It is fair to say that the character of the Northern Frenchman seems on the surface more akin to that of the Briton and possibly of other Northern Europeans but it would be a grave mistake to forget that the twenty-two miles of water which ensures that an Englishman is not a Frenchman equally ensures that a Frenchman is not an Englishman. There are, of course, other parts of France which, travelling by tunnel, will become more swiftly accessible to the British – Normandy, Brittany, the Loire valley – as, of course, will every part of France and all of the rest of Europe. It is not possible to forecast to what extent the Channel Tunnel will affect the distribution of British-owned properties in France; all that can be said is that the majority of those who do not need a tunnel to bring them to France –

the Scandinavians, the Belgians, the Dutch, the Germans – do not seem to stop north of the Dordogne. Indeed, as Dixie Nichols says in *Harpers & Queen*, 'Every Englishman who has ever flirted with the idea of buying a holiday property abroad, by which he means the Riviera . . .' and he has good reason for so doing.

It is fair to add that the further south one goes, the less does one find property suitable for restoration. But it is also necessary to add that restoring houses in one's own country, even with the benefit of the best of architects or surveyors, can prove to be a long drawn out battle with builders. It should not be forgotten that this kind of problem arises in every country but that it is considerably magnified if one does not know the language, is ignorant of local building regulations and, however swift the journey through the tunnel may be, cannot spend every weekend, let alone every day, personally wielding the whip. Of course, there are solutions but the purchase of delightful but tumbledown houses '*à renover*' should not be indulged in without the greatest circumspection and competent advice. Chapter 23 is intended to help those who agree that advice of this kind would be a good thing.

What must be remembered is that, although there has been a great deal of development in France as a whole, it has been on a totally different basis from development in countries such as Spain. There, much of the development has been undertaken by foreign countries for nationals of their own countries. Thus you tend to get predominantly German or British colonies. Most building in France has been undertaken by French companies with French capital and aimed if not entirely at the French buyer then certainly not with an eye to the foreign buyer only. Developments in France are by way of in-filling, on however grand a scale, and except in the Languedoc Roussillon, which is the subject of heavy Government subsidy, there are few or no completely *new* vacation villages.

The coastal region from the Spanish to the Italian border falls economically speaking into three parts from the property

44

buyer's point of view. From Perpignan to about Nîmes constitutes very roughly the Languedoc Roussillon and is the
cheapest; from there through Marseille to St Tropez (the
départements of the Bouches du Rhône and the Var mostly)
is the next cheapest, and from St Tropez east through the
département of the Alpes Maritimes is the most expensive.

It is unlikely that you will settle for the Languedoc Roussillon except on a secondary-home basis, beautiful and full of
history though it is. It has not been completely developed
and has certain climatic problems (the wind for one), but
nevertheless do not dismiss it too quickly. It is not difficult to
reach by air, and the *autoroute 'La Catalane'* passes right
through the centre of it. Its main drawback to the newcomer
is that it is difficult to see just how the development of the
area is going to pan out during the coming ten years.

The region from Marseille to St Tropez is one vast agricultural and wine-growing area which to a great extent has, until
recently, only been developed to about ten miles inland.
Development is now fast spreading further inland and away
from the coast a little, are the most lovely Provençal villages
perched on sugarloaf hills with fabulous views of pine forest
and vineyards before you. In summer it is very quiet, hot and
slow. In winter it can be disagreeably cold when the mistral
blows, and it is even quieter and slower. This is one of the
few areas where it is still possible for a foreigner to buy a
vineyard or an old *mas* or *bergerie* for conversion.

Although the *autoroute* is the least rewarding way of getting
to know the countryside, it does mean that you can spend the
day in Aix and be back in Cogolin, Flayosc or Cannes for
dinner.

Strictly speaking the Côte d'Azur begins at Cannes, though
the Var often claims to be part of it. The *département* of the
Alpes-Maritimes is the most developed area of France, and it
is extremely difficult to find either building land or an old
house to restore, though such things do still exist. A serious
search after the elusive owner of a desirable plot usually
uncovers a complicated family situation which cannot be
unravelled during the next twenty years or someone who is

simply not interested in selling but very content to sit on his property and watch its worth increase year by year. It is best just to accept that many French are like that.

Remember that there are parts of France which change radically with the end of the holiday period. These include virtually all the coast from Marseille to the Italian border together with the strip of land behind the coast which also comes to life only for the benefit of the holiday-maker. The same is, of course, the case with the resorts along the western coast. There are many who think that it is after the holidays are over that these places become if anything more pleasant. Vast parts of France (for France is indeed a vast country) suffer changes throughout the year dictated only by the passage of the seasons. It is evident that it is easier to find properties in the areas traditional for foreigners but it is a pity to overlook those parts of the country to which the non-French have not so far flocked. But sensibly, two questions should be asked – why has this part of France so far been avoided by the non-French, and is it a part which threatens too easily to become a ghetto? Remember that 'the natives' probably live where they do because they have little alternative whilst you have all the choice in the world. A delightful village may provide delicious wine but appalling weather, or may be easy of access but too remote for the city dweller to tolerate. Remember also that a sudden flocking by your compatriots to a newly discovered area will soon turn it from France into "Little ———" (whatever your nationality may be) and that is not acceptable to anyone looking for the real France. France is well served by road, rail and internal air services and a short course on geography and history before the visit to the estate agent can pay handsome dividends.

It is utterly pointless to give any firm indications of prices except in the most general terms. Often the cost of a studio or two-roomed flat in the best part of Cannes would purchase a five-bedroomed house just inland in the Languedoc Roussillon. The Alpes-Maritimes prices bear little relation to those in other parts of France since they are often more expensive than even Paris. And Monte Carlo, which is not in the province of this book, outdoes them all with the average flat price in excess of anything in France. Monaco apart, Cannes is the most expensive, followed probably by certain areas of Nice/ Villefranche and Beaulieu. Antibes is a mixed bag, as is Menton which takes in the very sought-after area of Roquebrune-Cap Martin. The area round St Tropez, including Cogolin, Port Grimaud, Ramatuelle and Cavalaire, is the most expensive in the Var. Away from the coast prices drop rapidly. The exception in the Alpes-Maritimes is the Grasse/ St Paul/Vence/Valbonne area which is often very expensive. Naturally a sea view commands a bigger price, as do flats and villas which belong to a marina complex.

Traditionally, new flats used to increase in value by about 10% per annum but this now seems to be a thing of the past. Nevertheless, it is unlikely that they will ever be a bad investment unless major currency readjustments occur.

Prices for older property are, of course, usually less and particularly for holiday purposes, one should not overlook these. It is true that the stamp duties on a purchase of these properties is much higher and possibly in really old flats decorative and possibly more serious work may be needed. However, bargains among older flats are much more likely to be found than if you are buying from a developer.

Those who harbour the dream of making their own wine must confine themselves to the Hérault, Gard, Var or, possibly, Vaucluse. There is no chance of purchasing something of this nature in the Bordelais or Burgundy unless you are using a multi-million-dollar consortium to do it. Those who enjoy shooting and country pursuits should plump for the Sologne (near Orléans), the Landes or the Auvergne and accept that the climate in winter leaves something to be desired. One can shoot in Languedoc and Provence, but it is not of the same quality. More or less anywhere in central France is good shooting country. *La chasse* is not the privilege of the rich only in France.

For skiers and mountaineers France has a massive choice, and they will not be deterred by the inclement weather. Summer in these mountain regions can be heavenly, and if you do not want to live there at that season yourself, it is easy to let your chalet or apartment to that tribe of people who believe implicitly in the '*cure d'air*'.

France's long coastline offers all sorts of marine pleasures from scuba diving and game fishing to windsurfing, to say nothing of yachting. "*La pêche est une industrie nationale*", the French announce proudly, and certainly it seems easier to go fishing in France than in any other country in Europe. Coarse or otherwise, the rivers in France abound with fish, and the local Syndicat d'Initiative will organize the inexpensive permit (which is not always necessary anyway) and tell you of the open and close seasons.

The main problem for someone coming to live in France is the sheer size of the country and the choice it has to offer. It is vital that you think about it most seriously since ultimately you will have to live with the choice you have made, and it should prove a happy one for you and your family.

For those who live permanently in France, or those who feel that from time to time they would like to behave as the French would do and take their holidays as do the French, the solution is easy. Few French go to the country. The tradition is to go to the sea. The whole of the south coast from the Spanish to the Italian border is by far the most popular area. Parts of the Atlantic coast are also favourites but they are by no means as popular as the Mediterranean. On the whole, quite a small proportion of the French holiday abroad. What must not be forgotten is that the month of August really does represent a total 'shut down' throughout France of everything except what is needed to cope with the tourist. It is preceded by July when the holiday resorts begin to fill up and is followed by September when the crowds are less and the visitors more discerning. For example, the best restaurants, even in the tourist areas, close in August. This must indicate something. Winter brings another holiday season, this time devoted to skiing. France is admirably provided with ski resorts mainly in the Alps with a few in the Pyrénées and new ones appear every year. Those in Savoie and the Dauphiné tend to be the most expensive, the Hautes

La Roque Gageac on the Dordogne

Domme and its bridge over the Dordogne

A typical scene in the Dordogne

Alpes and the Alpes du Sud are cheaper and cheapest of all are the Pyrénées. It is worth remembering that almost all of these places are delightful in summer for 'nature lovers' and those who shun the overcrowded beaches and most run a double season.

CHAPTER 4

Communications

AIR

Air France has one of the largest networks in the world, and you can fly from or via Paris to almost anywhere by jet, and by Concorde to New York.

UTA is the other French air-transport company which either duplicates or complements Air France services abroad.

Air Inter as its name implies, is the main internal air service and serves thirty-nine airports from either Paris Orly or Paris Charles de Gaulle. On page 54 is a table showing the main airports of interest to the non-French, their distances from the town centre and the areas they serve.

Air Inter (and Air France on its internal flights) operate a somewhat complicated system of coloured flights, red, white and blue (*vols rouges, blancs et bleus*).

'Red Flights' are the most expensive and open only to full fare-paying passengers or those with a commuter card (*carte d'abonnement tous vols*). This is a season ticket which gives thirty per cent reduction on red, white and blue flights on Air France, Air Inter and UTA in France on a specific route. This card also gives a reduction of twenty per cent on a first class rail fare on a journey which combines air and rail travel.

'White Flights' are open to all passengers and offer reduction for Air France/Air Inter commuter card holders (and SNCF holders where applicable) plus special cheaper rates for babies (free if accompanied), children, adolescents, families travelling together, newly marrieds, pensioners (sixty for a woman, sixty-five or sixty if retired for a man) and groups of more than five people. White flights can be taken in conjunction with blue flights – e.g. one can fly white to Paris and blue from Paris to somewhere else with a suitable adjustment in the fare.

'Blue Flights' are cheapest of all.

During the day from approximately 9 a.m. to 4 p.m. and 9 p.m. to about 7 a.m. next day most flights are either white or blue and therefore cheaper by about 20% to 35% on white flights and by 40% to 55% on blue flights.

On blue flights the times are less convenient, but discounts are highest of all.

There are no other conditions attached to these tickets, which are available for twelve months. Dates and times can be altered, though this may incur extra cost if you change from one colour flight to another.

Provided you are able to stay from between ten and thirty-five days at or near your destination, there are special cheap flights from Paris to Nice, Bordeaux, Toulouse, Lyon, Marseille or Corsica or vice versa. A return date must be given and should be adhered to. Absolutely NO changes are allowed of the commencement date you first book, but the return date can be changed by paying a twenty per cent penalty. The savings are considerable since the normal economy Nice–Paris return is 1,574 francs and only 670 francs on SPX flights for a ten-day period or 953 francs for one month.

Check-in times on Air Inter flights are twenty to thirty minutes before take-off.

All world major airlines have flights to Paris and many of them, particularly during the summer season, have flights to one or more of the following airports – Lyon, Marseille, Bordeaux, Strasbourg, Lille, Nice. When there is not a direct flight to the town of your choice, use Air Inter, which runs a frequent service from Paris to most large cities and towns in France with connecting flights between them.

There are many smaller airline companies (such as Danair and British Island Airways) who run flights into France, either scheduled or charter, and a good travel agent should be able to find the best value for you.

ROADS

France has almost 1½ million kilometres of roadway, and thus there is practically nowhere in the country that is difficult of access to the motorist. There are some four thousand kilometres of motorway (*autoroute*) with lovely names such as '*L'Aquitaine*', '*La Provençale*' and '*L'Océane*', and it is now easy to reach the Côte d'Azur from England, Denmark and Holland with only one night stop in or near Paris.

The main *autoroute* north-south goes from the Belgian frontier to the Mediterranean and on into Italy after leaving Menton. It is worth pointing out that Florence, Turin, Milan and the Italian Lakes are less than a day's drive from Nice or Cannes.

Roads are classified as follows:

Autoroutes

Sample Péages (as at 1st January 1990)

	Francs
Paris–Calais	79.00
Paris–Lille	50.00
Paris–Lyon	108.00
Paris–Orléans	34.00
Aix en Provence–Menton	78.00
Nice Airport–Ventimiglia	16.50
Bordeaux–Toulouse	75.00
Hendaye–Biarritz	19.00
Lyon–Annecy	50.00
Toulouse–Montpellier	86.00

Motorway toll prices usually increase every June but sometimes there is no increase in a year or sometimes the increase comes at another time. All that is needed is a dialogue with Minitel (see page 202) on 3615 Code Autoroute and you will get not only the toll prices, but also a useful map of the section of the *autoroute* you are intending to use, driving conditions, eating-places *en route* (on the whole better than those in many other countries, but very expensive) and a good deal of other useful information. The motorway system is constantly being extended (the Minitel map will show you what is new and what is under construction) and in general terms is excellently maintained. The standard of motorway driving, alas, is appalling.

Information of up to date rates can also be obtained at Association Française des Autoroutes, Paris (Telephone (1) 47.05.90.01.).

Routes Nationales: Main trunk roads going through towns and excellently maintained by the State. They carry a prefix N or RN and are coloured red on the maps and on tops of the milestones (*bornes*).

Chemins Départementaux: Coloured yellow on milestone tops and maintained by *départementale* authorities. Most roads in France are *chemins départementaux*. They carry the prefix D.

Voies Communales: Smaller and/or feeder roads maintained by small towns or local communes. They carry the prefix C on maps and on milestones.

Chemins Ruraux: Usually only found in deep deep country, and their condition often leaves something to be desired. If it is ever marked, it would carry the prefix R.

Voies Forestières: As their name suggests, these are forest roads and are marked with green on the milestones and carry the prefix F. Do not block any of these forest paths by carelessly parking your car. Access may be needed for a fire engine or tractor.

Roads with a '*Sauf Aux Riverains*' marker are usually private and for the sole use of the inhabitants of that area and their guests. Unless you fall into that category, do not use them as a short cut since you will be committing an offence.

ACCIDENTS AND BREAKDOWNS
The motorways and the larger *routes nationales* are patrolled by the police and/or the *gendarmerie*, usually on motorcycles.

On the *autoroutes* there are SOS boxes at staggered kilometre intervals – i.e. every two kilometres each side of the road. A knowledge of French is needed to explain your predicament at the other end (not all mechanics are good linguists – or vice versa!) On most other roads there are cafés

AIRPORT	DISTANCE FROM TOWN CENTRE	TRANSPORT METHOD	AREAS SERVED
BIARRITZ (Bayonne–Anglet)	8 kms from Bayonne 3 kms from Biarritz	Taxi Taxi	SW France to Spanish border – the Béarn, Gascony, the Basque country.
BORDEAUX (Bordeaux Mérignac)	12 kms	Airport bus	SW France not served from Biarritz – Gascony, Guyenne, Bordelais, Perigord and Dordogne.
FRÉJUS (St Raphael)	1–2 kms from town centre	Taxi	St Tropez Bay – *arrière pays* of the Var.
GRENOBLE (St Geoirs)	40 kms from Grenoble	Airport bus	Isère and skiing areas in Haute Savoie and Savoie.
HYÈRES (Hyères–Toulon)	4 kms from Hyères 21 kms from Toulon	Trans. Brondello bus Trans. Brondello bus	Hyères and Toulon, the Var coast and *arrière pays* which are not served from Nice or Marseille.
LYON (Satolas airport)	25 kms from city centre	Airport bus meets all flights Taxi-bus. Bus to central Lyon then taxi to final destination	Burgundy, Maconnais, Beaujolais, Bresse and Isère. Taxi-bus can be booked in advance. Price should be discussed in advance.
MARSEILLE (Marignane)	30 kms from Marseille	Airport Bus to Marseille or to Aix-en-Provence	Western Provence, Avignon area, Gard, Bouches du Rhône, Var coast up to St Tropez. A most useful airport for British people and not enough used.
MONTPELLIER (Fréjorgues)	8 kms from Montpellier	Airport bus	Languedoc Roussillon.
NANTES (Château-Bougon)	10 kms from Nantes	Airport bus	Brittany, Normandy, and the Vendée coast.
NICE (Côte d'Azur)	6 kms from Nice Centre	Airport bus Helicopter service – 7 flight daily	Côte d'Azur, Monte Carlo, Italian Riviera, St Tropez Bay area, the Var, Haute Provence. Connections to Cannes and Menton and Monte Carlo by special bus with connections on to the Italian Riviera as far as San Remo by Rapides Côte d'Azur and STP Riviera dei Fiori. Tel: 93.55.24.80 or 93.85.64.44. Monte Carlo/Monaco.
PERPIGNAN (Perpignan Rivesaltes)	7 kms from Perpignan	Airport bus	Eastern Pyrenees, part of Languedoc Roussillon. North-east Spanish coast.

54

with telephones or telephone boxes, but France has adopted the standard method of mitigating the vandalization of telephones by the use of cards and it is useful to have a French phonecard on one when going on a long journey.

The state of the roads such as roadworks in progress, snow, fog, ice, heavy traffic periods etc. can be ascertained by calling:

for the south of France	91.78.78.78.
for the centre of France	78.54.33.33.
for the north of France	87.63.33.33.

General motoring information can also be obtained from ASSFA (Association francaise d'automobile) in Paris on (1) 43.80.21.71. The British AA can also be contacted at Boulogne on 21.87.21.21.

There are large specialist organizations in France such as Europassistance, Gesa, Mondial Assistance etc. who all run an excellent get-you-home service covering the whole of Europe (except Russia and Albania). Once permanently resident in France, you should shop around for one of these assistance packages. None is cheap, but then neither is a tow or a breakdown in the middle of nowhere.

Finally, if you have the misfortune to have an accident, you must stay put until the police arrive. Unless your car constitutes a definite danger to the traffic (and not just merely an inconvenience), you must not move it until allowed to do so by the police. Having turned your car engine off, you must do the following:

Not smoke – (because of possible petrol leaks).

Put up your red triangle (obligatory in France).

Put on your hazard warning lights and if at night your dipped headlights.

Call the *gendarmerie* or police or get someone to do it for you.

Assuming you have not been hurt, start filling in your *constat amiable d'accident*. This latter comes automatically with your Green Card. You each hand over to the other this form to be filled in with details of the other party's insurance, name, address etc. It is not important whether you agree or disagree with each other. Each puts down his own version of the accident, and under observations you are quite entitled to put 'This man is lying' if you believe he is and it makes you feel better. However, as in any country, never admit liability. It is worth noting that a Green Card is obligatory in France even for citizens of Common Market countries. Green Cards purchased at the frontier give only the most basic cover – i.e. third party.

It should be noted that, if you arrive first at the scene of an accident in which people are hurt and do not call the police or an ambulance or give them first aid (if you are capable of doing so), you could be prosecuted for failing to render assistance under the French Penal Code. As in any civilized country, it is an offence to run away from an accident you have been involved in.

Throughout France, the number for the police is 17, and for the fire brigade 18. Both these organizations supply ambulances etc. NB. As in the United States you need a card or a minimum coin to get the dialling tone (at present 1 franc), and the moment the police or fire brigade answer, this is dropped back to you. From a private telephone the call is free. There is also no charge from one of the special SOS telephones found on motorways, on some main roads and occasionally on very lonely roads put up by some kind motor-manufacturer.

RAILWAYS

On 1st January 1938 the five major private railways of France were nationalized and henceforth were to be known as the Société Nationale des Chemins de Fer Français or SNCF for short. The State then granted a concession to a company of which it owned 51% of the capital and the remaining 49% was owned by the successors of the original five companies. This concession came to an end in 1982 and on 1st January 1983, SNCF was reconstituted as a public enterprise entirely in the ownership of the State.

Over one-third of the lines are electrified, and the remaining lines use diesel engines. It has almost 35,000 kilometres of railway, but compared with countries like Germany and Great Britain the density of line is considerably smaller, i.e. one kilometre of railway for sixteen square kilometres compared with Great Britain which has one kilometre of line per eleven square kilometres. On the other hand it has the longest network of all Western Europe. The density of passenger traffic is astonishing. In Paris on New Year's Day for instance 375,000 main line passengers are handled. Every day between six and seven o'clock in the evening the Gare St Lazare in Paris handles 1,250 passengers per minute on the suburban lines.

The main-line services all radiate from Paris ('*Grandes Lignes*'), following the routes of the old five companies. The west and south-west of the country are still rather poorly served compared with the north, east and north-east. There is one fast main line to the Mediterranean via Lyon to Marseille and on to the Italian frontier. The TGV network (Train Grande Vitesse) continues to be extended and includes services to Lille, Dijon, Besançon, Lausanne, Beaune, Chalon sur Saone, Le Creusot, Macon, Lyon, Bourg en Bresse, Geneva, Annecy, Chambéry, Valence, Avignon, Montpellier, Marseille, Toulon, Nice, Rennes, Nantes and generally to the south-east. To give an indication of the time saved by using this service, the journey from Paris to Lyon now takes two hours instead of double that time and from Paris to Montpellier, 4.30 hours instead of 6.25 hours. Seats must be booked in advance at least 30 minutes before departure and can be done either by telephone, by Minitel (see page 202) 3615 code SNCF or at a booking office or by using a most ingenious little computer which is installed at almost every station of any size, irrespective of whether it is visited by a TGV or not. The booking fee is minimal. Approximately one-third of the trains also carry a small supplement but otherwise normal fares apply. None of these trains has sleeping cars.

Compared with British Rail, SNCF offers an impressive number of services beyond merely transporting people and freight from station to station. For the physically handicapped who have to travel by train many of the main-line stations have services which are specially equipped, and most stations have folding wheelchairs. Many main stations have specially adapted lavatories and carriages specially designed for the handicapped are included in many trains running between many towns including Paris and Brest, Lille, Toulouse, Hendaye, Tarbes, Nice and Grenoble and from Nantes across France to Lyon.

For those who want to travel by train with their car, which is a somewhat restful alternative to a long motorway journey, there is a considerable network of trains called 'Motorail' throughout France. Ideally, you should get the booklet called *Trains Autos et Motos accompagnées* which can be obtained from any French station and, out of France, from the French Railways office in most capital cities. Basic information is also given in English. The list of stations served is considerable and it is unlikely that you will want to end up somewhere which is not either directly served by one of these trains (TAC for *train auto-couchettes*, TAJ for *train auto jour*, TMA for *train motos accompagnées* and SAE for *service autos-express*) or by a station within reasonable distance of your destination. It is desirable to book well in advance, especially at holiday time. It cannot be said that this is the cheapest method of travel; indeed, over the years, it has become more and more expensive. But it is worth comparing the cost against that of motorway tolls, meals, petrol and, for journeys across France, the cost of a night's stay *en route*. Depending on distance and/ or the number of people travelling and/or the size of your car, there is a breakeven point. Remember that if you are entitled to one, the use of the card issued in your county which is the equivalent of the *Carte Rail Europ S* (see page 61) does make a considerable saving in cost.

All the TAC trains are, of course, available for night journeys without a car. Some of these are TEE or TEN trains and start or finish out of France. Some trains with sleepers and couchettes do not take cars as well. Full details of all these trains are also readily available and, of course, Minitel will answer enquiries if you do not want to make them personally, although in many of the larger stations the Information Offices can manage English and usually two or three other languages.

MAIN TYPES OF TRAINS

Apart from suburban lines, SNCF operate the following types of trains: 'Omnibus' is a train which stops at every station on the route. 'Rapide' is a little faster and stops at many stations on the line. 'Express' is not always that fast but stops at a limited number of stations clearly posted up on the platform and often on the train itself. Certain express trains have restaurant cars or bars – *'Trains corails'* for instance which have coral-coloured doors. No extras are charged. The most expensive are the TEE 'Trans-Europ-Express' or TEN 'Trans-Europ-Nuit' which are first class only, require reservation and incur a supplement on the normal first class fare.

SPECIAL SNCF CARDS:

Whenever you get a SNCF card, you will be given a calendar which shows the red, white and blue periods. At every station there is a board which indicates the ruling period. It is essential to consult this board before beginning your journey because the cheap periods are related to those in force at the beginning of your journey, irrespective of the fact that it may continue into another (and full fare) period. If you are caught travelling at a discount in a period not allowed by your card, you will not only pay an additional fare but also a heavy fine (on the spot!). In very general terms, blue periods, which are cheapest, are those from Saturday noon to 1500 hours on Sundays and from Monday noon to Friday 1500 hours. This gives approximately 250 days per year of cheap travel. Cards are available for first and second class but generally speaking not on the Parisian suburban system. Where cards require a family relationship, such as marriage, those living together but not married may get from their local *mairie* a *certificat de concubinage* which solves that problem.

Carte d'Abonnement (season ticket). The cost depends on whether you want a go-anywhere card (*Carte de libre circulation*), which is the most expensive, or an ordinary season ticket which depends on the kilometres covered. Worth it if you use the railways a great deal. It can be paid for by monthly instalments. All students and apprentices get a 50% reduction. A photograph is required for this card and the production of your passport or *carte de séjour.*

Carte Demi-Tarif (Half-Fare Card). This is similar to a season but offers greater advantages since it gets progressively cheaper for each member of the family. On a hundred-kilometre journey a six-month season is paid for by the tenth journey. It can be modified during its period of issue or cancelled. The card can be obtained at any railway station for a small fee and requires a photograph.

Carré Jeune. For people between the ages of twelve and twenty-six, this card gives a 50% reduction for four single or two return journeys started in a *période bleue* and a 20% reduction for each such journey started in a *période blanche.* It is valid for one year and covers four return journeys. Its cost is 160 francs.

Carte Jeune. This card is available from 1 June to 30 September. It is available to all young persons between 12 and 26 and provides a 50% reduction on all journeys begun during a blue period. It has additional advantages such as a free couchette on journeys in France, 50% reductions in West Germany, Spain, Portugal and a 30% reduction in Italy and a 50% reduction on the ferry between Italy and Greece. The card costs 160 francs and when applying for one, you will need a passport photograph.

Carte Inter-rail. These are available to young people currently at the cost of 1,490 francs. They allow free travel over virtually the whole of Western Europe and within France at half price for the period of one month. There are two variations of this card available, the *Card Inter-Rail + Bateau* which costs 1,790 francs and which allows free travel on certain journeys by boat and *Carte Inter-rail flexi* which costs 1,430 francs. This latter card is intended for those who are not travelling continously and allows up to ten journeys in one month. It must be remembered that the Inter-rail card is international and can be bought in any of the countries which grant these facilities. The country where the card is purchased can allow only a 50% reduction on its rail system so it is worthwhile considering where you buy it. Of course, if by reason of your age you are entitled to a *Carte Vermeil* and you are intending to travel only in France, it is cheaper to use that card which costs considerably less than a *Carte Inter-rail*.

Billet 'Séjour'. This ticket gives a 25% reduction providing you are travelling at least 1,000 kilometres either in the form of an outward and return journey or as a circular journey, the return journey not being undertaken until a Sunday or part of a Sunday or a Bank holiday and provided that each part of the journey must be started in a *période bleue*.

Carte Vermeil. This card is available to men and women over sixty. It currently costs 125 francs and is valid for a year from the date of issue. You do not need to be a resident of France to obtain one: all you need is to prove your age by production of a suitable document. This card entitles you to travel throughout France at 50% of the normal fares at all times provided you begin your journey outside a peak period. The holder of a *Carte Vermeil* may obtain for 50 francs a *Carte International Rail Europ S* which entitles the holder to the same benefits as the *Carte Vermeil* in eighteen European countries. This card can only be obtained in the country in which you obtained your *Carte Vermeil* or its equivalent in that country.

Carte Kiwi. This card costs 350 francs. It allows a person under sixteen together with those who accompany him (minimum one person and maximum four persons) to travel at 50% reduction for journeys begun in *périodes blanches* or *bleues*. Brothers or sisters of the cardholder who are also under sixteen may buy this card for fifty francs and no charge is made if they are under four. It also kindly allows the family dog or cat to travel free of charge.

There are many other cards and reductions available from SNCF, but for the majority you need to be resident in France or a civil servant or both.

BUSES AND COACHES

Certain towns give free bus travel to pensioners on production of a card issued by the bus company on production of a passport, identity card or *carte de séjour* and proof of residence by the applicant. In some places, this can be proved by the production of a telephone or electricity bill or a rent demand or receipt but a number of towns allow this facility only to those who can produce a receipt for local general Rates (*taxe d'habitation*). Enquiries should be made at the main bus station of the town in which you live or at RATP in Paris.

Both in Paris and in the provinces, books of tickets can be purchased at discount prices for the Métro (where applicable) and the bus services. Often a card, issued by the bus company as above, is required when buying pensioners' tickets which are even cheaper than the normal discount tickets. These books of tickets can be purchased at either the bus station, tobacconists or certain banks such as Banque Populaire (in all its forms throughout the country). Sometimes LOTO booths sell books of bus tickets also. Whether travelling by train or bus, all tickets must be validated in the machine provided at the entrance to the platform or in the bus. It is illegal to travel without validating your ticket. The verb in French is *composter un billet*. In the case of non-card tickets, the corner of the page of *the ticket you are using that day* should be put into the machine. Sometimes this is well nigh impossible.

Coach travel. France has an excellent coach service throughout the country. Enquiries should be made at the local *gare routière.* Coach travel is usually more expensive than travelling by train but sometimes considerably more convenient and comfortable.

POLICE AND GENDARMERIE

For the foreigner coming to France the *police/gendarmerie* system appears rather more complicated than it actually is.

Cities, most medium-sized towns etc. have their own police force – *la police municipale* or *le corps urbain*; the terms are more or less interchangeable. All police are under the control of the Ministry of the Interior (Home Office). The policeman you see in the streets is an *agent de police.*

In most cities or largish towns the *police nationale* are also present. In practice most of the day-to-day work is done by the *police municipale* (dealing with housebreaking, traffic control and accidents, etc.), whereas the *police nationale* concern themselves with higher things. However, when you lose your wallet or passport you are usually directed to the *Commissariat de Police (Nationale)* which can muddle a foreigner. Frequently, local telephone directories do not distinguish the two types of police adequately and you may well find you get little help if you happen to ring the wrong police force.

As in the UK there are many different branches of police. In France the *police judiciaire* are more or less the equivalent of our CID. All visitors to France will have seen the notice *"Police de l'Air et des Frontières"* as they come through Immigration. Police also carry out certain customs duties and these will have the word *'Douanes'* on their uniforms.

The CRS (*Compagnie Républicaine de Sécurité*) was founded in 1958 by General de Gaulle for special duties and acquired a somewhat sinister reputation from a British viewpoint after the 1968 student riots in France. Usually the mere presence of their black uniforms tends to exercise a salutary effect on the crowd.

Police ranks in descending order are: *Directeur, Principale,*

Brigadier-Chef, Brigadier, Agent de Police or *Gardien de la Paix*.

The *gendarmerie* is a military organization and as such comes under the direct control of the Ministry of Defence. Each *département* in France has its own *Gendarmerie Départementale*. In places too small to warrant a police presence, the village *gendarme* takes on detective and police duties. Otherwise the gendarmerie has three main divisions, *Air, Maritime* and *Terre*. In the latter are included many of the *motards* seen patrolling the main roads and *autoroutes*, and usually the helicopters seen above crowded holiday routes are piloted by the local *gendarmerie*. The *Gendarmerie de la Montagne* who patrol the mountains are the people who organize rescue operations and helicopters for those who have accidents. They are all crack skiers, needless to say. The *Gendarmerie Maritime* perform the functions of the coast-guards, lifeboats, river police etc. Frequently they carry out customs work as well. In certain areas there is also a *Police Maritime*, but they are less commonly seen than the *Gendarmerie Maritime*.

CHAPTER 5

Buying and Selling Homes

There will be few people who buy homes in France who have not been involved in at least one property purchase in their own country. In France, the notary has the monopoly of conveyancing but it is vital to understand that his function is essentially limited to preparing the document which transfers the property, ensuring that the parties involved understand it and seeing that the stamp duty and registration fees on it are paid. Indeed, he is personally liable for that duty, which is why he will not complete a purchase without having money to cover those disbursements in hand. The notary will, of course, investigate the seller's title, make planning enquiries, see that there are no mortgages on the property or, if there are, will clear them off immediately after completion. He is not, however, a 'handholder' and those who in their own country are used, when buying or selling property, to the large doses of aid and comfort beyond the bounds of pure law will not easily find this in France.

The notary is one of the largest tax gatherers in France and his conveyancing monopoly stems from that function. He is, in fact, a government official and enroller of all official documents. Of course, he deals with a lot of other non-contentious work, which in other countries is done by the solicitor or attorney. But his uses in the French legal system are such that it is not always easy to get from him the sort of advice which the non-French buyer really requires on coming 'cold' to France and which is more often than not practical rather than legal. It must also be remembered that there is a limited number of notaries in France – one cannot just set up in practice where and when one wants. Whilst those in large towns may have some knowledge of the law of your country and speak some of your language, it is unreasonable to expect that apart from those few exceptions they will be any more knowledgeable on, for example, UK or US or Danish law than would a country lawyer in Britain, the States or Denmark be on questions of French law. Make no mistake, a knowledge of both French law and of the law of your country is much more frequently needed than might be imagined for buying or selling property in France or indeed for any transaction in France where a foreigner is involved.

There is another fundamental difference between the notary and the lawyer dealing with property transactions in certain other countries, where separate representation is the keystone of the system. For example, in Great Britain, a solicitor cannot, with minimal exceptions, act for both seller and buyer. In France, one notary very frequently acts for both parties. This has come about because the notary – together with his brother notaries throughout the country – is, too all intents and purposes, the equivalent of the land registry in France. A comprehensive system of local land registry offices exists in France. This is made up of the *Cadastre* and the *Bureaux des Hypothèques*. The former is a tax-registration system designed to ensure that the French fiscal authorities know who owns what land. The latter, as their name suggests, deal with mortgages but also register land transfers, rights of way and other burdens on land. But these offices do not 'vet' transactions except as to formalities. That is the duty of the notary, in whose files the original document of sale remains permanently recorded.

It is not usual in cases of flats or houses for a notary to become involved with any transaction prior to the actual transfer of the land. Unlike the situation in certain other countries, he does not usually deal with the purchase contract or anything which goes before it. His task is formalist, and if an error is made in an *acte de vente* (conveyance), only the courts can decide on questions of title. Errors are rare, but, as in any country, they do occur from time to time. Had two notaries been employed, perhaps such an error could have been avoided. Certainly, experience has shown that to become involved in any action in the French courts over land is a tragedy.

However, it is a fundamental rule of French conveyancing that it is the buyer who has the prerogative of choosing the notary to act in the transaction. Not unnaturally, if you, the buyer, choose to use notary X and the vendor wishes to use notary Y, he will not wish usually to agree to your choice, particularly when in the case of a new block of flats it is *his* notary who has done all the legal spadework beforehand. Although a buyer always pays the notarial fees, the involvement of two notaries does not increase his costs, for the two notaries have to share one fee. Few developers will tell you of your rights in this matter it being customary for the seller's agent merely to insert the name of the seller's notary in the sale contract as the only notary involved. If it is possible to imagine an even less likely situation when this would be told to you, it would be on the sale of land or an old property for conversion in the country. Such a transaction is bound to be fraught with all sorts of legal problems, and the conservative make-up of the French country dweller would not allow him to believe in the fiction that there is any notary better than his own who can, if necessary, 'slip one over'. Even if a signed contract provides for one notary only, the buyer may still insist on using another notary of his choice.

It is really a matter of considerable skill for a buyer to decide which notary to use, and suffice to say it is not a decision which a non-French buyer should be expected to make unaided. It is now possible for every Notary to deal with any transaction anywhere in France; this was not the case until quite recently. Enlisting the aid of a local expert who speaks a language in which you are fluent, the local Consulate and banks are all methods towards the solution of this problem.

Remember that a developer has a development to sell. He has spent considerable money on publicity, and you are his target. Remember also that the attitude of sales offices and estate agents particularly in the South of France and other tourist areas is not quite as sober as one might always wish. They are assuming that you are hooked once you have found something which pleases you. That means that many buyers seem to be either at the end of their visit to France or bemused by the sun and beautiful surroundings or just plain tired out. Even if none of these states applies to you, you are probably overjoyed at having, at last, found something and are fearful of losing it. You are ripe to be told that, if you do not sign at once, you may find that you will indeed lose it or the price may increase. Both could possibly be true, but neither is so urgent a reason that you should allow yourself to be forced to sign a binding contract without some form of advice first. Always remember that a *'réservation' is a deposit* and *not* a payment made to the seller to 'reserve' the property for you until you make up your mind to buy or not. That payment is, unless the contract contains special conditions, irrecoverable.

Some of the better estate agents and sales offices offer a cooling-off period. Some do not. Those who do not should be treated with a certain amount of caution. Even in the case of those who do, would you sign blind a contract in your own country without the advice of your lawyer?

The special conditions referred to above relate primarily to mortgage loans towards the purchase price. If they are inserted into a contract in a proper form and you do not get the necessary loan, you can get your deposit back. French law has given added protection to the buyer in this respect, but even if the danger of the seller not making the buyer aware of his rights in this matter is now less than previously, the law is quite complex, and your knowledge of the language and the legal system needs to be considerable to understand what is being put to you (Chapter 13 deals in more detail with mortgages).

Never sign a contract which includes any reference to the payment of agents' commission without prior advice. In most parts of France, the seller pays the agent's commission, but in some parts, notably the north-west and south-west, notaries frequently undertake the work of estate agents and are entitled to commission. It is also customary in these areas for the buyer to pay part or all of the commission.

It may seem that this advice is angled at the novice buyer rather than at those who have lived in France for some time before deciding to buy. This is because the non-French who have lived in France know that such assistance as you have been recommended to seek is indeed necessary.

A further word on estate agents is desirable. There are a number of highly reputable estate agents operating in France – particularly in Paris and the south and south-west – who are nationals of your country or who have close connections with your country. There are also other professional people of various nationalities whose reputation is impeccable. Naïve though it may seem, it must, alas, be said that having the same nationality as yours is of itself, in a few cases where property is involved, no guarantee of integrity or capability.

The vast majority of non-French buyers purchase new flats. A number buy new houses. Of course, there is a considerable market in other properties where you are not the original buyer from a developer. It is still also possible to find land on which you can build, and old properties for renovation become available principally in the north-west and south-west of France. To endeavour to cope with the problem that this type of property poses without advice must be evidently so stupid that no further comment is necessary. The French are at the same time enamoured of the written word and fearful of 'putting it in writing'. On the other hand folk are quite kind, particularly in the country, and are very happy to please – but not on paper. It is impossible when negotiating, or for example dealing with planning problems, to cope with this kind of outlook without local expertise.

If you are buying a new house or flat, you will very possibly be buying '*en état futur d'achèvement*' (on plan). This is a common method of purchasing property in France. You may find that a large part of a development has already been sold in this manner even though it is still only at foundation stage, when it is difficult to imagine the finished product. In many cases, however, you will find that there is already one phase of the development completed and sold, so that, although the flat or house you choose exists only on paper, you will be able to see a comparable finished property.

The law lays down very strict rules about purchases of this nature, designed to protect the buyer. Briefly, the times at which stage payments may be asked for and the percentages of the total purchase price they represent are well defined. Completion of the building in accordance with specification is the subject of a bank or similar guarantee, and stage payments are payable against architects' or similar certificates. It is not uncommon to find that stage payments are asked for more frequently but in less amounts than the law prescribes, but so long as the maximum total part payments at the permitted stages are not exceeded, this is in order. A final payment of 5% of the purchase price is made when the property has been completed, inspected and found to be in order and the keys are handed over. The law provides for guarantees for defects in building which in certain circumstances extend up to ten years after completion of the building or in the case of relatively minor defects up to two years.

There are obvious advantages of buying in this manner. From a practical viewpoint it allows you often to choose the decoration and colours you prefer for wallpaper, paint, tiles, etc. From the price point of view you will almost certainly be buying something at today's price which will have increased in price to subsequent buyers. A contract can provide in very limited circumstances for revisions of the purchase price but this is comparatively rare and increases are controlled by law. Moreover, you are not required to find all of the purchase price in a lump sum. Completion of the purchase itself takes place after the usual interval of time after contracts have been signed (which is never less than one month), after the draft conveyance has become available, and the amount that you pay on completion is of course governed by the stage to which building has progressed at that date. No problems arise on getting mortgages for this type of purchase. A contract may not provide for interest in excess of 1% per month for the late payment of any stage payment.

You may also sometimes find that an investor (who is often an estate agent as well) has bought a number of flats or houses in a development, possibly at a reduced price for such a large purchase, and is prepared to sell one of these at slightly under the then market price. You then take over the property from him, paying him on completion the amount of the stage payments he has paid to date plus his profit, and you then pay direct to the developer the remaining stage payments. This type of transaction is quite tricky and needs very careful watching.

If you are buying a flat, you will certainly be buying *en copropriété* (see Chapter 8). Try to find out as soon as you can what your service charges are likely to be. Obviously this is not easy if you are buying a flat in a block still far from completion, but the question should be pressed. Where there is a resident *concierge*, the service charge will reflect this to a noticeable degree, and a communal heating system also puts up the price, all the more so because you will then be paying for heating even when you are not there to use it. Scales of approximate service charges per square metre exist, but these will give you only a rough guide since they cannot take account of every circumstance. If you are buying from an existing owner, insist that you see his last service charge account. If you are buying a new flat, try to establish that the block contains such things as adequate security provisions, proper central temperature control for hot water and central heating, and fire-precaution equipment in the boiler rooms. If it does not, you will find that, at some stage in the future, these may have to be installed, and the cost will fall on you and the other flat-owners.

As has been said, the preparation of the *acte de vente* is done by the notary, who in his capacity as a recorder of the transaction requires both parties to be present at completion. *They need not be there in person* but each can appoint a representative to attend on his behalf. In the case of a non-French buyer, be he a private individual or a company, this is done by giving a Power of Attorney. There are considerable advantages to this. In the first place, if you are not, or do not want to be, in France at the time of completion, it saves the cost of a special journey. In any event, it is more usual than not to give the date for completion of a sale as 'on or before the . . .'. Fixed completion dates, which are rare, seldom hold good. In part, this is because one is at the mercy of various branches of the Administration which function in their own good time. This is another reason for using an Attorney rather than fixing a visit to France for completion; you will almost certainly arrive too soon or you will have to make what may be an inconvenient journey at very short notice. Secondly, unless you are a fluent French speaker, and one with a reasonable knowledge of legal French, the exercise will be a lengthy mystery to you. Documents are never finalized until actual completion, and a good deal of alteration may be done whilst one waits – and waits. In the country this can be made an excuse to retire for a coffee or a drink but does not lessen the confusion if the buyer has no idea what is going on or is required of him.

Another problem is that what may seem to the Notary a run-of-the-mill problem may not be told to a buyer until he actually reaches completion. This can be true of such things as unexpected rights of way, water and drainage rights, party walls, rental agreements and other things which affect the property. The Notary may assume that you have been told about such things which may well not in fact have been disclosed to you. When faced with this kind of situation for the first time at completion, it is very difficult to know what to do. A suitable Attorney should have already been through the draft *acte de vente* with the Notary and advised you of anything he thinks you ought to know about.

Among other things, he must cope with the lack in the UK and many other countries of *état civil* (see Chapter 10) and particularly in the UK or in any country whose law is based on Anglo-Saxon law, that legal and social puzzle, the lack of the system of community of property on marriage. Some very efficient notaries have been known to have official translators present at completions, whose knowledge of the law of your country is negligible and of its legal language therefore dangerous. This usually results in what, in their absence, at worst, can be a comedy of errors, turning into an extended farce. Your local adviser will prepare for you a Power of Attorney. If you are out of France, it requires signing at a French Consulate in your country (see Appendix A) or before a Notary Public in the UK or the States or his equivalent in other countries. Remember that if you do not sign before a French Consul, the Notary Public's signature must be 'legalized' in the appropriate way by the affixing of the Hague Convention apostille; this is something he should deal with for you. Without this, the Power is valueless in France. If you are in France, you make the Power before a French notary. Supplied with a Power of Attorney and other necessary documents such as (on occasions) birth and marriage certificates and (always) passports or photocopies of passports, completion attended by your attorney becomes a painless experience.

Remember, however, that in France a Power of Attorney is required for each transaction. The Power you give for the purchase cannot normally be used to give instructions to your bank in France for your attorney to obtain the cash for completion. You must give separate instructions to your bank to enable this to occur.

The French very rarely seek the advice of a surveyor when they buy houses or flats. Indeed, the profession of a chartered surveyor does not exist except in the form of the *geomètre* who is literally a measurer of land. Certainly, the contract 'subject to survey' is unknown. There are one or two English surveyors to be found in France – more in Paris then elsewhere but your local adviser probably knows of one. You should always use his services when buying on plan before making your last stage payment and on the purchase of any country property; in fact, you would be well advised to do so on any purchase. You will not lose a property because of the delay before signing a contract and if you are threatened that you will – be even more wary.

It is not essential to have a bank account in France merely to purchase property; it helps immeasurably. The comments on the chapter on banking should be carefully followed.

It is now no longer necessary to impress the purchase price of property with a non-resident source in order to be able freely to export the proceeds of sale of that property in the future.

Whilst in most cases you will certainly benefit from suitable local advice, there are a few very special cases where it is vital to have it, however well you feel you can cope with the system on your own. For example there are schemes for the reduction of French tax liability which are perfectly legal but which involve a knowledge of French law and possibly the law of some third country. Do not be tempted to buy from sellers who have set up such schemes or to create such a scheme yourself without full advice. Remember that French law does not recognize Trusts, and the owner of land registered at the *Bureau des Hypothèques* is, in France, considered to be the beneficial owner for all purposes. Sometimes it is necessary or useful to buy as a trustee or as a nominee for, say, a non-French company. You must be advised as to the effect of doing this before becoming involved in a transaction of this type.

For purchasers from countries where the type of joint ownership exists under which the property bought passes automatically to the survivor on the death of one of the owners (as, for example, in the UK) it is useful to know that this type of ownership also exists in France, although the French themselves rarely use it. In all fairness to the notary, since for legal and social reasons this method of buying is frowned on by the French, it would hardly occur to him to ask a husband and wife if they wished to buy in this way and you may find more than mild disbelief on his face if he is asked to arrange such a purchase. In fact, without a local expert to guide you, you may never succeed but the importance of such an arrangement – and it can be important – is to be found in Chapter 10 under Rules of Succession.

Finally there is the 'under the table' transaction where you will be asked to pay part of the price in cash, and the total price to you will (it will be alleged) be less or, if you will not agree to such a suggestion, the transaction is 'off'. This will usually happen only in the case of 'old' properties because new developments are largely financed by banks, who, of course, monitor the sales prices. Such an arrangement is, of course, designed primarily for the benefit of the seller, either because he wishes to avoid having to disclose to the tax authorities that he has more capital than he has or thinks that he will clinch a deal by reducing for the buyer the stamp duties which all agree are monstrously high. Sellers will, of course, tell you that it is for your benefit because by hiding some of the price you will pay less stamp duty, which is perfectly true and a great temptation when that tax runs normally at the rate of nearly 8%. It can, however, hardly be said that it is a good beginning to living in a country to become involved at the outset in a fiscal fraud. The problem is that such transactions do occur in France, and some notaries and similar people dodge the issue by 'not wanting to know' and so avoid becoming implicated themselves.

The author's considerable experience in dealing with this problem has not helped him find any satisfactory answer to what is basically blackmail and it is absolutely essential that any purchaser to whom an 'under the counter' proposition is made gets advice from his local adviser. It is worth adding that not only do both parties to a conveyance have to certify that the sale price shown in it represents all the money passing from buyer to seller, but, if the authorities think that the price is a fraudulent undervalue, they can seek to 'upgrade it'. They can also exercise the right during a period of six months from the date of sale to 'buy in' the property at the price shown in the conveyance plus 10%. How easy then is it likely to be to get back the 'black' cash paid by the buyer to the seller, of which there is no record? This is because there is no way that any Court will support a fraudulent transaction, and the honesty of a seller who has proposed this method of payment must remain in doubt. That right is not frequently used but, when it is, it is amazing how (for a short period) disclosed sale prices increase. Many estate agents will and, to the author's certain knowledge, do tell foreigners that it is buyers who are responsible for this method of cheating the French tax authorities – Swiss bank accounts, Bahamas, Channel Island companies etc. Do not accept this. In many cases, the suggestion does come from the seller. The best thing the author can do is quote the heartfelt cry of a leading Notary on the Côte d'Azur that it is both untrue and unfair to assume that simply because much of the French property sold to foreigners is in the south that therefore the sellers are fraudulent. That goes for all parts of France and basically the story that every transaction in France is done at an undervalue (or even many of them) is a myth.

The cost of buying property is dealt with in Appendix F. It is intended as a rough guide only, and the only safe rule is to ask the right person at the outset what the costs of any particular transaction will be.

Having successfully completed the purchase of your property, do not forget that every home needs water, telephone, electricity and possibly gas and insurance. A guide to the 'link-up' costs of these utilities and some useful hints will be found in Chapters 15 and 19, which merits careful study if you wish to avoid any surprises.

There is less to say about selling property, but what there is is important. You must observe the rules about agents you intend to employ, which you will find earlier in this chapter and in Chapters 6 and 7. It is always wise to get local advice about the standing of the agent you intend to use. See Appendix F as to the commission a seller may pay. It is not true that the buyer is liable for commission. What sometimes occurs is that the agent asks the seller whether the sale price he hopes for is before or after payment of commission and if the answer is 'after', the agent will, if he thinks it will stand it, then increase the selling price wholly or partially to include the commission. But it is still the seller who pays the commission out of what he receives. What is unfortunate for the buyer is that this increase of price, which does not represent any property value, carries stamp duties etc. as part of the price he is paying. It is difficult to get round this problem. You will not know what to do but your experienced local adviser may be able to hive the commission from the price.

As you will have seen from the procedure on the buying of property, your sale contract would normally be drawn up by the agent you have chosen to deal with the sale. On the whole you would be advised to get this document prepared by your local adviser, who will decide whether it should be an informal document or a formal one made before a *notaire*. Whilst on a sale the choice of *notaire* is less important than on a purchase, you are well advised to insist on your own *notaire* acting for you (i.e. the one who acted for you on the purchase), and this must go in the contract. If this is inconvenient for you, ask your local adviser to recommend you to another *notaire*, but you must be able to hand him a copy of your *acte de vente* or at least give him the name of the previous *notaire* acting for you and the date of purchase. Take note of the following important practical points:

1. Normally, you will not get the proceeds of the sale for quite some time. Some notaries pay out in about fourteen days or even less but some not until registration of the sale has been completed. There are technical reasons for this – strange to the UK seller who is used to getting the proceeds of sale from his solicitor on the day of the sale or at least on the following day but quite acceptable to the French who are used to it. In theory, it is possible to sell in the morning and use the proceeds to buy in the afternoon but the chain of transactions, so usual in the UK, is not known in France and the suggestion of such a transaction will almost certainly be met with a refusal. It would involve enormous organization on the part of all the notaries involved and they are simply not prepared or able to cope with it. Besides, as has been said, completion dates provided for in contracts are very seldom adhered to. What do the French do? Few are anxious to take out bridging loans (see page 155). They stay with mother during the intervening period or add to their expenses by staying in a hotel. Incidentally, the *notaire* save to a minimal extent does not get interest on the proceeds of sale held by him; nor do you. The French state does.

2. On a sale service charges are apportioned by the *syndic* (see Chapter 8) and anything due to the *copropriété* on the

date of sale will be retained by the *notaire* and paid over. You must therefore be prepared to tell the *notaire* if you agree the amount said to be due. Remember that, if you are paying on account of the current year's service charge, there is just a possibility that you will have overpaid and there is a refund due to you.

3. *Taxe d'habitation* is a personal tax and is not apportionable on a sale. The burden rests with the person who was in occupation on the 1st January in the year of the sale. *Taxe foncière* is a tax charged on property and is technically apportionable on a sale. In practice, the results of such an apportionment seldom apply – at least in the case of non-French sellers.

4. Read with the utmost care the comments on Capital Gains Tax and TVA (insofar as it relates to property) which you will find in Chapter 14. You could be in for some nasty shocks if these comments are only relayed to you on the day of completion.

CHAPTER 6

Renting Property

In 1981, the Socialists, full of the joys of being the first left-wing government returned to power for a number of years, produced a number of laws which in 1986 the right-wing government on its election promptly altered. One such socialist measure was a Landlord and Tenant Act – la Loi Quillot, named after the Minister who was responsible for it – which introduced wholesale rent control and security of tenure for tenants where previously such protection had applied to only a very small section of rented property. It must be admitted that that part of the Law which dealt with the granting of leases and their contents was a not unwelcome innovation. It had been, and doubtless will remain, the custom in France to push printed forms of leases under the noses of would-be tenants on a take-it-or-leave-it basis and it was (and indeed still is) extremely rare for lawyers ever to be involved in the granting of leases of private dwellings. This is virtually always done by the estate agents.

That part of the Law which controlled rents and made it difficult for landlords ever to get rid of their tenants was destined to produce just such results as exist in the United Kingdom, where landlords are inhibited from letting their property and would-be tenants, unless they are foreign diplomats, visiting professors or companies, are frustrated in their search for accommodation to rent. Indeed, it did produce those results and it became extremely difficult to find houses or flats to rent other than for very short holiday periods.

It is interesting to remember that living in an *immeuble* or block of flats has been a well-established habit in France for nearly three hundred years, long before it became fashionable or convenient elsewhere in Europe. The mushroom development of flats in cities and large towns which took place throughout Europe in the twenties and thirties took place in France well before the First World War. Although there is a trend towards ownership, not far short of one half of the population of France lives in rented accommodation. Moreover, the letting of flats by individuals as a form of investment is still a common hedge against the day of retirement and it was, therefore, more the control of rents imposed by the Loi Quillot than the security of tenure for tenants which appalled the French. Although companies do build blocks for letting, the fact that so many landlords are private individuals results in a massive 'absentee landlordism' with the management of flats and houses which are let by agents, whose quality is rather more variable than it should be. So it is that a tenant normally has contact only with his landlord's agent, who is invariably on time with his demands for rent but seldom interested in his tenant's problems. Remember that the French landlord, like every other Frenchman, is very conscious of his rights but less of his obligations and arguments between landlord and tenant are best avoided. Hence, as has been said, many of the provisions of the Loi Quillot which have been left unaltered by the new Loi Méhaignerie are undoubtedly of benefit to the tenant.

The problem now is that the letting of flats is currently governed by two laws – the Loi Quillot for leases granted before 23rd December 1986 and the Loi Méhaignerie for leases granted after that date. Inevitably, there are transitional provisions which apply to the renewal of Loi Quillot leases but in the interests of simplicity this chapter deals with leases under the current law, except where specific reference is made to the old Loi Quillot.

The Law applies to lettings of private dwellings and lettings but not to 'holiday lettings', furnished lettings, sub-lettings and a few other types of lettings, which, with the possible exception of garages or parking-spaces let separately from a dwelling-house by a different landlord, are not likely to interest you. The definition of a 'holiday letting' is somewhat obscure. Originally it was thought that it should not in any event exceed three months, but a French Court of Appeal decision has said that essentially to be a 'holiday letting', the tenant must have a principal place of residence elsewhere. Hence, if you have come to France for good but sensibly have decided that before buying anything you would like some time to look around, you may find it difficult to get a 'holiday let'. It may be useful to be prepared to produce with confidence a non-French address as still being your 'home'.

All the provisions of the Law are *d'ordre public*, that is to say there is no answer to a failure to abide by them and the parties to a lease are not able by consent to 'contract out' and agree to other arrangements.

The basic rules as to the contents of a lease are as follows:

1. The lease must be in writing but need not be a notarial document. However, if the lease is not in writing, it is not void but either party can insist that it is reduced to writing.

2. Every lease must contain a full description of the premises let, its permitted user, a list of fittings and fixtures of which the tenant has the exclusive use and of those of which he has the use in common with others, the date of the commencement of the lease, the rent and any provisions for its review and the times of payment of the rent.

3. If there is a rent review clause, this can take effect only once a year and the rent revision is linked to the Cost of Construction Index. As a matter of interest, this Index which stood at 100 at the end of 1956, was 821 at the end of 1984 and 929 in October 1989. A rent receipt is not obligatory but must be supplied to a tenant at his request.

4. The tenant may not be required to pay his rent by direct debit or by providing promissory notes payable at future dates. Provided that rent is not payable in advance at more than two-monthly intervals, the landlord may ask for a deposit equal to two months rent. Such a deposit must be returned within two months of the end of the lease less any amount properly due to the landlord.

5. In addition to rent, the tenant may (and normally will)

be required to pay what will usually be a large proportion of the landlord's service charges and local Rates and a small tax on leases, known as *droit de bail*. Service charges are normally paid by fixing a monthly sum on account and once a year there will be an adjustment supported by extracts from the service charge accounts which the landlord will receive as *copropriétaire* (see Chapter 8).

6. Certain provisions are illegal and, if inserted in a lease, are unenforceable. Thus, no tenant can be required to insure with a company of the choice of the landlord, though he may be under an obligation to insure (see Chapter 15). A tenant may not be required to give inspection of his property except during a period of two hours on working days. A lease may provide for forfeiture for non-payment of rent or service charges or failure to insure but not for breach of any other obligation.

7. If the property let is a flat in a building owned *en copropriété*, the landlord must give to the tenant certain details of the *règlement de copropriété*.

8. All costs of the granting of a lease are to be shared equally by landlord and tenant.

9. Tenants must '*user paisiblement*' their flat or house – a phrase which sounds too charming in French to translate and which must be readily understandable to even the poorest speaker of French. They must, of course, respect the user clauses. The landlord must give quiet enjoyment and is responsible for keeping the premises in a state suitable for the purposes for which they are let. They are also liable for defects other than those caused by the tenant in carrying out works agreed to by the landlord. On the other hand, a tenant is responsible for 'tenants' repairs' which basically relate to the proper use of the premises for the purposes for which it was let, other than those made necessary by reason of the age of or inherent vices in the building, accident or *force majeure*.

10. Leases are unassignable without the consent of the landlord but there is no obligation on his part to give this. Sub-letting also requires the consent of the landlord who is

entitled to know the rent under the sub-lease. Sub-leases are not governed by the Loi Méhaignerie.

There is one very important point, which has also been changed by the new Law. Under pre-1987 leases, it was obligatory to have a Schedule of Condition (*Etat des Lieux*) prepared at the beginning of every letting and annexed to the lease. Now, this is no longer obligatory but if this is not done by agreement, either party may require one to be prepared by a *huissier* (see below) at the joint cost of both parties. If none is in fact prepared and annexed to the lease, the landlord cannot at the end of the term, claim that the premises were in a good state of repair at the commencement of the lease. It cannot be overemphasized how essential it is from a tenant's point of view to have this Schedule prepared before taking possession.

In connection generally with the repairing liabilities of landlords and tenants of flats, a good deal of confusion arises because much which falls within the liability of a landlord is the ultimate responsibility of the *copropriété* of the block. Water streams through the ceiling of the top floor flat damaging not only the ceiling, walls and floor but also the tenant's effects. When approached, the landlord will probably try to fob-off the tenant with the suggestion that he get in touch with the *syndic* of the block who will repair the roof and pay for the redecorations and damage to the tenant's furniture. Do not agree to this. Certainly, the ultimate liability, i.e. to the landlord is that of the *copropriété* (in which the landlord will share), but the tenant has no standing whatsoever with the *syndic* and should insist on enforcing the direct landlord/tenant liability arising under the lease. The landlord will also try to persuade the tenant to claim under his own policy which again is not the proper course of action (see Chapter 15). In fact, the landlord will do all he can to calm his tenant whilst avoiding the outlay of any cash to achieve this. Do not agree to any such manoeuvres and insist on your rights directly against the landlord. If the damage suffered is more than minimal, it may well be worthwhile calling in a *huissier* to make a *constat*. A *huissier* who, among other things, acts as a Bailiff and Process Server, will also prepare reports on various situations such as accidents or damage done to property. Since these reports are considered by the Courts to be incontrovertible, to have one made at an early date effectively prevents landlords from denying the extent of damage for which they are liable, whilst the threat of having one made, often spurs a landlord into action.

It remains to consider perhaps the most important points – the length of your lease, the circumstances in which you can renew your lease and in which the landlord can get you out. Here the Laws differ considerably and both are complicated. If you have doubts about your rights and obligations, then consult your local adviser. Briefly, the position is as follows:

Under the new Law

1. No lease may be granted for an indefinite period and it must be for a minimum period of three years. During that period, the landlord cannot obtain possession except, of course, for the reasons mentioned above.

2. There is one exception to this rule. A lease may be for less than three years if the landlord is a private individual and by agreement the lease contains a provision enabling him to retake possession before the end of the three years (but not before the end of the first year) for 'family or professional reasons' e.g. to provide a home for his daughter who is going to be married. If that happy event takes place as intended, the tenant must go, but if someone has 'been left in the lurch waiting at the church', the landlord may, if his daughter's prospects are still bright, once but only once carry forward the date for possession.

3. At the end of the three-year term, either the tenant is 'out' and the landlord is 'in' or the term is renewed for another three years. If the landlord is prepared to renew the lease, he must serve a notice with the new terms at least six months before the end of the lease. If the tenant accepts these terms

or other terms are negotiated by agreement, the tenant must accept at least three months before the lease comes to an end; failure to keep to this time limit is taken as accepting a notice to quit.

4. A tenant may at any time during the lease give it up provided that he gives three months' notice of his intention or, in the case of a change or loss of employment or if over 60 and for reasons of health, one month's notice only.

5. If neither landlord nor tenant do anything within the time limits imposed, the original lease is taken as having been renewed for a further three years at the same rent and on the same terms.

Under the old Law

1. Leases, depending on a number of circumstances, were for a minimum of three or six years. Their rents were controlled.

2. Assuming that such leases come to an end normally, new leases of the same property will, of course, be dealt with under the new Law. However, there are two special transitional provisions. In the case of leases of property in conurbations of more than 1 million inhabitants, these will apply until 1995; in smaller places, the date is 1991.

3. If an old Law lease comes to an end during the transitional period, the landlord may by a six months' notice propose a rent fixed by reference to rents of other similar properties in the neighbourhood during the last three years. If the tenant agrees, a new lease is entered into at that rent but its effect is spread by equal instalments over three years. If the tenant does not agree, either party can put the case to a local Tribunal which will propose a new rent and if the parties do not agree this rent, the rent is finally fixed by the Court. Any increase over the old rent is also spread over three years.

4. The old Law gave landlords certain special facilities to obtain possession. These are now limited. He may do so, if he or close members of his family want to live there. He may

also do so if he wishes to sell the property but in this case, the tenant has the right to offer to buy the property and to ensure that if the terms are offered to him were unacceptable, the landlord, having obtained possession, does not sell elsewhere on easier terms. In neither case can these rights be exercised if the tenant is aged more than seventy and in receipt of less than a certain income unless the landlord finds the tenant suitable alternative accommodation or is himself aged over sixty.

If you are properly advised at the outset, so that you know exactly what your rights and liabilities are as a tenant, there is no reason why you should not be the contented tenant of a contented landlord. You simply must not expect to find that the law is the same as it would be at home and get hot under the collar when you are caught out. Perhaps most important of all, you should keep strictly to two rules. Make a friend of your *concierge*; this applies to owners as well as tenants. If your French is not up to animated conversation, do the best you can. She knows all that goes on and much that does not; it is in her power to make life hell for you or smooth over many of your problems. Legislation has given the *concierge* at least a day and a half off every week and she will normally take from Saturday midday to Monday morning. Do not expect to get anything out of her during that period. The cost of protection from – or, if you prefer, the way to the heart of – your *concierge* usually runs to about 400 to 500 francs at Christmas (whisky is 'in' and much appreciated) and unending patience listening to all her woes when she buttonholes you as often as she can in the entrance hall of the block.

The second rule which cannot be too often repeated is that all communications in France, to whomever they may be sent, from your landlord's agent to the President of the Republic, must go by registered AR post. No letter sent by ordinary mail ever arrives because the recipient knows that you cannot prove that you sent it. This is one of the sadder aspects of the French character, which is assiduously nourished by a grateful Post Office.

CHAPTER 7

Letting Property

There is undoubtedly a market in France for furnished lettings on a short-term basis. The season (in the south) runs from about the middle of April to about the middle of October, but it is not unusual to find people who take their holidays at other times. Read very carefully what is said in Chapter 6 on holiday lettings and if you are in any doubt, get advice. The first decision to make is how you are going to find your tenants. To some extent, clearly this is a matter for personal preference, but the following comments should be of assistance.

1. You can advertise in newspapers at home, which will normally restrict your tenants to residents of your own country. *The Herald Tribune* is a useful international paper. For UK residents, the Sunday papers, local papers with wide circulations such as the *Yorkshire Post* and magazines such as *The Lady* have produced good results. The advantage of tenants from your own country is that you are going to meet them yourself and make your own judgement whether they will prove to be satisfactory. You can take your rent in advance – and a deposit for breakages and other expenses which the tenant should bear – but, of course, you will have no one in France to check these tenants out, read the electricity meters, see what the position is about the telephone (see Chapter 18), ensure that the flat is clean for the next tenant and that everything that ought to have been left behind has been left behind. How serious this may prove to be depends on the tenants you have, and many will be admirable and come again and again without any trouble. It is a dangerous rule to follow that all your tenants will behave as well as you

would. If you want to find out what rent you should charge, which depends of course on the month in which you are letting, you have only to phone a local agent, describe to him your own flat and ask what sort of a rent you should pay if he could find you one similar for the desired months. Be fairly precise about the locality, whether you are '*pieds dans l'eau*' or overlooking 'le golf' in an expensive area. You will not need to add anything on to the rents he quotes, for to you, a prospective tenant, he is quoting the highest he dare.

2. You use the services of a French agent. This has the advantage of catching the tenants who do not read your country's papers and the vast number of searchers for flats as well as holiday-makers who are possibly booking up for next year or have come early to book for later in the year and do not live in your home country. It is evident that you will, of course, have to pay the French agents' commission, which will be in the region of 10% to 15%. The current scales appear in Appendix F. Some agents will, as part of that commission, 'manage' the flat for you, see tenants in and out, see that all is clean, deal with laundry (if unadvisedly you do not require your tenants to bring their own linen, towels etc.), have breakages mended, read meters and cope with unsatisfactory tenants. Some agents will tell you that they will do this and do not do it. Some are not prepared to undertake this task at all. However, the real disadvantage is that all rents which a French agent collects ought to go through his books and may well get paid into your French bank account, where there is a record for all to see of these rents. It is worthwhile considering if this is desirable.

3. There are international agencies who deal with the letting of properties on a worldwide basis. Commission varies from agency to agency, but the rents they collect will be paid to you out of France or wherever you wish. However, most of them suffer from the disadvantage that they will not provide services in France so that, from that aspect, it is as though you were letting from your own country. Be careful also with some of these agencies. Many book on a deposit only, so that you think you have a summer full of bookings, only to find

that would-be tenants are prepared to lose their deposits and at the last moment you have a gap of unoccupied weeks. Equally, because some have a very wide net, they can find tenants at the last moment, when you or local agents cannot.

4. The management of certain blocks of flats, particularly those who sell flats in the block 'on time', offer a letting service. It is up to you whether you use their services. Much should depend on whether you are satisfied with the way the block is run, for which you pay service charges, and whether you think that they are more interested in their commission than in your rent. In the most general terms, this is perhaps the least satisfactory way of letting.

5. Finally, there are a number of individuals or small organizations, of non-French origin or non-French based with representation in France, who will undertake to deal with the management of your property during your absence. This may run to a total looking after your flat or house or may be limited to finding tenants for you and doing all the things which you would do if you were on the spot every time a tenant came in and left. Obviously, you can find your own tenants as well, so long as you do not let the dates clash with those which have been found for you. All rents collected will be paid to you wherever you want, and there is very little doubt that in many cases this is the best way to deal with your lettings.

Unfortunately, it is not very easy to find these organizations and people. The best method of contacting these 'managers' is either through your local adviser or your local national association (see Appendix B) or your bank in France (see Chapter 13). In any event, you would be ill-advised to entrust the letting of your flat to anyone without first checking their *bona fides*. Mediterranean Property Owners Association (see Chapter 8) is one of the organizations which can undertake or arrange for this kind of management.

It is, of course, possible to let on a long-term basis, both furnished and unfurnished. In any area where there is a tourist season, rents are naturally lower out of season, and therefore any letting which covers both in and out of season will not command the inflated rents which can be charged to the tourist. Such periods will almost inevitably not qualify as 'holiday lettings', and you may well feel that the risks involved (see Chapter 6) are too serious to contemplate. When thinking of letting your house or flat, please trust no one but a competent adviser in France.

If none of this deters you, it is almost inevitable that you do come in touch with a local estate agent to find you a tenant. There are more of these in France than there are pubs in the UK (particularly in the south) and they are not only at street corners. One wonders how they all make a living, and, indeed, it needs only a slump in the property market for them to go out of business like flies. Whilst they are all required to be 'qualified' and those who handle clients' money are required to effect Fidelity Bonds, do not consult any without first enquiring carefully as to their competence and trust-worthiness. A long let implies that the agent you instruct will be managing your house or flat. In very general terms, do not use the agents who manage the block and advertise that half the fun of buying a flat is the income you can get from it. They are not usually suitable for the task you have in mind. An additional safeguard is, as usual, the friendly *concierge*.

Watch extremely carefully what happens to any deposit cheque to cover breakages, telephone, electricity etc. given to a French agent by your tenant. It is common for agents to put them in a drawer and not pay them unless at the end of the tenancy it is necessary to use them and if it is not, to give them back to the tenant. This is unlawful and can lead to unfortunate results to your detriment. Insist that the cheque is in your favour and paid in immediately.

A true story may not be out of place. It is profoundly significant, well outside the bounds of this chapter. An English lady had a flat, previously let and which became vacant shortly after the *Loi Quillot* came into effect. She was warned of the possible problems if she relet it. "That's all right," she said. "I would only let it to an English tenant, and he would go whenever I asked him to." There seems a possibility that it is not only the British who are sentimental about their fellow nationals.

CHAPTER 8

The Condominium

The system of *copropriété* or condominium is not unique to France. It is common in certain parts of the United States and in certain other European countries but it is to all intents and purposes unknown in Great Britain. Virtually every foreigner will acquire his flat and sometimes also his house in France as a *copropriétaire*. An older system, which involved the buying of shares in a company which owns a block of flats and where the ownership of the shares gives the right to occupy a flat in the block, is nowadays rarely used, and it is the system of *copropriété* which prevails all over France. The effects of the system are, to some extent, social as well as legal because they bring the co-owners together into a group in which it is desirable that they all get on well with one another and that they all pull their weight as co-owners. The present law on *copropriété* was laid down in detail in 1965 and subsequently added to in 1967 and 1985 and it helps to be conversant with the pecularities of the French system.

In Britain and in other countries where flats are bought on long leases, whatever arrangements are made about the maintenance of the block as a whole and the payment of a service charge to cover the cost of that maintenance and the provision of amenities, the block itself does not belong to you and the other flat-owners in the block. You pay rent to a landlord, and it is between him and you that the link exists which deals with what you may and may not do in the flat and the block and how, apart from keeping in his good books, you are constrained from annoying your neighbours and they from annoying you. Sometimes the landlord himself will deal with the maintenance of the block and collect the service charge, and sometimes he will pass this task over to a company which belongs to him. There is also the method of making all the flat-owners shareholders of a company and making the company responsible for keeping the block in good order when it receives the service charges. But in no case are the flat-owners directly themselves personally owners, not only of their own flats but also of the whole building. On the contrary, in France this is precisely the result of owning a flat *en copropriété*.

It is very unlikely that you have not at some time or other had service charge problems. Laws in various countries designed to protect tenants from service charge abuses show how difficult a problem service charges can be. Basically, you will have the same sort of problems in France, but the difference is that at home, many of you may be members of a tenants' association keeping a statutory wary eye on the landlord or his managing agents; in France your eye is on yourself and your neighbours and the managing agent appointed by your own side – the *copropriété*.

The *copropriété*, made up as it is by all the owners of the flats in a block, owns that part of the block which is not within the definition of 'a flat'. Basically it owns the main structure, foundations, roof, land on which the block is built and all parts of the block and its surroundings which are used in common by all flat-owners – approach roads, gardens, lifts, drains, gutters, swimming-pools and tennis courts and any other amenity which the developer has wanted to provide. The *copropriété* functions through a *syndicat*, which is made up of all the owners in a block. It is not a company and not a partnership but which has a legal life of its own, and the *syndicat* itself can only function through a *syndic*.

Here again, there is another important practical difference in the French system. Over the years, there has grown up in France the profession of the *syndic*, whose sole job is to manage blocks of flats and similar property. He is seldom a qualified surveyor with experience of problems in fields wider than just the management of blocks of flats. Of course, there are *syndics* who are excellent at their work, but the word *syndic* has acquired the same sort of reaction from his audience as has the music hall mother-in-law and tends to be greeted by howls of rage or moans of despair. As usual, climatic conditions have their effect, and the warmer the weather, the less efficient the *syndic*. What is curious is that although many French flat-owners are anti-*syndic*, only quite a small proportion seem to attend meetings of the *syndicat* and express their opinions in public. Perhaps this is a good thing, for it is not unknown for blows to be exchanged at meetings, and some have ended with an unexpected swim in the pool for the *syndic* and a number of irate *copropriétaires*. Luckily, there are fewer pools in the north than on the Côte d'Azur. It is in fact the rule rather than the exception that a quorum fails to attend meetings, which then have to be adjourned to a later date when those then present form the quorum. The temper of those who do attend such meetings (often at awkward hours on awkward days) can be gauged from the not uncommon practice of prolonging the totally abortive proceedings merely to argue fiercely why there was no quorum.

It is not only blocks of flats which are owned *en copropriété*. A development of houses in a *lotissement* or estate will obviously have a number of things used in common by all the house-owners. The roads on the estate, the drainage system, swimming-pools and tennis courts will all belong to the owners of the houses *en copropriété*, but clearly the service charges will relate to many less expenses and therefore be much lower, though the problems may be just as tricky. The faulty installation of the main drainage system affects all the houses and needs a concerted effort on the part of all the house-owners, through the *syndic*, to have it repaired. Since often many of the houses are occupied only on a part-time basis throughout the year, absent owners do not make for pressure on the *syndic* and the rectification of leaking drains or dirty swimming-pools.

You should not imagine that the system does not work, but how well it works and what surprises you get depend on how well you and your co-owners know your rights and liabilities.

The rules and regulations for the use of your flat and what may and what may not be done in your block are contained in the *règlement de copropriété*. It also contains all there is to know about the functioning of the *syndicat* and, on the face of it, is a formidable document. The real problem is that, whilst in countries where the lawyer acting for you would do more than just prepare the purchase document, all that is in the *règlement de copropriété* would be given to your lawyer before you signed any contract and be digested by him and explained to you, in France this does not happen. French law requires that every conveyance (but not every contract) on the purchase of property bought *en copropriété* must contain a statement that the buyer has had prior notice of the *règlement de copropriété*, and such a statement results in his being bound by its contents. It is extremely unlikely that any *bureau de vente* will provide you with a copy before you sign a contract to buy, and although you are undoubtedly in order to refuse to sign the conveyance if a copy has not been given to you a reasonable time in advance, unless you have a good knowledge of French language and law, reading through its many pages will not give much reassurance. This is one of the important things your local adviser will deal with for you.

Règlements de copropriété vary very much in length, depending on whether you are left to read the laws of 10th July 1965 and 17th March 1967 or whether many of their clauses are set out in detail. Normally, however, this document will contain:

1. A statement of the numbers of your *lots*. These will refer to your flat, garage, cellar and anything else included in the property you buy which becomes your personal private property. The numbers do not always tally with the number of your flat or garages and are usually taken from the developer's original plan. Each *lot* will have a *quote-part* given to it, which is usually shown as a fraction of round numbers, such as ten thousand or a hundred thousand, and tells you the proportionate part of the *copropriété* which you own. The calculation has been done at an early stage of the development based on the value your *lots* bear to the whole *copropriété*,

taking into account the area and situation of your *lots* in the block but not the use to which they are put. Your proportion of service charges is based on your *quote-parts*, and they also tell you how many votes you have at meetings of the *syndicat*.

2. A list of general and special expenses relating to the management and maintenance of the block. You will find that whilst your *quote-part* fraction applies to general expenses, a different fraction may apply to special expenses. This is because not all flat-owners have or need the same amenities, such as the use of a lift (if your flat is on the ground floor), and therefore these special expenses are shared out only by those who actually use them. In this way, you will see what are the items comprised in your service charge.

3. There will be rules for the collection of the service charge. They are usually collected twice or three times a year on account and adjusted when the annual accounts have been passed by the *syndicat*. Perhaps not unexpectedly, there is a tendency to overcharge for payments on account, and overpayments are carried forward to the next year as credits.

4. Rules and regulations applying to the use of your flat and to the common parts of the block will be set out. On the whole they tend to be reasonable but unusual provisions do turn up. Strangely, it is rare to find any prohibition against keeping animals in a flat without the *syndicat*'s consent, which is common enough in some other countries. To redress the balance, let it be said that the French are great 'abandoners' of their pets, particularly when they go on their extended summer holidays. Many flats may be used for professional purposes, which includes the right to have a nameplate in the entrance hall or outside the building.

5. Your obligations towards the *copropriété* as a whole and your co-owners will be set out, and on the whole these need careful study.

6. The regulations for the meetings of the *syndicat*, when meetings are held and who may call them, what things may be dealt with at meetings and how you vote, together with a lot of other administrative provisions are all spelled out in some detail.

A vineyard in La Marne

Returning from the *boulangerie*

Market day at Crémieu in the Rhône Valley

7. The precise powers of the *syndic*, how he is appointed – and removed – and the control which the *syndicat* has over him are explained, as are his duties and how he must prepare and render his accounts.

8. The insurance cover effected by the *copropriété* for its own benefit will be indicated. This is a very important point which, if not fully understood, can lead to disappointments. This is dealt with in Chapter 15 on Insurance.

9. In some cases, there will be special rules about letting, selling, leaving the flat unoccupied for any length of time and certain other situations, included at the whim of either the developer or his *notaire* or possibly inserted by the *syndicat* from experience.

There are generally no rules which forbid letting, for if there were, no one would buy. However, it is essential that every tenant be made aware of all these rules and regulations (see Chapter 6), although in the case of very short lettings this may not be so important. Nevertheless, it is worth remembering that the tenant of a co-owner can be sued directly by the *copropriété*, although there is no direct relationship between them. By the same token, a tenant can sue the *copropriété* if it fails to do what it is liable to you to do and which a tenant is entitled to expect from you (see also page 83).

The guarantees you get from a developer are mentioned in Chapter 5 on 'Buying and Selling Homes'. It is unlikely that you will be the only one in a block to suffer from some defect which affects only your flat, wholly within your 'private' area. It is much more probable that such a defect will be in the structure or the drains or in some part of the block which belongs to the *copropriété*. Defects do not abound, but they exist, and it is here that the *syndicat* can really come into its own and all co-owners ought to play their parts. Many *syndics* are appointed by the developer at an early stage so that the administrative set-up exists as soon as the first sale takes place. It follows that it may be irksome for a *syndic*, who should be the creature of the *copropriété*, to pursue a developer to whom he owes his job. There are special procedures for prodding *syndics* who are dilatory, and in smaller blocks it is now becoming quite common for one of the flat-owners, who is possibly a retired civil servant and therefore particularly well qualified for the task because of the peculiar outlook of the French *fonctionnaire*, to take on the job of *syndic*. It is also a good sign if the *syndic* happens to live in the block even if he is a professional or, as is sometimes the case, if he 'receives' regularly in some office in the block.

No one can accurately estimate service charges for a new block, and sellers of 'old' flats notoriously lie about them. It is wise to assume that selling agents and *bureaux de vente* will underestimate. What is essential is to make certain that on the one hand you get what you are asked to pay for and on the other that you do not pay too much for what you do get.

A word is necessary about heating and water charges. There is now a tendency for new flats to be heated individually. This is highly desirable, since it avoids your having to share in central heating costs in a block in which you may only be living occasionally – and in seasons when you do not need heating. Water is not charged for by a standing charge or water rate but by the amount consumed. The custom is for the *syndic* to agree with the water company at the beginning of every year the probable amount of cold water which will be consumed in the whole block and for that amount to be available at a specially low rate. If that agreed amount is exceeded, a penal rate is charged for the excess. A careful watch should be kept on the *syndic*, since all depends on the accuracy of his estimate. Hot water is charged either by adding an amount per cubic metre consumed by each flat-owner to cover the cost of heating the cold water or is split out among the flats on a *quote-part* basis irrespective of the amount consumed and naturally this cost increases every year. Some flats have individual hot water systems, which is also a good thing. Otherwise in blocks which are only partly occupied or occupied mainly as *résidences secondaires* the cost of heating water from a central source to occupied flats is increased because there is so much cold space through which the pipes must pass.

One cannot guarantee the quality of management, and in the long run the *copropriété* gets what it deserves by keeping the *syndic* on his toes. Do not sit and suffer either at the hands of the *syndic* or at the hands of one or two of your neighbours, and to do this you must be properly advised on what your rights are. The correct method of communication with the *syndic* is by registered AR letter, not only because the law frequently requires it but because it is the only way you have of proving that you wrote at all. The *syndic* is as liable to dodge problems by failing to receive a letter as is any other office or organization in France.

The need for specialized help with service charges, *syndics* and the problems which can arise in connection with ownership *en copropriété*, has led to the formation of Mediterranean Property Owners Association (see Appendix B) with fully qualified representation in France, which will, for an annual fee, take these burdens from your shoulders. Thus, whether you are in residence or away from your flat, you can always get advice. It will act as your proxy and represent you at meetings of the *copropriété* and in dealings with the *syndic*, and you may well find that this is an effective and not expensive answer to any worries you may have or fear you will have.

CHAPTER 9

Time-sharing

Time-sharing first appeared in France in 1967 under the name of *multipropriété*. Since then, this method of 'ownership' has been sold under such varied names as *spacio-temporelle-, tri-, poly-, inter-, pluri-* and *time-propriété*. Some who advertise this type of 'ownership' are more scrupulous than others and refer to *multijouissance* or *multivacances*, but the magical word used or implied is always *'propriété'* or 'ownership'. Typical sales prospectuses will tell you "Without touching your capital, you can become the owner of a flat" or "Remember you are buying a real right of ownership which your children can inherit", but the print which adds "And yet your flat will cost you only a fraction of what full ownership would cost you" tends to be several sizes smaller.

The social background to time-sharing is by now well recognized. Many people like to feel that they too have a second home (and abroad) but cannot afford its all-year-round use. In any case, they may well want to use it for only a few weeks in every year – in summer for the sun or in winter for the snow. The idea is an excellent one in theory. How excellent it is in practice, is another matter.

Since the appearance of time-sharing in France, the lawyers have been much concerned at the very vague legal arrangements which can be used to grant the right to occupy a flat for a given period of time in every year. This is the position where there is a block of flats wholly given over to time-sharing but it is far more obscure when the seller of time-shares himself only owns a few flats in a building which is otherwise occupied by ordinary flat-owners who are *copropriétaires*. However, early in 1986 an attempt was made to clarify the legal situation, although it is difficult to see whether it can do much to help.

It seems likely that anyone who already owns a time-share in a flat will not be affected by the new law and it is by no means obligatory for new time-share sales to make use of the new arrangements. Hence, existing time-sharing owners and those who buy under the old scheme must realize that what they have bought or are buying does not give *pleine propriété* (full ownership) of anything. You own a *'jouissance'* which is no more than a personal right to occupy the flat at certain times in the year. It is therefore not a right registrable at the equivalent of the Land Registry in France and is no more than a contract between you and the person or company granting the right and in French law is of no value against third parties. The right is therefore not an immovable, is not treated as land and will pass under your Will according to the law of your domicile. In France, you will almost inevitably be a sort of licensee of a person who himself is a *copropriétaire* of a flat in a block. You and probably twenty-five other people are therefore involved in a flat in which the 'full owner' is himself involved as a co-owner with all the other co-owners of flats in the block. There are problems enough in blocks of flats where no time-sharing is involved. It requires little imagination to see how wrong things could go when you, as a time-sharer, have no rights against the owners of the other flats.

The new law envisages the formation of a *société civile*, which is not a limited company and really has no equivalent in English or other Anglo-Saxon legal systems, which will sell shares giving the right to occupy a flat in the building which it owns for certain periods during each year. There is a slight advantage over the old system in that although the right to occupy the flat is still only a *jouissance*, in addition you own the shares which give that right and through those shares you will have a say in the management of your and all the other flats occupied on a time-sharing basis. In fact, the arrangement is very much like that of *copropriété* described in Chapter 8, in the sense that all the time-sharers in the block can appoint

Managing Agents of their choice and can dismiss them. Each time-sharer can vote at meetings of the company and has as many votes as his flat and period(s) of occupation give him. Thus, presumably, a big flat gives more votes than a small one and two time-sharing periods in a year or one longer one will give more votes than one short period. Each time-sharer will pay a proportion of the total cost of managing the block in which is the flat in which he has a time-share.

It will be seen that, under this system, as under the *copropriété* system of the full ownership of flats, it is highly desirable to be present or be represented at company meetings and it is understood that in view of this change in the law, Mediterranean Property Owners Association (see Appendix B) has extended its activities to act as representatives of owners of time-shares in France.

However, not much imagination is required to realize that even if there were no legal problems in time-sharing, its pleasure depends to a very large extent on the quality of management of the flat you are occupying. Periods of occupation seldom give more than a day between occupants, and all must be cleaned, swept, changed and replaced where necessary before you move in. Not all time-sharers are as neat, tidy and well behaved as you are. What will you do if 'your' flat is not ready for you when you arrive? What happens if there is a fire or flood? What are your rights in respect of the common parts of the block (which include the main structure and not just the gardens and the swimming-pool) when the 'owner' of the flat in which you have a right of occupation has to cope with the *syndic* who manages the whole block on behalf of all the *copropriétaires*? How, under the old system are your service charges worked out and to what extent have you, under the new system, played your part in controlling these? Whilst under the new system, provided everyone pays his service charges, such a thing should not happen, what happens if you buy under the old system if the person from whom you bought goes bankrupt or into liquidation?

Put shortly, whether you occupy your flat on a time-sharing

basis as a shareholder of a French company when your shares give you the right of occupation or whether you occupy the flat as a licensee, it is essential that you are told to the last particular what your position is. All the more so because the amount you are paying for your 'ownership' will seem comparatively small whilst, given the right conditions, this type of 'ownership' may seem to have great advantages.

Certainly, you can sell your time-sharing rights, you can 'lease' them and technically you can raise a loan on them, although that exercise is not worth engaging in. You can also often exchange your period of occupation for one elsewhere, which is a service most developers feel they need to offer to attract buyers.

When you are dealing with sellers of time-sharing in France, you must distinguish between those who are selling a whole block on this basis and those who are selling some flats on an ordinary outright basis and some on time-sharing. Logically, you should get better management and fewer problems if the whole of the block is sold on time-sharing. If on the other hand you are buying from a non-French source, you may be surprised to see how many flats and in how many places all over the world are offered to you. Do not imagine the sellers own the blocks or even large parts of them. They probably own one or two flats in each block, so their portfolio is perhaps less impressive than at first appears.

It must be said that certain sellers of time-sharing have appreciated some of the problems involved in France and have attempted to overcome them by interposing non-French companies or by other devices. How successful these attempts may be must depend on how ingenious their creators have been, but if you are buying in this way, the assistance of someone knowledgeable in French law and the law of your country is a 'must'.

If all the comments in this chapter seem rather negative, the reason is simple to discover. The body of French lawyers recognize that time-sharing is here to stay and is probably a good thing. French law really cannot satisfactorily accommodate this type of 'ownership', and so long as this situation exists, it is unwise to buy without knowing all the pitfalls. After all, if your teenage children hung about with skis turn up in January to find your flat in chaos or still occupied or inundated or littered with demands for wholly unexpected payments, it does help to have an idea of what to do next. Indeed, in a small way, the more enquiries you make and the more advice you take, the more you will be helping to achieve a change in the law in France to the benefit of all time-sharers.

There has recently appeared on the market a novel form of time-sharing, called *bi-propriété*. This involves full ownership with another person, each for six months of the year. This type of ownership is based on the ownership of undivided shares in the property, through the medium of a *société civile*. There is no reason to suppose that, from a practical point of view, the scheme may not be attractive, for one has a half year's use of the flat, which can be let, and presumably the price of one half year is not necessarily the same as the other half year. In theory, part of the purchase price can be raised on mortgage, and the half share bought can be sold. Certainly, what is bought represents true real property. All that can be said is that anyone who buys this type of property without the most careful advice from someone conversant both with the legal snags in France and with the effects of undivided ownership of land in that country richly deserves the headaches and surprises which await him.

CHAPTER 10

Family Law

Quite apart from the advice which you will have been given on a number of problems in connection with your move to France, it is useful to have some idea of some of the basic differences between the law in France and in your own country in family matters. Even if you are not for the moment setting up in France for good, some of the events referred to in this chapter could affect you.

Two preliminary words of warning. Since this chapter is intended to be of use to you whatever country you may come from, it is not possible, except very rarely to compare the position in France with that 'at home'. This makes it very important that, whilst the explanations given in this chapter are those which from experience seem to call for the most attention, you should never try to apply the rules to your own personal situation without proper advice. Your road is being signposted for you, but it is easy to misread signposts, and even if you take the right turning, it is easy to misjudge the distance down the road you should go.

DOMICILE

In most countries, domicile means the country which you intend should be your permanent home. Nothing gives the lawyers, the accountants and the Tax Authorities greater scope for argument than domicile. It is one thing when you are alive and can express your own opinion, even if sometimes the Taxman tends not to believe you. It is quite another thing when you are dead, and quite a lot of death duties may turn on where in fact you were domiciled. Of course, you knew exactly where you were domiciled – where there are few taxes and death duties to pay. Do try to make certain that the tax authorities in France and in your own country have every reason to agree with you. As you will see from Chapter 14 on taxes in France, whatever may be the definition of residence applied by the tax authorities of your own country to determine whether you are liable to tax there – and in some countries the definition can be quite artificial – in France you will be caught for tax if your 'tax domicile' is in France. Life is not made any easier by the fact that in French '*domicile*' also means the address at which you are living at any particular moment. You will see also that the way in which your assets can be dealt with by you in your Will and the way in which they will be dealt with if you leave no Will depends on your domicile, and in this context '*domicile*' means your permanent home or, if it does not sound too gloomy, the country in which you intend to die. Remember also that in some countries (as in the UK), husbands and wives can have separate domiciles, although they are happily living together though that is not quite the position in France. There is only one useful piece of advice which can be given. Make certain when a Frenchman talks to you of '*domicile*' that you are quite clear what he has in mind, and make certain that everything about domicile, in whatever language it has been said, has been fully explained to you. If you do not, you may live to regret it, and the fiscal authorities of one and possibly two countries will rejoice.

WILLS

The rule is the same in every country – never make a Will without expert advice. There are three kinds of French Wills.

1. *Testament olographe*. This type of Will must be in the handwriting of the person making it and must be signed and dated by him. No witnesses and no other formalities are required. Indeed a witness may well invalidate such a will since it will not then be written exclusively in the handwriting of the testator. At best, the inclusion of one or more witnessess will probably lead your heirs into long drawn out litigation, a thing devoutly to be avoided in France.

2. *Testament authentique*. This is a Will in the form of a

notarial document which is dictated by the person making it to a *notaire* and witnessed by two *notaires* or by one *notaire* and two other witnesses.

3. *Testament mystique.* A will of this kind is drawn up by or prepared for the testator and, after it has been signed by him, is placed in an envelope in the presence of two witnesses and given to a *notaire*. The *notaire* inscribes on the envelope a memorandum that the envelope has been handed to him and that the testator has declared to him that the envelope contains his Will.

Only advice can let you know which kind of Will is suitable or necessary for you. Normally a *testament olographe* will suffice and certainly would be good enough to cover a single property owned in France. In the cases of the other two types of Will, there are certain formalities relating to the witnesses of these documents which are very strict and which, if not complied with, render the Will void. Note that in France marriage does not automatically revoke a Will.

A word about the safekeeping of Wills made in France. If you wish to leave these in France, it is preferable to leave them with a notary or your local adviser and not to deposit them at banks.

EXECUTORS

The functions of an executor under French law and under English and other Anglo-Saxon systems of law are totally different. Under the latter, an executor becomes the owner of all the assets of the person under whose Will he is appointed, subject to his obligation to pay all debts and death duties and then distribute the balance in accordance with the terms of the Will. In France, the property of a person dying passes directly to his heirs in the way in which it has been laid down by his Will. If an executor (*exécuteur testamentaire*) is appointed, his duties are supervisory only, and it is the obligation of the heirs, if they accept the inheritance, to pay the debts, whilst each heir is responsible for his own death-duty liability. It is possible to give 'ownership' of certain types of property (never land or rights in land) to an executor, but this ownership cannot last for more than a year and a day from the date of death. In the case of a non-French person making a French Will, where there are beneficiaries who are not living in France of, say, jewellery, furniture or investments, the appointment of an executor is probably a good thing. Non-French people who are used to the methods of dealing with an estate in their own countries may find that things tend to move rather more slowly in France. The work is done by a *notaire*, and whilst obviously there are exceptions, there seems to be a tradition in France that the winding-up of estates should proceed at a pace which would be wholly unacceptable in many other countries.

There is no procedure in France equivalent to obtaining probate in for example, the UK, the US, Australia, New Zealand or Eire. A *Testament olographe* or *mystique* must be handed to a *notaire* (a *Testament authentique* is already a notarial document) for filing among his records, and he sends a copy to the court in the district in which the estate is being administered. Wills do not become public property in France as they do in, for example, the UK. There is a central Registry of Wills in which all Wills coming into the possession of, or made by a *notaire* must be registered but this is not open for inspection by the public after the death of a testator as in the UK.

RULES OF SUCCESSION

In theory, under the laws of some countries, you can dispose of all your belongings by Will as you wish, and if you feel that the proverbial Cats' Home merits your bounty more than your nearest and dearest family, you can provide for the purchase of unlimited tins of cat food and leave your children's larder empty. This theoretical liberty has, however, in many countries been somewhat circumscribed, and certain members of your family who have been 'cut out' can apply to the judge to be 'cut in'. Not so in France. For very many years and as a matter of public policy, the law absolutely requires you to leave a proportion of your estate to your descendants or ascendants, the former taking precedence over the latter. So, if you die leaving two children, they must inherit at least two-thirds of that part of your estate governed by French law. If you have three or more children, the proportion rises to three-quarters. Your surviving spouse has no such rights for he or she has rights under the system of community under which you are married. Additionally, he or she can either be given outright one-third or one-quarter of your estate, depending on the number of children or parents you have, or nothing outright but a life interest in all of your estate. If your surviving spouse has such an interest, then he or she is entitled to the income from your estate whilst he or she is alive, and the capital goes to the children only on his or her death. There are ways and means provided for unscrambling this and dividing out the capital, and of course if you have no family who are entitled to this entrenched part of your estate (*réserve*), you are then free to dispose of your worldly goods as you wish. As a general rule, French law allows a person of non-French nationality to make a Will provided it is in a form which is valid according to the law of the country of his own nationality. However, again as a general rule, whatever your nationality or domicile, land in France must pass on your death in accordance with French law: assets other than land pass in accordance with the law of your domicile. Hence, quite apart from the tax problems, it is very important to be quite clear on where in fact you are domiciled. Domicile, as opposed to nationality, also is important when you come to revoke Wills.

In Chapter 5, reference was made to buying property in joint names. The significance of this is that it is probably the only way in which one can avoid the impact of the French rule of the *réserve* on your house in France. Where property is bought in France *en tontine* such persons as children or parents who otherwise have a right to share in it on your death will not, save in fairly unusual circumstances which can hardly ever apply to English buyers, have that right and it will pass entirely to the surviving owner. This arrangement will not save death duties (see Chapter 14) but it may produce results which you prefer.

ETAT CIVIL

It is extremely difficult to explain the 'feel' of the *état civil* of a Frenchman. It is of importance to the national of certain countries because, apparently, he does not have one. This, in fact, is not so: it is just that he does not carry around with him evidence of his civil status from time to time in a neat little book as the French citizen does, as snugly as the snail carries his house. Nor is he asked to prove it in his own country as frequently as the Frenchman is in France.

The system is a self-perpetuating one and stems from the *livret de famille* which is given to a couple on marriage (this being the moment of the creation of a new family unit) and which reunites in one book all the information about the couple which would be found by searching the birth, death and marriage registers, which in many countries have no cross-references one to another. So, the details of the births of the couple are shown and of their marriage. As their children are born, these details are added, as are adoptions, divorces and any other events which affect the civil status of the family. It is an offence not to keep the *livret de famille* up to date. On death, the document must be handed in, and on divorce two copies will be made and given to each party to the marriage. It is, of course, possible to obtain copies of birth, death and marriage certificates, if these are required, from the local *mairie* at which the registration took place.

For the preparation of virtually every formal document and in many instances besides, proof of one's *état civil* is obligatory. It is therefore very useful to have in France birth and marriage certificates for oneself and all the family, and it is sometimes necessary to have information about the births and marriage of one's parents. Evidence of divorce is also useful and should be by means of a suitably certified final decree of divorce such as, in the case of any one divorced in England, a sealed certified Decree Absolute obtainable from Somerset House in London.

Most *notaires* in large towns understand the reticence on the part of the non-French continuously to remind themselves of their civil status and most have heard of the uncivilized lack in some countries of the *régime matrimonial*. Where you come across wide-eyed disbelief, gentle explanation is all that is required, coupled with a sheaf of all the necessary documents from your own country. Beware, however, the French legal document which tries to give you the equivalent of a French *régime matrimonial* if you come from a country where this does not exist. The results can vary from irritating to dangerous. As has been said, the French are a formalist nation, and the written word and the official signature will take you far, particularly if there is a rubber stamp or seal added. There are certificates in profusion available from the *mairie* or *préfecture*, all of which are useful or requisite (these include Certificates of Good Behaviour and Certificates of Concubinage) and for many of which your *état civil* is required. Many documents are issued free. Some require a *timbre fiscale* (revenue stamp) and when these cannot be bought from the local tobacconist, they are to be found at the *préfecture* or *sous-préfecture* or *recettes locales des impôts* (local tax collector's office) but never at a post office.

BIRTHS

It is obligatory to register all births in France, irrespective of the nationality of the parents or whether they are in the country permanently or temporarily. Registration is done at the *mairie* of the district where the birth takes place and must be done within three days of the day of birth, Saturdays, Sundays and holidays excluded. Anyone present at the birth may register it, provided he is in possession of a certificate of the doctor or midwife attending the birth. There is no registration fee payable, and the certificate is normally available forthwith.

It is advisable to register the birth of a child of non-French parents at your local Consulate. This will avoid considerable difficulties when a passport is required for the child (see Appendix B).

So far as the French law is concerned, the child of non-French parents who is born in France has French nationality only if the laws of the country of the nationality of his parents do not attribute their nationality to him. It is therefore extremely unlikely that the child of non-French parents will be French by reason of his birth in France. However, if one of the parents of a child born in France is himself or herself of French nationality or, if of another nationality, was born in France, that child has French nationality. He may repudiate this nationality during the six months preceding attaining his majority (eighteen years of age) provided that the parent who was not French or born in France has not in the meanwhile acquired French nationality. Again, it is unlikely that this set of circumstances will arise, but do not forget that military service exists in France and is obligatory for all French male citizens.

DEATHS

Deaths must be registered within twenty-four hours of the event. A doctor's certificate is necessary, which is obtained from a doctor retained by the Local Authority who will visit the house, but otherwise the doctor attending the person who has died will suffice. Since you cannot hand in the *livret de famille* of a non-French person who has died, you should take his *carte de séjour* or equivalent document. No coffin may be closed within twenty-four hours of death (or remain open for more than six days), and it is closed on the authority of the local *mairie* where you register the death. It is customary in France for coffins not to be closed until just before actual burial so that family and friends may 'pay their last respects'. If you feel that this does not accord with your wishes, you must give the undertakers the most precise instructions to close the coffin as soon as this has been authorized.

Contrary to the custom in certain other countries, it is not usual to give instructions about burial or cremation in French Wills but in a separate letter or document, preferably kept separate from your Will. Wills in France are not normally read until after a funeral has taken place.

The burial of bodies in France, except in a few towns and rural communities, is the task of the Local Authority. Most

Golf at Anglet, near Biarritz

A quiet day's fishing in France

Typical countryside near le Beausset in the Var

of them license a firm of undertakers to carry out this function, and you are advised to leave all formalities to them, once you have given them your instructions. Cemeteries in France also belong to the Local Authorities, and there are now no separate Protestant or Jewish cemeteries. However, parts of many cemeteries have over a period of years become used only by certain religious groups, and no problems need arise on this score. France is, of course, a predominantly Catholic country, and hence in the case of a Catholic funeral one need only get in touch with the local parish priest. There are also large French Protestant communities. A list of churches will be found in Appendix C, but if it is necessary to arrange a funeral in a place far removed from any of the towns shown, you will undoubtedly get assistance from one or other of the Church of England vicars. Appendix C also gives a list of synagogues in the larger towns in France. Again, if funeral arrangements have to be made too far away from any of these towns, it is suggested that you get in touch with the Consistoire Centrale, 17 rue St Georges, 75009 Paris (Tel. (1)45.26.02.56.), who will either make all the necessary arrangements or put you in touch with the right people.

Cremation has not, for religious reasons, been very popular in France until very recently. This attitude is now changing. There are now crematoria at Amiens, Bordeaux, Clermont-Ferrand, Grenoble, Le Havre, Lyon, Marseille, Montpellier, Mulhouse, Nantes, Nice, Orange, Paris (one in central Paris and one in the suburbs), Rouen, Strasbourg, Toulouse and Lille. More are envisaged. Documents required to enable a cremation to take place vary slightly from place to place but normally are only the request in writing of the person who has died that he wished to be cremated or the written request of the person dealing with the funeral formalities together with the certificate of a Local Authority doctor that the cause of death does not pose any forensic problems.

Considerably more use seems to be made in France of the chapel of rest (*reposoir*) than in certain other countries. This may be because hospitals have less space or homes are smaller, but it is not unusual to have the funeral service at a *reposoir*.

This can be particularly suitable in, say, the case of a death in a town far removed from a crematorium or where a suitable place of worship does not exist. *Reposoirs* are 'licensed' for any Minister of Religion to hold a service.

Death certificates in France never show the cause of death. If therefore you wish to have a body transported to another country for burial, there may be problems on this score. However, undertakers in parts of France where there is a fairly large non-French population know how to deal with this difficulty, and Consulates will advise in other cases. Otherwise, no particular problems arise.

The cost of funerals, in respect of such minimum items as the law requires to be provided, is controlled by the *commune*. In some cases, other items normally (but not required by law to be) provided for a funeral are also controlled, but in the case of some *communes* they are free of control. It has been estimated that the average funeral in France costs about 20,000 francs (probably more if the deceased was of a faith other than Catholic) whilst the cost of a funeral which complies only with the minimum legal requirements would cost about 3,800 francs. Hence it is that for death duty purposes, the maximum which may be taken as a deduction for funeral expenses is currently 3,000 francs only. Except in cities and other parts of France where there are cemeteries with still unused ground, most burials take place in horizontal vaults. Plots (where available) and vaults may be reserved for periods which vary considerably according to the area involved and vary from a right in perpetuity to a right for as little as five years. The cost of these reservations also varies considerably. It is also possible to be buried in *terrain communal*, in individual graves with suitable stones. These graves are maintained by the Local Authority free for a period of five years, after which the body is either placed in a common grave or reinterred in a private vault if the family so wishes and has acquired a concession.

The export from France of any item in the estate of a person who died in that country normally gives rise to no problem. When the items in question are being sent to another EEC country, all that is required is the production to French Customs of the notarial document proving the legacy and that the recipient's home is in the country to which the goods are being sent. Export should take place within one year of legal possession of the goods being obtained by the legatee, but may take place on a number of occasions throughout that year. A detailed inventory of the goods in question with individual valuations signed by the exporter should accompany the notarial document. Normally, the same rules will apply for export to a non-EEC country but enquiries should be made as requirements do vary from country to country.

The import of inherited goods into the UK tax and duty free is a concession available to any person normally resident in the UK and to a non-profit-making organization incorporated in the UK and carrying on their activities there. The concession can also apply to persons living in another EEC country who desire inherited goods to be sent to the UK but special application must be made to Division A6 of Customs Directorate. Very much the same evidence as is required for the export of the goods from France is needed to obtain the UK concession on their import into that country. This is not surprising since both sets of rules follow the same EEC regulation and further information will be found in Notice 368 issued by Customs and Excise in the UK.

MARRIAGES

All marriages celebrated in France are civil marriages, and no place of worship is registered for marriages. If you want a religious service of marriage, this must take place after the civil ceremony, and you will have to ask the priest or minister concerned what documents and information are required, since these are purely religious requirements. It is unlikely that they will differ much from what is asked for in most countries.

It must be remembered that certain French rules apply to the French party to a marriage even though they may not apply to the non-French party. The capacity for the non-French to marry is determined by that person's national law. Such a person may be asked to produce a certificate from his Consul or, if the procedure exists, from some authority in his own country, proving his freedom to marry. In addition, a birth certificate is required which ought not to be subject to the rule that it must not have been obtained more than three months previously and which in the case of many countries needs neither legalizing or translation by the Consul. If one party has been divorced, see earlier in this Chapter under *état civil* and if your former spouse has died, arm yourself with a copy of a death certificate.

1. Boys may marry at eighteen and girls at fifteen. The age for girls may be reduced by the Court for suitable reasons. If the intended bride is over fifteen but under eighteen the consent of both parents is required and must be produced at the ceremony. The consent of a surviving parent will suffice but if both parents are living and cannot agree, the law presumes that they give their consent. There are rules permitting the consent of grandparents, if parents are dead and even more remote consents but there is no provision for the Court to give its consent to override a refusal. If therefore a consent, parental or other, was obtained in another country to permit a non-French person to marry in France, it would be as well discussing with the Consul how best to formalize that consent.

2. A widow cannot remarry within 300 days of her husband's death unless she produces a medical certificate proving that she is not pregnant. The same rule applies to divorced women.

3. In cases of extreme urgency, it is possible to shorten the period between the publication of the banns and the date of the marriage.

Where one or both of the parties are not French, the following is an indication of the major formalities involved. It is, however, well worthwhile checking all these with the *mairie* where you intend to get married and with your own Consul.

1. Notice should be given to the *mairie* of the *commune* where one of the parties either has his permanent residence

or will establish residence for a continuous month following the publication of the banns. It goes without saying that some form of identification (passport for the non-French) must be provided to satisfy the French that you are who you say you are.

2. The publication of banns is obligatory. These must be published for ten days prior to the ceremony at the *mairie* where the marriage will take place and also where each party has his or her residence.

3. If one of the parties has no residence in France, he or she must arrange for banns to be published in his or her place of residence out of France and provide proof that this has been done and no objection to the marriage filed.

4. For the publication of banns in France, it is necessary to provide a medical certificate (paid for by Sécurité Sociale) which is not more than two months old.

5. Each party must provide at least one and not more than two witnesses, details of whom must be given to the *mairie* when giving notice of the marriage.

Your marriage is likely to be recognized as valid in most countries, though you should check this at home first. You may, however, be given after the wedding ceremony a document by the *mairie* exonerating the French authorities from all responsibility if in fact this is not so. The form is standard and is to cover countries where there are special formal requirements which are not necessary in France.

There is no fee for a marriage in France. Copies of French marriage certificates are obtainable only from the *mairie* where the marriage was celebrated. The ceremony is very short – a précis from the Civil Code dealing with the duties of a married couple is read and the standard question "Do you . . . ?" is asked. If both answers are "Yes", the parties are declared to be married. If a religious ceremony is to follow, it is customary to delay the exchange of the rings until then, but the bride may be kissed, but, by tradition, no more!

Consuls of some countries have powers to celebrate marriages and some do not. British Consuls stopped rendering this service when the romance of a wedding and honeymoon in Paris became too popular and now limit their marriage functions to countries where it is very difficult to get married in any other way.

A marriage in France automatically results in your marriage being subject to one of a number of '*régimes*' which govern the manner in which the two parties' property is dealt with during the marriage, on divorce and on death. There are a number of *régimes* prescribed by law and within limits, variations are available. If you marry without such arrangements being made, the system which will affect you is automatically provided by French law. It is the '*régime légal*' which distinguishes between property owned by the parties individually and property owned by them in common. What each spouse owned before marriage and what each acquired by inheritance or gift during the marriage, is owned individually. What is acquired during the marriage with their common funds, belongs to them in common. There is one special provision – '*les biens réservés*' – which are assets acquired by the wife from her earnings in her own profession or job. These belong to the wife. There are special rules about the liability jointly or separately of debts contracted during the marriage. Under this '*régime*', each party manages his own property, but the husband is '*chef de la communauté*'. So, in the case of the sale of the family home, even if it belongs exclusively to one party and the sale price goes only to one party, both spouses' signatures are required to the sale document.

If you are married in France, then the rules of whatever '*régime*' applies to you governs all land or rights in land you own in France, wherever you are domiciled, and all your assets if you are domiciled in France. Hence you are likely to be asked at the *mairie* if you have appreciated the significance of these rules and to be advised to ask the appropriate expert if you have not.

Marriage under French law is without effect on the name of either spouse who specifically retains his or her name as shown on his or her birth certificate. Each spouse may use the name of the other spouse by joining it to his and a wife may, as is currently the case, substitute her husband's name for hers. But the French are at pains to point out that this is 'usage' only and has no legal effect which is why in all documents the wife of Mr X is shown as Mrs Y (maiden name) wife of Mr X.

Marriage of a non-French citizen to a French citizen entitles the former to acquire French citizenship by simple declaration after six months of marriage provided the parties are still living together as man and wife, which must be proved by the French equivalent of a Statutory Declaration and supported by production of such things as a rent receipt (presumably in both names) or a bank statement (presumably a joint account). Other documents less naïve in content are also required including (which will be difficult for the British) a certificate of a 'clean record'.

A charming afterthought is provided by the *Code du Travail* which provides that every employee is entitled to four days' paid holiday on his marriage whilst the happy couple's parents, if they have not retired, are entitled to one day's holiday. However, the French are realists and if you get married during your regular paid holidays, you cannot add on four days, which leaves couples with the choice of a four-day honeymoon or (impossible thought) the loss of something to which they *'ont le droit'*.

ADOPTIONS

Under French law, adoptions may be 'full' or 'simple'. The former confers on the adopted child all the rights of a legitimate child. It confers also the right to use the name of the adopter or, if the adopters are married, the name of the husband. Any person over the age of thirty may adopt a child, but an adoption by a married couple can take place only if the adopters have been married for five years and are living together at the date of the adoption. There is no minimum age limit when the adoption is that of a spouse's child. Adopters must be fifteen years older than the child being adopted, but the court can reduce this age difference. No child over fifteen may be adopted without leave of the court in special circumstances, and the consent to his adoption must be obtained from a child over thirteen years of age.

'Simple' adoption effects a far less fundamental change in the circumstances of the child. He usually keeps his original name, to which is added the name of his adopters. He remains part of his original family, with all his original rights to succession to property: he acquires only limited rights of succession in his new family. However, full parental rights are vested in the adopting parents, such as the consent to marriage. There are no restrictions as to the nationality of adopting parents. A 'full' adoption is irrevocable, but a 'simple' adoption may be revoked by the court. In very general terms, the procedures and enquiries in France are what one would expect in countries where adoption is hedged round with safeguards. Obviously, in countries where there is no equivalent of 'simple adoption', such an adoption in France would not be recognized. Full adoptions in most 'civilized' countries will be recognized in most other 'civilized' countries but it is safer to make enquiries of the two countries involved. France has a system for birth certificates designed to avoid showing if a child is adopted but it has to fit in with the French system of *état civil*; hence, similar kinds of birth certificates issued in other countries may not be sufficient and if there has been an adoption in your family, it is wise to bring with your bundle of documents the Order of the Court making the adoption and not just the birth certificate of the child involved which was issued when the adoption took place. Children not of French citizenship adopted by French citizens may acquire French citizenship by simple application of the adopting parents.

DIVORCE

In France, the Courts will entertain divorce actions if one of the parties is French or if both parties have their habitual residence in France. There is no specific time limit other than that needed to satisfy the Court that the 'habitual residence' is genuine. It is a peculiarity of French law that in the majority of cases, a wife, on divorce must revert to her previous surname unless her husband or the Court authorizes her, for special reasons such as her custody of a child of the marriage or a justifiable interest in its continued use, to continue to use the surname of her ex-husband.

The basic grounds for divorce in France are the following:

After six months of marriage, the parties may by consent ask for a divorce. No grounds need be disclosed, and all that is required is that the parties must be agreed as to 'the consequences' (e.g. maintenance, division of property) of a decree. The petition can even be presented by a lawyer acting for both parties. The judge meets the parties and tells them to think it over for three months, and if at the end of that period they are still of the same mind, a decree must be granted.

If a petition is filed by one party to the marriage on the grounds that married life has become impossible, and this allegation is admitted to the judge by the other party, the court must pronounce a decree without going into the allegations in any way. The resultant decree is treated as a divorce where the parties are equally to blame for the breakdown.

In cases of more than six years' separation or a similar period of incurable mental illness, a petition may be presented, and if the allegations are accepted by the court, a decree will be granted unless the other party to the marriage can show that a decree would involve exceptionally grave moral or material consequences for that party or the children, having regard to the length of the marriage or the age of that party or of the children. Equally, if a decree in the case of incurable mental illness would adversely affect the party who is ill, a decree will be refused. Such a petition can be defended on the grounds open to him or her as general grounds, and if the defence succeeds, a decree will be granted on those grounds.

There are also general grounds for divorce such as used to exist in England before the 'breakdown of the marriage' encompassing ground was introduced – adultery, cruelty etc, including the commission of certain criminal offences.

All the usual by-products of divorce, such as alimony, maintenance and custody are dealt with in very much the same way as in most other countries. The courts take a severe view of failure to pay maintenance and among other things the Criminal Code requires a person paying maintenance to keep the recipient advised of his address.

Judicial separation (*séperation de corps*) exists in France. The grounds are the same as for divorce, and a decree of judicial separation may be converted into a decree of divorce.

It may well be that there is a choice of countries in which non-French nationals living in France can commence divorce proceedings and it is important that advice should be sought if this unhappy circumstance arises. Final decrees of divorce made in France will be accepted in most countries as valid divorces, though since there are exceptions to every rule, again advice should be sought. Maintenance orders made in most countries can be enforced in most other countries and there are special rules applicable to Common Market citizens under the European Judgments Conventions, which need careful consideration in appropriate cases. Where children are concerned, it is sensible to consider which country's courts should have ultimate control of their welfare. Remember too that the French court is no happier than any other court at children within its jurisdiction going out of the country without either the consent of your ex-spouse or of the court; this is a point to bear in mind if you want to send children 'home' to school rather than have them educated in France.

NATURALIZATION
To obtain French citizenship by naturalization as opposed to acquisition by marriage, one must live in France for at least five years and satisfy the authorities that one is of good character and has a sufficient knowledge of the French language. In this context, it is difficult to define exactly what 'living in France' may mean but as a rough and ready guide, if one has established fiscal residence in France, this will probably suffice even if one does not spend every day of the period in the country. The period can be reduced if one has attended certain French centres of higher education or has rendered special services to the Republic.

An application for naturalization, which currently takes about eighteen months to process, is made initially to the *Préfet* of the *Département* in which one resides. He usually passes the file to the local Mayor for investigation and interviews and if all seems in order the application is sent to Paris with the *Préfet's* recommendation. The Minister's decision is wholly discretionary and no appeal lies from a refusal to grant such an application. A grant of naturalization gives French nationality to the applicant, his or her spouse and children under eighteen.

CHAPTER 11

Cars and Driving

Before taking up permanent residence in France, it may be worth considering whether purchasing a new motor car in your own country, free of VAT and car tax, would be worthwhile in your particular circumstances. The French Customs allow most incoming nationals to bring in their car free of tax and VAT at the time of acquiring their permanent residence in France provided these have been paid in the car's country of purchase. However, so far as the British are concerned, the French seem sometimes unable to differentiate between a pink (tax unpaid) log book and a normal one. So though there is always a possibility you will have to pay *ad valorem* tax and VAT (for it will not be a new car) there is also a chance you will not be charged anything. It is, therefore, worthwhile for the British to consider buying a tax-free car, provided the basic prices are lower than those in France and, even if one cannot import it free, paying *ad valorem* import duty six or eight months later. The car tax today is 28%, and you should add approximately 300 francs for Customs expenses etc. Moreover, many cars for export, and particularly French, are of better quality with many added refinements as standard rather than as optional extras in their country of origin. For the same reason, British cars are a better bargain in France than in the UK. It must be stressed that this is a once-in-a-lifetime privilege and cannot be repeated some years later when changing one's permanent residence from the north of France to the south-west of the country for example. The car must be at least six months old and capable of passing the French vehicle test. It does not need to be a left-hand drive, but a right-hand drive car might be somewhat difficult to sell later on, and certainly it would incur higher insurance charges. Yellow lights are compulsory on French cars but in the case of American cars, where the lights cannot be changed, non-yellow lights will be *tolerated* and you should get a certificate to that effect as you will be constantly stopped by the police.

From the British end, the purchase of a tax-free and VAT-free vehicle can be made by any person who intends permanently residing outside the UK for a period of more than twelve months. In the case of someone about to take up permanent residence in France, permission will be granted to use the car in the UK for a period of not more than six months. After that date the car will be liable not only for full VAT and car tax but also to forfeiture. Therefore choose your dates carefully, and preferably have your car in France or any country other than the UK a little before the date due for its final export. A road-fund licence for six months will have to be purchased unless you come into the scheme as an overseas visitor (i.e. you have not been in the UK during the previous two years for 365 days in all or during the six previous years you have not been in the UK for more than 1,095 in all.) The burden of proof will be on you. If you are such a person, you can drive the car in the UK for up to twelve months and without a road-fund licence.

Your new car MUST be purchased from the motor manufacturers or the sole-selling agent and not from your local distributor, who cannot operate the scheme. If you are at the time of purchase a normal UK resident, you will complete VAT Form 411, and if you count as an overseas visitor it will be VAT Form 410. You should be most careful that the correct form is completed since your entitlement period in the UK depends on your resident status.

Only the purchaser may take delivery of the vehicle. You may take your chauffeur when accepting the delivery, and he may drive it, but no employee, and no other person, except someone who is himself eligible to acquire a car tax-free, may drive this car. No employee may use the car for his personal use. You will receive a pink log-book on which it will be shown that you have paid neither VAT nor car tax, the amounts of such taxes and the date for final export of the vehicle. Short journeys abroad may be made provided you can export the car by the due date. The car should be insured for its full sum including the VAT and car tax, since if it is in an accident or becomes part of a 'write-off' insurance claim, such amounts will become payable. Most non-UK manufacturers run special insurance schemes for British-registered cars which include a year-round Green Card giving comprehensive cover which will solve your insurance problems until you get French plates.

If for any reason you have to delay your departure from the UK, the full VAT and tax become liable unless you can keep the vehicle in a garage or parking-lot somewhere abroad. Of course, every country has its own rules about the export of cars and you should make careful enquiries before embarking on such a venture. Danes, for example, purchasing new cars for export MUST get the vehicle out of Denmark within twenty-four hours of purchase. It probably pays a Dane to garage his new car out of Denmark (but not in France) for the six months prior to his taking up residence in France.

From the French end you must simply satisfy the Customs people that you intend to take up permanent residence in France. Your *compromis de vente, attestation notariale d'acquisition* or *bail* will serve as proof. Even though you may have a Customs clearing agent, you should be personally present at the clearing of your car. Almost certainly the French Customs will require a photocopy of your pink log-book and a sight of the log-book itself. The car will be (somewhat cursorily) examined to make sure the engine and chassis numbers etc. match up with the log-book, a chit will be made out to the *Service des Mines* and you will receive, either immediately or a little later by post, a *certificat de douane.*

After this formality has been completed, you then go to the concessionaire for your particular make of car (you will find them in the Yellow Pages or your local telephone directory, or your Customs clearing agent will advise you) and hand them the log-book, your passport and the *certificat de douane.* The concessionaire will then hand you back your own papers plus a whole new sheaf of his own. Do not throw any of these away; even though they may look like waste paper, they are all precious. He will then demand payment – but it will be a nominal sum. You then go home and await events, taking these papers with you.

Depending on the time of year and the region in which you live, you will eventually receive a demand from the *Service des Mines* to present your car for examination. Remember to take all the documentation given to you by your concession-aire.

Your car should be in a condition to pass a roadworthiness test. The British should ensure that their car headlights have been re-aligned for driving on the right hand side of the road. Unaligned lights and non-yellow lights are frequent reasons for failing this test. Your car, in any event, should have been purchased with French specifications in mind, and although the test is a simple one, it would be well to make sure your car is capable of passing it before presenting yourself. On passing the test you will be given a temporary *carte-grise* with which you can obtain, at the local *préfecture*, *sous-préfecture*, *mairie* etc. (your concessionaire who did the documentation will tell you where to go), your permanent *carte-grise* or log-book for the car. Before you get this, insure your car with a French company or get your previous company to note the change of number shown on your temporary *carte-grise*. *Until you have received a new Green Card, do not run your car on French plates.*

Once you have the *carte-grise* (which will show the vehicle as 'dédouanée' and which means you cannot sell it for six months) and your new Green Card, purchase a *vignette* (which is the French equivalent of a Road Fund Licence and is calculated on the horsepower of the vehicle) from your nearest *Perception* (to be found in the pink pages of your local telephone directory). Stick this high up on the right-hand side of your windscreen. You will be stopped by the police constantly if you stick it elsewhere. If you import your car after 15th August in any year, you do not need to get a *vignette* until the following November. Then, and *only* then, purchase from your concessionaire a set of French number plates. Usually these are made on the spot and delivered at once.

French law requires that changes of residence are notified. If you are remaining in the same *département*, then a simple visit to the *préfecture* or *sous-préfecture* or *mairie*, depending on where you live, is all that is required, and there is no charge. If you change *départements*, a new *carte-grise* will be issued, together with a new set of licence plates. This is obtained again at the local *préfecture* etc. depending on where you live, and you should hand over your previous *carte-grise* and show them your passport or *carte de séjour*, plus some proof that you are either the owner or the lessee of your new property. You will be required to fill out a special form and perhaps, but not necessarily, will be asked for a *certificat de résidence*, which is something you go and do for yourself at your local new *mairie*.

It is an offence to run a car with its old number plates for more than three months in a new *département*.

If you lose or have your *carte-grise* stolen, then you should tell your local police station or *gendarmerie*. They will give you a special certificate which will enable you to get a new *carte-grise* for which the steps are as explained above. In the case of a woman who marries, there is no need to change her name on her *carte-grise* — it can remain in her maiden name.

If you want to import a foreign-registered car into France (not under the scheme above) TVA will be due. This currently runs at 28% on all cars no matter from which country they come. In addition there will be Customs duty on all cars from outside the Common Market. Certain countries have agreements with the EEC and pay less duty. The highest percentage is for Japanese, US and Australian cars. These percentages often change. As before, all cars imported into France must complete and pass an examination by the *Service des Mines* before acquiring French number plates and *carte-grise*.

Insurance of motor cars etc. is dealt with in Chapter 15. It should be noted, however, that a car's papers should be carried at all times. It is obligatory to stick on the windscreen of all French registered cars the *vignette d'assurance* which is issued to a car owner when he renews his motor policy. Green Cards, which are issued except in cases where cover is limited to third party, fire and theft only and the car will never leave France, should be kept with the *carte-grise* and *vignette* receipt, since the *vignette* can easily be, and often is, stolen. This receipt is your only proof that you have paid the tax and your sole method of obtaining a new one free of charge. Never leave your car unlocked during November and December or your *vignette* may be stolen. However, this aside, many people leave their cars with the doors unlocked but with the steering wheel locked and with absolutely nothing of value inside. This avoids vandals breaking the windows to see if there is anything worth stealing in the car, for this type of theft is very common in certain parts of France.

SELLING A CAR. Once your car has completed the six-month period before it can be disposed of, you may sell your car. If you trade it in with a garage when buying another car, they will complete the formalities for you. If you are selling it to a private individual, you will need to fill in a *certificat de vente* (which is obtainable at any *préfecture*, *sous-préfecture*, *mairie* etc.) in duplicate giving one copy to the authorities and one to the purchaser of your vehicle together with your *carte-grise* crossed through and marked '*Vendu à Monsieur XYZ de*' (address) and sign it and date it. Hand over the car and its *vignette* and receipt for the *vignette*.

If the car you are selling or transferring is more than five years old, it must first undergo a technical inspection commonly known as an *autobilan*. There are fifty-two items to be inspected and the certificate issued is valid for six months. However, it is valid for only one transfer and each subsequent transfer requires a further *autobilan*. There are certain exceptions to the need to obtain this certificate such as when the vehicle is transferred to a legatee on the death of the owner or when the car is more than twenty-five years old and is registered as a *véhicule de collection*.

However, if the car, even though it is over twenty-five years old has a normal *carte-grise*, this inspection is obligatory.

PURCHASING A NEW CAR. The selling agents will arrange for a *carte-grise* to be issued to you.

PURCHASING A SECOND-HAND CAR. Application must be made to your *préfecture*, if not in person then by post, and it must be done within fifteen days of the purchase. Present the *certificat de vente* you will have received, and the cancelled *carte-grise* together with your passport or *carte de séjour*. If you have purchased the car from someone not resident in your own *département*, then you will also require a '*certificat de non-gage*' (i.e. that there is no hire purchase outstanding on the vehicle) before you can obtain a new *carte-grise* for the car. Since July 1985, all second-hand cars over five years old must be accompanied by a valid *autobilan*. There is absolutely no difference between the second-hand car market in France and the second-hand car market anywhere else. 'Let the buyer beware' is the best motto in France also. Your local *préfecture* can check on hire purchase outstanding on a car, or the *préfecture* which issued the *carte-grise* if the vehicle is registered elsewhere. The charges for the above services vary according to whether the person is the seller or purchaser and whether the acquisition involves only one *département* or two, but it would be safe to say that they are all nominal. Before you drive away in your newly acquired car, do make sure that you have a valid insurance certificate in *your name* from your own insurance company.

The *vignette* (an annual tax charged on all motor vehicles according to their age and horsepower) is due for payment in November of each year and during that month are obtainable from almost every tobacconist. Failure to pay by the 1st December incurs a penalty of 3% for the first month and 1% for every successive month. Those purchasing new cars at any other time of the year will have their *vignette* apportioned by the *préfecture* and those buying second-hand cars should make sure that a *vignette* goes with it. Otherwise, in general terms, *vignettes* cannot be apportioned, or paid for by instalments and must be paid for in full. If you lose your *vignette*, duplicates are issued free of charge. You should go to any *Recette des Impots*, provided you have the receipt for the lost one; failing this, you must go back to the issuing office, which will have a record of your payment.

For the year 1989/90, the average *vignette* for a 5/7 CV car (1,000 to 1,500 cc) under five years old varies depending on the département from 300 to 475 francs. Cars over five years old pay approximately half the normal *vignette* rate.

CAR HIRE. Car hire is expensive in France when compared with certain other EEC and West European countries. Special offers are made for weekend hire, particularly out of the tourist season, and it must be remembered that a great deal of this extra expense is due to high insurance rates, which in turn, as in the UK are due to 'fiddles' perpetrated by certain dishonest persons and garages.

There are many car hire companies in France and, like anywhere else, Hertz and Avis are the most expensive with local companies being considerably cheaper. However, it should be borne in mind that only the big companies offer such services as airport or hotel pickup and the possibility of hiring in one place and returning the car to another place and even in another country. Therefore, if you only want a car as a runaround locally, choose one of the cheaper companies. For those who are regular visitors to France, it is worthwhile thinking about buying a small (secondhand) French-registered car and keeping it in France. You must however remember that it will need turning over from time to time by a kind friend and if you want to avoid paying a penalty (see page 130) that same kind friend must buy your vignette for you in November if you are not there yourself to do this.

It should be remembered that if you keep a hired car for a period longer than is written in the hire contract, the insurance will lapse and you are therefore committing the offence of driving an uninsured car. In such a case you must notify the hirer that you want to prolong the period of hire (by telephone is sufficient). If you do not, you also run the risk of the Police being notified that the car is stolen.

DRIVING IN FRANCE

The most important piece of recent legislation is that throughout most of France (and shortly throughout the *whole* of France) children of sixteen will be allowed to drive. Albeit at 90 kilometres per hour only but a lot of damage can be done at that speed. This means that there will be a greater percentage of poor drivers on the road in France than ever before. They will be just as arrogant, rude and pushy as their elders and betters, probably more so. *Moi d'abord* is the motorists' motto in France no matter what the age – or indeed the cost.

Although there are constant discussions on the possible dangers of allowing priority to those coming into a main road from the right and although this law has recently been brought into some disrepute, it is, nevertheless, still the law, and anyone ignoring it courts a great deal of trouble. Be particularly vigilant at intersections where often a right-hand entry is hidden to an oncoming main-road driver. The French often seem to wish to maintain their rights even at the cost of their own vehicle. There is no longer any priority at roundabouts (traffic circles) and this is usually marked clearly. It is, however, very dangerous to rely on French drivers overcoming their natural desire to get in front of everyone else and, to be fair, the *priorité à droite* rule dies hard.

Only on routes where there is a yellow diamond on a white ground does the driver have priority over all others entering the road, from the right or not, but everyone should be careful to note any panels which temporarily remove the priority from him. This frequently occurs before bridges, level crossings and the like. Driving as a resident, rather than as a tourist, demands a rather more careful and vigilant attitude. The French police feel particularly strongly about the order in which cars arriving at four corners of an intersection may cross. If you intend to live in France on anything but the most temporary basis, it would be well to purchase '*Le Permis de Conduire*

Français' from any bookshop or driving-school since it is a mine of information on how the French should drive. That they do not drive in the exemplary fashion demanded by this endearing little book is certainly no fault of the *Service National des Examens aux Permis de Conduire* but of the average driver's basic attitude once behind the driving-wheel. There he becomes powerful, omnipotent even, and in his excessive impatience to get from A to B in an unreasonably short time he is easily made furiously angry and liable to act intemperately. As in many countries, women in France tend to be better drivers than men, particularly when there are children in the car. There are exceptions to prove the rule, but fifty per cent of French accidents are occasioned by people in a hurry not observing the priority-of-traffic regulations.

For those about to take up residence near France's frontiers:

The Italians are just as impatient drivers as the French but are, usually, far more in control of their vehicles. They are also by nature considerably more polite to other road-users.

The Spaniards are less impatient and infinitely more polite and are terrified of the really ferocious fines imposed by their police for traffic offences.

The Germans are very fast, very impatient but withal fairly law-abiding and disciplined, particularly when they think they are being watched. The Swiss are very like the Germans.

The less said about Belgian drivers the better. It is salutary to remember there are a large number of Belgians driving on Europe's roads who have never taken a driving-test in their life.

These indications of national behaviour behind the wheel should always be kept in mind when driving in France, for it is a country which abounds in foreign drivers. To the list should be added, therefore, the gentle, unhurried driving of the Scandinavian, the snail-like pace of the Dutchman, who seems to carry his home with him everywhere he goes, and the particular danger of the British driver, who, for all his innate good sense, is on the wrong side of the car on the wrong side of the road and is therefore a permanent hazard to other road users.

It is worth pointing out that it is a recognized French driving-technique to accelerate at all pedestrian crossings if a person is about to step off the pavement. Pedestrians should make sure that all cars are actually stopped at the red light before crossing on their green one. Even then a wary eye should be kept open for motor-cyclists, who tend to jump red lights as though such things do not apply to them. This is particularly important at corner crossings.

At some time or other everyone in France has seen an old lady literally harried off a pedestrian crossing or watched a car actually accelerate *round* a person crossing the street. Lots of the elderly carry blind persons' white sticks, but the French driver seems to scent out the really blind, and the merely frightened and infirm must shift for themselves with no help or consideration from him.

Finally it is worth noting that for many traffic offences your driving-licence is taken away from you for anything from a minimum period of eight days for having gone over a red light twice (an endorsable offence and a record *is* kept) to six years for having been involved in an accident where someone was killed. You can also get your licence taken away for speeding or for deliberately not obeying a policeman. At least once a year, if not more often, penalties are increased. This seems to have a minimal effect on French driving behaviour.

The suspension of a driving licence is frequently dealt with initially by a *commission* made up of representatives of the local authority, the *Préfet*, the Police, the *Parquet* (State Prosecution Service), a motoring organization and others, and this is not a Court of Law. You may be represented and this would be advisable if you are not fluent in French. There is no appeal and a decision will be reached even if you are absent. The *commission* can decide to take no action, or suspend your licence for a period of time. It is then open to the *Parquet* to institute or not to institute proceedings. It must be remembered that criminal proceedings of this kind are merged into civil proceedings if what was involved was an accident and there is a claim for damages. It is vital never to leave the scene of an accident in which you are involved or think you may have been involved (see chapter 4) since *'fuite'*, however trivial it may seem to you is considered very serious and can lead to prosecution in higher Courts and consequently stiffer penalties.

Do not rejoice because you are driving on a non-French licence, which cannot be confiscated. You can be forbidden to drive on that licence in France, and such an Order is computerized and treated just as a suspension of a licence, should you be caught driving your car in France during the period of 'suspension'.

Judging by the number of illegally parked cars in French towns and cities, the average French driver is either a hardened gambler or a very rich man. The more so as he is not covered for damage to his car while it is parked illegally, to say nothing of getting a car out of the pound *(la fourrière)* and in time! You are allowed between ten and forty-five days to do this depending on the circumstances or the car is sold.

Driving a car without a proper driving licence can cost from 2,500 to 5,000 francs and/or ten to thirty days in prison. Driving an uninsured car will cost 2,500 to 5,000 francs. Simple illegal parking (which is rife) can cost 75 to 200 francs but if it also causes an obstruction (which is equally rife) so that the car is liable to be towed away, the fine (exclusive of the cost of recovering the car) is from 1300 to 2500 francs. Failing to stop at a red light (of which a vast number of Frenchmen are guilty) costs from 1300 to 2500 francs. It is absolutely essential for the safety of the non-French driver that he recognizes this French inability to distinguish red from green and never crosses on a green until he is certain that there are no cars about to cross his bows.

The most common speeding offence is doing more that 110 kms/hr on the motorway in wet weather or when it has been raining. Remember the road remains wet and possibly muddy for some time after the rain has actually stopped and this limit remains in force in such circumstances. The next most common offence is exceeding the 130 kms/hr ordinary motorway speed limit. In an attempt to reduce this type of dangerous offence, it has even been necessary to set up roadside tribunals which can impose 'on the spot' fines which are frequently over 1,000 francs. A single example will suffice. In a drizzle, a Porsche was caught doing 180 kms/hr on the *autoroute* near Lyon: the driver was fined 1,110 francs on the spot and told to open his wallet. There was no question of saying he was without money. If you are genuinely without money the Police in some parts of France will take a cheque or Eurocheque or you will pay a bit extra for not having paid on the spot.

The breathalyser exists in France. It is called *le dépistage*, or *Alcooltest*. You are not allowed to drive with more than 0.80 gr. per litre of blood (*0.8 gr. pour mille dans le sang*). The breathalyser is always followed by a blood test or a further test by a doctor. Refusal of any or all of these tests incurs further penalties. If the *Alcooltest* indicates you have more than the permitted amount of alcohol in your blood, you will not be allowed to continue driving your car. Between 0.80–1.20 gr. per litre will incur the suspension of your driving-licence for up to three years. Over 1.20 gr. per litre and three years suspension is automatic. Drunken driving also alters your insurance cover. See Chapter 15 on Insurance.

The speed limits in France are written up at all the frontiers, at airports for people who have just arrived and hired a car and at most yacht marinas and harbours. They are 45 km/h – approximately 28 m.p.h. in town; 60 km/h – approximately 37 m.p.h. in built-up areas; 90 km/h – approximately 56 m.p.h. on normal two-way roads; 110 km/h – approximately 68 m.p.h. on dual carriageway and 130 km/h – approximately 81 m.p.h. on the *autoroutes*. As a result of a terrible accident in 1982 at Beaune, when many children in a coach were killed, a new motorway speed limit was introduced. As soon as you need to use your windscreen wipers because of rain, you must reduce your speed to 110 km/h. As one would expect in France, a survey has shown that few drivers obey this rule, but one hopes that a steady imposition of penalties will alter this typical disregard for others which is continuously met with on French roads. You can also, in certain circumstances, be 'caught' for speeding when driving at a speed considered dangerous in view of the prevailing traffic conditions. Foggy weather is a classic example.

As well as the newly qualified driver being limited to 90 km/h (as shown on the back of his vehicle), drivers are limited to a maximum of 90 km/h when using snow chains or studded tyres or towing a trailer or caravan. It is an offence not to display a ninety-kilometre disc on the back of your car when using snow tyres, snow chains or studded tyres or when towing a trailer or caravan. Special tyres are authorized only between 15th November and 15th March except in certain areas near high passes. If special equipment is required to use certain roads, the driver is not given a choice but must comply or he will be committing an offence. Chains can often be hired for short periods, but anyone who lives in a snowy district would be well advised to purchase his own equipment.

So far as driving licences are concerned, French law has now changed. The moment you are in possession of a *carte de séjour*, you MUST change your driving licence for a French one. Your local *Préfecture* issues the new licence and no test is needed though a minor medical test is usually required. French driving licences are not for life and must be renewed (and paid for again) at the requisite time. British nationals wishing to keep their driving licence must write to the DVLC at Swansea SA99 1AB, Wales for a duplicate, remembering that you must pay for this and must give a British address to which it can be sent. An address c/o a bank is acceptable.

French law now requires that the car's papers be kept with the car for on-the-spot checking. Failure can result in a fine and/or sequestration of the car until you can prove your ownership. You must also always have your driving licence with you.

The driving groups of French licences differ slightly from those of other countries. For the average car driver this does not matter but care should be taken if you wish to drive certain other categories of vehicles over 3.5 tons, delivery trucks or vehicles with more than eight seats. Heavy goods vehicle (HGV) licences cannot be automatically exchanged.

If you have any doubts, enquire at your local Police station or *gendarmerie*.

Seat belts must always be worn in France. You may find when importing your car into France seat belts will be required in the back also, although it is not compulsory to use them. It is now the law in France that young children may never sit in the front seat of a car.

CHAPTER 12

Boats

The Côte d'Azur has been a Mecca for boat-owners, both power and sail, for many years. Numerous marinas and harbours cater for boating on the west coast of France, but it is the south coast which draws so many boats from so many countries. Between Marseille and Menton, marinas, often only a few miles apart, offer moorings for boats from twenty to two hundred feet. Some are old-established like Cannes, which was classified as a safe harbour with the completion of the Jetée Albert Edouard in 1904. Others, such as Port Grimaud, Cogolin and Marina Baie des Anges near Antibes, have been completed in the last few years. The older harbours now often have modern facilities, and moorings for over a thousand vessels are commonplace.

If you wish to make use of any of these marinas on a permanent basis, there are three aspects to consider – location, price and availability. If your visits to France are usually by air, you will not, by choice, find yourself a berth in the area of St Tropez or Toulon on the Var coast. They are difficult to get to from the airport at Nice despite the fiction put about that everything is forty minutes by road from that airport. In summertime particularly it is a long and tedious journey, and the train takes you only to St Raphael. You can fly into Marseille, from which the journey is somewhat less long but to which there are fewer flights. On the other hand, berths are on the whole cheaper than those within easier reach of Nice. If you bring your car, then location is less of a problem, but there remain price and availability to consider.

The cost of a berth varies, of course, according to the boat to be accommodated. The real difficulty is finding a berth and then, not unreasonably, a berth which is in a place which pleases you. There is only one way to achieve this. Come by car to France or hire a car once you arrive and drive from one end of the coast to the other. Come preferably out of season, when there are few visitors about and there is time to give attention to your needs and enquiries. All enquiries about berths are made to the *capitainerie* at each port.

In 1982 the French imposed a Ports Tax of quite staggering proportions on boats using French ports. The result was a wholesale departure for other countries, so that the authorities decided to repeal or not collect the tax (they were not quite sure which), and boats have come back. Hence a berth will again be fairly difficult to find.

Once you have found a berth, you will need someone to look after your boat when you are not there. This service ('*gardiennage*') is provided by countless firms and individuals to be found easily in any of the ports. The problem is to find a *gardien* who will do his work faithfully and adequately and will take as much care of your boat during your absence as you would if you were there. It is impossible to lay down any hard and fast rule about such a choice, but it is worth asking locally or possibly from other boat-owners who know the area or who, if you are lucky, also have a boat in the same port. Certainly do not use the firm which advertises itself the most obviously in the port or the local ships' chandler merely because they are the most easily found.

There are very strict Customs rules and regulations about boats belonging to non-French owners using French ports. There are always a number of flagrant attempts to avoid the rules. The French Customs have powers which are considerably wider than those enjoyed by the French police, and although it is not likely that they will use these powers to the full in the case of genuine inadvertence or even for the first offence, they can, in addition to confiscating your boat, impose a fine of double the tax you have incurred but not paid. Since many non-French boat-owners enjoy a considerable tax concession, it is worthwhile paying heed to the rules, and it is impolite to the French, who do not enjoy these concessions, not to do so.

Irrespective of whether you have bought and used a boat in your own country so that you will have paid the equivalent of TVA on the boat or whether you have bought the boat for export, you may as a non-resident in France have your boat permanently in France free of TVA subject to certain strict rules. They are quite likely to change suddenly and possibly without you being aware of this. So the most important rule of all is to check the up-to-date position with the French Customs at the port where you are berthed. Your *gardien* ought to know but some are more 'on the ball' than others. Customs Clearing Agents (*Transitaires*) are also an excellent source of information. The basic rule is that the boat may not be used for more than six months in any twelve month period. This six month period need not be continuous but may be made up of shorter periods, so long as they do not exceed six months in all.

TVA becomes payable in France on your boat if:
(a) you become resident in France
(b) you make use of your boat for more than 6 months in any 12 month period
(c) your boat is chartered to a French resident irrespective of where the charter may have been fixed
(d) your boat is chartered to someone, whatever his nationality, if the charter has been fixed in France.

In order to avail yourself of this freedom from TVA, you must obtain from the local Customs Office a *titre de séjour*. This document, which is, of course, available only to non-residents, proves your boat's freedom from TVA but although it must be renewed *annually*, does not enable you to avoid the payment of TVA if you use your boat for more than the total of six months in every year. The arrangement, which is novel and seems a bit loose, is probably designed to cut down administrative work for Customs and, particularly on the South Coast attract, by the reduction in previous formalities, boats from neighbouring Italian marinas.

If the owner of a boat is a private individual, no other special rules apply except that if you have friends aboard and neither you nor a close member of your family is also aboard, you may have considerable difficulty in proving that you have not chartered the boat to your friends. In such circumstances, it is best to give them some simple document (in French) showing that they are using the boat as your guests and not paying any hire. If they are friends of friends or strangers, whom in fact you are charging, make certain that they have a simple charter document (again in French) with them, which proves that the arrangement was made out of France and that the hire is payable out of France.

If a boat is owned by a company, the company must make an application on Form EFT for the boat to be in a French port. This application has nothing to do with TVA. You must attach to the application a formal French document (*acte notairé*) which proves who is the person who has the right on behalf of the company to use the boat. Others may be aboard in port but if anyone other than the person mentioned in the *acte* takes the boat to sea, it will be deemed to be on charter. This is a new rule, likely to be strictly enforced, since the use of companies as owners of boats has in the past lead to wide abuses of the rules and regulations. Since TVA is currently at 18.6%, such concessions as are available are widely used. Their use is rigorously controlled. If TVA should become payable, it is charged on the value of the boat when imported. Owners from Common Market countries who are armed with an Export Certificate from the Customs Authorities in the country from which the boat has come do not have to pay the 2% French Duty on entry.

In theory, it is possible to arrange for the payment of these taxes oneself; in practice, it is not, because the Customs authorities will not deal with you direct. You need the services of a '*transitaire*' or Customs clearing agent, and it is to your advantage to use one. Their fees are small. The Customs authorities will not 'agree' the value of your boat for TVA purposes: they will only accept or reject the value put to them. Your agent will know far better than you what value will be accepted and, having agreed it with you, will organize it with the Customs authorities. If your boat is not on the list of makes held by the French Customs, you will have to have an expert valuation made, before the value can be put to Customs for agreement. Your *gardien* can look after this for you.

The TVA paid, you may then freely arrange charters in respect of the boat or, of course, use the boat in circumstances not permitted if the boat is in France but relieved of the payment of this tax. If, however, you have paid TVA on your boat because you are using it for more than six months in the year, you should make certain that all the charters you arrange are organized out of France and the hire is paid out of France. In no circumstance should the charter be to a resident French charterer. If you do not do this, you will be treated as carrying on business in France, and the owner of the boat, be it you, an individual, or a company, will have to register at the local *Registre de Commerce*, and you will then fall into the French tax net and the charter hire is liable to TVA. There is no reason why your charters should not change over at the port in France where the boat is berthed or indeed anywhere else in France, but you or whoever else arranges the charters should have this very important rule in mind and see to it that evidence of the arrangements made is always available if asked for.

Difficulties can arise over the purchase of moorings at Marinas. Usually they are bought not by buying the mooring itself but shares in a company, the ownership of which gives the right to use the mooring. Stamp duty on share transfers is relatively low (for France); it is very much higher on purchases of the moorings themselves. Watch out – stamp duties are payable locally and some stamp duty offices (including the office in Paris which deals with non-residents) take the view that the transaction is a true share transfer and some that it is really a transfer of the underlying asset of the mooring and stampable accordingly. It is hinted that to send the document to be stamped at an office where it is known that the lower rate will be charged might be treated as a deliberate 'fraud', notwithstanding that not the slightest element of 'fraud' is involved, since presumably the same stamp duty policy prevails all over France. If this is true, it is an extremely French attitude but one which may prove expensive if proper advice is not obtained.

It is assumed that those who read this chapter have some experience with their own boat and know how to get it to France. If you have no such experience and are either a first-time buyer or buying purely for investment and not for your own pleasure, you will clearly not attempt to sail the boat to France yourself. It can come by road, though in some cases there are problems with bridges and overhanging trees. If it is less than 3.6 metres high, it can often come through the canals. If it has to come by sea, you will find that an experienced skipper is essential, and if you do not feel that you qualify for that description, you will find that the manufacturers from whom you have bought the boat will be able to put you in touch with a suitable skipper.

So far as insurance is concerned, you will probably be covered for your local waters and for an occasional summer voyage. All you need do if you bring your boat to France permanently is to call your broker and tell him, so that he may make the necessary arrangements. No disrespect is intended to the yachting community, but there are few areas of business where roguery can better flourish. Brokers, repairers and the like of repute will support this view, and only such persons should be used when buying or selling or having repairs done. All that has been said assumes that the owner of a boat is a non-French national or company. For those, the importance of the following comments cannot be too highly stressed. When buying or selling a boat, by all means use the services of a broker to negotiate the deal (but see below!). Preferably do not let him deal with the transfer itself. A great deal can be said on this subject; suffice it to say that brokers are not lawyers and you would not ask your lawyer to find you a boat. Merely because the document of transfer looks simple, it is a dreadful error to make light of the transaction. This is particularly the case where you are buying a boat on the French Shipping Register because, as you are not a French

Market scene at Bandol, Var

View of the Promenade at Bandol, Var

Roman Theatre and Arena at Arles

national, it will not remain on that Register. There is no reason why brokers in France should know anything about non-French Registries. Nor are they able to advise you on some of the finer points which are or ought to be involved, which may well extend to tax and other questions requiring considerable skill, the very existence of which is quite beyond any broker. Get your local adviser to deal with the documentation of the sale or purchase. Examples of what can go wrong, which range from the stupid to the horrific, are numerous. Many seem to stem from the assumption on the part of brokers in France that all foreign boat-owners are 'on the fiddle'. This is simply not so but this assumption if not firmly corrected can cause a great deal of trouble and needless expense.

A final word of warning, which one would have thought was not necessary to boat-owners but which sadly most certainly is. There is a goodly number of honest and helpful brokers, both French and non-French. Delightful though it may be to find someone who speaks your language or comes from your own country, fluency in your language or your nationality are not guarantees of honesty and it is the few who are dishonest who give all a bad reputation. Do check out the broker you intend to use with your local adviser or bank.

CHAPTER 13

Banking and House Purchase Loans

1 January 1990 saw the abolition in France of Exchange Control and with it the distinction between residents and non-residents for Exchange Control purposes. But it is worth noting that, in a somewhat back-handed manner, the French government has freed from control what its citizens do with their assets against the right to require them to disclose if any such assets are held out of the country. How this will be enforced remains to be seen. It is to be assumed that this is a situation which will not affect overmuch the non-French citizen living on a permanent basis in France to whom special rules have always applied. Generally speaking, provided that he paid French tax (subject to such relief as Double Tax treaties may afford him) on income arising from non-French sources, he had considerable liberty freely to own capital assets out of France.

It is, perhaps, kinder to say that the banking system in France is dissimilar to, rather than less efficient than, the system in many other countries. There are, in any event, certain rules which are peculiar to the French system and without knowing something about these, certain transactions can produce unexpected results. It is highly desirable to try to get a 'run down' on the most important of these rules at the outset and this applies whether you are resident or non-resident in France. It is unlikely that a French bank will explain these to you and even if you ask them specifically to do so, they will probably not know what are the differences between the system you are used to and the French system on which you need guidance. At least two 'British' banks take the trouble to do this to new non-French customers but as by no means all English-speaking people open accounts with these banks, a close study of this chapter is a 'must'.

The British seem best served by their own banks in France. Including branches, there are over sixty such banks in France, split fairly equally between Paris and the Provinces. The Americans are also well served in Paris, with about twenty banks but they are very thin on the ground in the Provinces. There are a number of Canadian banks in Paris but none outside; there are two or three Dutch banks in Paris and a few elsewhere. The Danish Bank, Copenhagen Handelsbank, has a Representative Office in Nice and this will undoubtedly be of considerable assistance to Danes and other Scandinavians living in the South of France. Certainly no nationality is so well represented by its banks on the Côte d'Azur as the British. As a general rule, they are likely to provide a more useful service to the non-French customer than a French bank, if only because they can accurately translate French banking terms (which like all foreign technical terms can be very confusing) into English.

In addition, you will find that these non-French banks have a considerably wider international knowledge than the average French bank and are likely to be more flexible in their ways. Do not forget, however, that all banks operating in France are subject to Banque de France regulations and general French banking law and should not be placed in embarrassing situations because you are trying to use their services as though you were in your own country.

Notwithstanding the abolition of Exchange Control, the French government has kept the rule that everyone, whilst they may bring in or take out cash in any amount, must declare to Customs on arrival or departure all amounts in cash in excess of FF50,000, whether in French notes or its equivalent in non-French notes. It seems not wholly improbable that if a very large sum of cash were paid into your bank account, the bank might ask to see a Customs declaration. There is no restriction on the use of credit cards out of France, although for reasons explained later in this chapter, it is probable that you will prefer not to use a French Card.

It is not absolutely essential to have a bank in France at the time completion takes place but it is highly undesirable that cash required for completion in France should be sent direct to the *Notaire* dealing with the transaction. This, of course, is not because the *Notaire* is not trustworthy but because for highly technical French banking reasons, this can result in the French State having the interest-free use of your money for anything up to four weeks, whilst it cannot be made use of for your purchase. It is absolutely essential to get your local adviser or your own bank to cope with this problem. In the case of a purchase by stage payments, it is obviously best to have a bank account in France. Use your own account but instruct your bank to accept your local adviser's instructions to make stage or other payments in connection with the purchase as they become due. This will avoid a lot of correspondence to and fro and developers prefer to deal with a purchaser's representative in France than with the purchaser direct. They also prefer French cheques, for foreign cheques cost a lot to clear.

There are a number of practical hints about the running of your French bank account, to which you should pay heed.

1. On the opening of every bank account in France, the bank in question is required to confirm with the Banque de France that the person opening the account is not under an *interdiction* (see 8. below). In this way, there is a central record of all accounts in France.

2. The clearing system in France can be slow and it is unsafe to trust your statements to show your up-to-date cash position. Curiously, there is a tendency in France not to rush to pay in cheques so that they can take a long time to figure on your statement. Some, but by no means all, banks seem to obtain their statements from a central source and these tend, by the time they reach you, to be out of date or repetitive. French banks use the 'value date' system, which means that although the cheque you pay in today is shown as a credit to

your account at once, it does not qualify to be drawn against until it is cleared. It is the same as the English 'uncleared funds' with one very important exception. Bank drafts are not treated as cash and need clearing as though they were cheques.

3. There seems to be difficulty in getting cheque books as speedily as in some other countries and it is advisable to keep a spare one always on order at the bank.

4. If there is a discrepancy between the words and the figures on a cheque, it will be deemed to be for the amount shown in words.

5. You cannot give a post-dated cheque for, whatever the date shown on the cheque, it is payable on the day of presentation. Cheques cease to be valid one year and eight days after their date of issue.

6. You must distinguish on paying in between cash (*espèces*) and cheques (*chèques*) and whether the latter are drawn on a bank in the same town (*sur place*) or in another town (*hors place*). All cheques require endorsement, even when paid into your own account or when drawn in favour of yourself – (*moi-même* is the correct formula). You cannot endorse a cheque over except to a bank, or a savings or a similar institution so there can be problems about a friend 'cashing' a cheque for you. Specimens of a cheque and a paying-in slip are shown in Appendix J.

7. Normally all cheques issued by banks are crossed and are not freely negotiable. Banks may issue 'open' cheques but in such cases must, if so requested, supply the tax authorities with the names of the persons to whom such cheques were issued and the numbers of the cheques. In addition, stamp duty of FF 5 is charged per cheque. The object, of course, is to discourage transactions which are difficult to check on and bearer cheques are very rare. For other efforts on the part of the tax authorities to contain the Frenchman's innate aversion to paying tax, see Chapters 5 and 14.

8. The law in France about 'bouncing' cheques has always been ferocious. At the last count about one in every 1,500 cheques issued in France 'bounced' and nearly three-quarters

of a million Frenchmen were under the rules forbidden to operate bank accounts. A recent relaxation in these rules, designed to acknowledge that inadvertence rather than fraud accounted in a number of cases for this seemingly high proportion, has resulted in the position now being as follows. If your bank will not for lack of funds meet a cheque you have issued, it will send you a registered letter so advising you. This immediately prevents you from issuing further cheques. You then have thirty days in which to put the matter right and if you do so within that period, your account can again be used. But if you find yourself in this situation for the second time within a period of twelve months, you will then be forbidden to issue cheques for a period of one year and must return your cheque book to the bank (and all other cheque books to other banks where you have accounts even if they are in order). You are then under an *interdiction* and banks allowing such customers to open or operate an account are in trouble. It follows, therefore, that if during an initial thirty-day period when you can recover the position, a second cheque 'bounces', this will involve you in the twelve month ban. The ban applies to the 'innocent' holder of a joint account and, of course, to anyone holding a *procuration* to operate an account. The blocking of an account is reported to the Banque de France, where it remains on file for two years and any violation of the ban is reported to the Police. However, it is not quite as bad as it may seem for the ban can be lifted if it is possible to show that you had no control over the events which caused your account to be in debit (e.g. an error on the part of your bank) or if you can show that within two months of the ban being imposed you paid directly to the payee of the cheque the amount for which it was drawn.

What is so important to note is that the thirty day notice counts from the day it is sent out by the bank and is operative whether you receive it or not e.g. because it has been sent to your holiday home address in France and you have left the country. Obviously no bank with which you have good relations will not advise you if it sees you are running short of cash and it knows that it will have, for example, to meet standing orders for telephone or electricity bills but it is necessary to exercise care when issuing cheques because, as has been said, statements accurate though they may be, may well not reflect your true cash position. This advice is not intended to suggest that you are a 'bouncer' of cheques but quite awkward situations can arise if you are not familiar with the system. On the other hand, it has advantages. French cheques, unsupported by cheque cards, are accepted virtually everywhere, although proof of identity (passport or *carte de séjour*) is normally required cheques on company accounts are not normally accepted.

9. A corollary to the law on *chèques sans provision* is the rule about 'stopping' cheques, which needs careful attention. For practical purposes, there are only two cases when by law you may 'stop' a cheque – if you have lost your cheque book or if it has been stolen or, of course, if you have been told by someone to whom you gave a cheque that he has lost it or had it stolen. The law as to what you may do if, for example, you have given a cheque in payment of goods, which when they are delivered turn out to be not what you ordered or are not up to standard, varies from country to country. In France, if this happens and before you give irate instructions to the bank to 'stop' the cheque you have given, consult your local adviser or you may well find that you have landed yourself in considerable trouble.

10. It is not unusual for banks in France to pay interest on current accounts. It must be added that whilst it is not standard for French high street banks to require customers to keep a minimum balance on their accounts, bank charges are relatively high. However, there are some banks (including at least one 'British' bank) which do actively discourage customers who do not keep what seems to be quite a high minimum balance on their accounts. This can be particularly irritating if for most of the year your account is quasi-dormant and comes to life only from time to time. As one would expect, the French are not anxious to be paid with a foreign cheque, which costs a lot to clear and before opening an

account with a bank in France it is worthwhile asking if you are expected to maintain a minimum balance.

11. Deposit accounts (*comptes à terme*) are, of course, available in France. Normally, if these are opened in French francs, there is a minimum amount which banks will accept but other rules may apply for other currencies, if you are non-resident. You should consult your bank manager. If such an account is in French francs and you are non-resident in France for tax purposes, you will currently not be liable to suffer French Withholding Tax. For UK residents who now find their deposit interest in the UK paid to them after deduction of tax, it is worth remembering therefore that interest on a non-resident deposit in a bank in France will be paid to you gross. This may be useful if you have set cash aside for a flat or house purchase in France or if you are paying stage payments.

It is, generally speaking, a bad thing to close your bank account in your home country unless you have been advised to do so for special reasons. It is certainly going to be cheaper if you can avoid the need to change currency back into that of your own country when you visit it and there are certain other obvious advantages.

It is folly to throw in your credit cards which have been issued to you out of France. Access/Mastercharge, Visa/Barclaycard, American Express etc are all accepted in France and should be paid for from your non-French accounts. French credit cards are somewhat less useful. In the first place, all you spend in one month will be automatically debited to your French bank account. It is true that you pay no interest for this facility (there is a small annual fee) but this is a trivial compensation compared to the benefits available to you with, for example, the UK or US credit card. In the second place, although currently French credit cards can without limit as to the amount involved be used out of France, there is no guarantee that this freedom will be maintained. However, if you travel a great deal and pay for your journeys with a French *Carte Bleue* (Visa), you get automatic and very worthwhile insurance cover for the flight or other journey.

If you are in any way dependent on transfers of cash to or from your French bank account, it is absolutely essential to insist that the instructions you give for the transfer are scrupulously adhered to. The 'loss' of cash on a transfer between countries has to be suffered only once to be believed. The impossibility of tracking it down whilst it is in the maws of the system is beyond description. The simple answer is to let the manager of your receiving bank know exactly where the cash is coming from and, if possible, the route it is taking. All is easy if the two banks involved are in the same group – or it should be – but get your two managers together on the telephone if you can. If you are transferring between different groups, insist that the remitting bank send the cash to the branch or correspondent of the receiving bank in the country of the remitting bank for it to transfer out of the country. In that way, the cash will get into the system of the receiving bank immediately it has left the coffers of your remitting bank and the manager of your bank in France will know how to question his own system. Some banks will refuse to do this but it is worthwhile trying hard to persuade them to agree.

A final word of advice. If you find it quite impracticable to use the service of a 'foreign' bank in France, because you live deep in the Ardèche or in the Cotentin for example, remember that your local *Crédit Agricole* or *Banque Nationale de Paris* will be as used to foreign transactions as will the branch of any bank in any small market town in any country in the world. Why not use both – a local French bank for day to day business and a 'foreign' bank for your more important and international transactions? The latter can always keep your account in the former 'topped up'. The system of drawing facilities on the basis that one bank will cover another bank up to an agreed limit does not exist in France.

You may borrow in France towards the purchase of property in that country. You may borrow in French francs or in any other currency. In general terms, you may borrow as much as a lender considers that your financial position will allow but some impose limits for 'holiday homes' as opposed to your permanent home. On the whole, a typical maximum period for a loan will be fifteen years but longer can be obtained from certain lending institutions. In very general terms, if you want a loan towards the purchase of your house or flat, consult your bank manager in France or local adviser at the outset. If your own bank cannot assist, it will probably pass you on to a lending institution with which you can safely deal. In some cases, you will find that you can get a pretty swift decision; in some cases, a decision will take what seems to be a long time. Try always to tie up your loan in principle in advance of signing a purchase contract. Although by law, such a contract must include a condition that if you are buying with the aid of a loan, you may get out of the contract if you cannot get your loan (see Chapter 5), obviously your seller will not allow you to include a reference to a totally impossible loan and if you cannot get one, he is entitled to try to get one for you. Hence, if your purchase depends on your getting a 90% loan, you will not get one and you will not be able to make the obtaining of such a loan a condition of your contract. You must know more or less what you can get before signing your contract, which will state the amount you are seeking.

Loans for the purchase of property are of two types. Either you repay every year a fixed proportion of the loan and interest on the diminishing capital, so that repayments get smaller each year; or you pay a series of equal amounts over the agreed period. English and many other readers will recognize the latter type as the typical Building Society mortgage. It is almost inevitable that the lender will require you to take out a Life Assurance Policy but this is a sensible thing to do anyway and adds little to the cost of the loan. You must also ascertain what penalty (if any) you may have to pay for early repayment of the loan, since this is not uncommon in France.

The question of the rate of interest charged by your lender depends to some extent on the proportion which the loan bears to the total purchase price and the length of the loan. As a general rule, it is said that the best rate can be obtained for a loan of about 50% of the purchase price for a period of

15 years but this is based on statistics and must not be taken as gospel. There do exist loans at differing rates of interest, rarely indexed by being tied to some external norm, but quite frequently indexed by arranging for a lower rate to apply for the opening years of the loan and a higher rate thereafter. For those who think that their French is adequate, Minitel (see page 202) can be used to provide useful information about loans. The Minitel number is 36.15 and the code PAR. For those who are subject to income tax in France, loan interest is an allowable relief.

As is not unreasonable, if you want to repay a loan earlier than the date on which final payment is due under the loan agreement, you must pay a 'penalty' usually of several months interest which is the equivalent in England of giving so many months notice of early repayment. The amount of such 'penalty' is limited by the Loi Scribner. In addition, a lender may insist that if you make early repayments, none can be less than 10% of the amount borrowed but this must be stipulated in the loan agreement.

You can get bridging loans (*prêts-relais*) in France, but they have certain disadvantages. They are not normally granted for less than one year. Usually, only interest is payable until repayment of the loan out of the proceeds of sale of the property you are selling but sometimes interest can be rolled up and paid together with the capital sum borrowed. Another problem is that whilst sometimes a lender will be content to take a charge on the property you are selling (and some will want a charge on that which you are buying), others will want a charge on both properties and this can considerably increase the costs. There is nothing equivalent to the Solicitor's undertaking to pay over proceeds of sale to the provider of a bridging loan with makes the transaction so easy in England. Full mortgages are needed and *frais de dossier*, i.e. the cost of receiving and considering the application for the loan and ultimately the cost of removing charges from the Land Registry are not inconsiderable.

The next question to consider is not an easy one but should not, for that reason, not be asked. With perhaps an eye on the UK joining the European Monetary System and possibly with other things in mind, what is the best currency for me to borrow in? It is, of course, pointless trying to compare French interest rates with those in other countries, though people who are brave – or foolhardy – may 'take a view'. There are really two things to consider. If all your income comes to you in a currency other than French francs, is it perhaps a good idea to borrow in that currency and avoid exchange risks? On the other hand, interest on loans in (say) Swiss francs is very low and attractive but what happens if the Swiss franc rises in value against the currency out of which you are repaying the loan? You may lose on the exchange rate all you have gained on the interest – and more.

There are two other ways of financing a purchase in France; either might be helpful. You could borrow in your own country and simply use the money in France. At least you are paying for your loan with your own country's money; interest rates may be lower and you might be able to get tax relief on a loan secured in this way. Or you might get your bank at home to give a guarantee to a French bank, on which you will get your loan in France without any difficulty. Unfortunately, there are very few banks which will lend directly on the security of property in another country but they do exist; it is to be hoped that this may one day become commonplace.

It does pay to think internationally and not only in terms of mortgage arrangements in your own country. It also pays to get the best advice you can and ideally this seems to be a joint effort on the part of your own bank at home and your bank or local adviser in France, since each is expert in its own country. Above all, however, do not as a general rule allow property developers, sellers or their agents to negotiate loans for you. They cannot be aware of your personal situation and are interested only in selling to you.

CHAPTER 14

Tax in France

France, like every other country, is liable to change its tax laws and the rates of its taxes at the drop of a hat. You should therefore check all figures and rates quoted in this chapter as well as the bases of taxation referred to before applying any of this information to your particular case. The law and rates of tax in this chapter are those in force at the date given in Apppendix H.

The Inland Revenue system in France is part of the *Ministère du Budget* and it is with the local tax offices that you will normally be in touch. You file your *déclaration fiscale* (tax return) with the local *inspecteur*. Various forms are used, depending on the nature of your income and cover additionally such things as TVA and Capital Gains Tax, if any of these misfortunes should apply to you. TVA and stamp duties are collected by the *Recettes des Impôts*.

The French would be the first to admit that the administration of their tax system has not been very satisfactory. Recent efforts to remedy this have not been without some success but the system still creaks and, for those who are used to other systems, it may seem very unsupple. It is often extremely difficult to get anything other than a straight 'yes' or 'no' to a question and this tends to be a 'no' at lower levels if the question is at all unusual. This, however, is wholly in keeping with the lack, when dealing with the *Administration* in any of its forms, of that useful grey area which admits of neither 'yes' nor 'no' but of negotiation. Moreover, it must be admitted that the French are by tradition given to tax evasion on a fairly large scale and are therefore dealt with by their Revenue accordingly.

The basic taxes in France for individuals are:

1. Income Tax. French law distinguishes between *impôt sur le revenu* (earned income) and *impôt des revenus de capitaux mobiliers* (unearned income).

2. Capital Gains Tax. This is known in French as *régime des plus-values des particuliers*.

3. Death Duties. Known in French as *droits de succession*.

4. Gifts Tax. Known in French as *droits de donation*.

5. Wealth Tax. *Impôt de la solidarité sur la fortune*.

6. Land Tax and Communal Tax. Known in French as *taxe foncière* and *taxe d'habitation*.

Liability to French tax falls on two groups of people. On the one hand, those who have their 'fiscal domicile' in France are liable to tax on world-wide income. On the other hand, if you are not so domiciled in France, only income arising from French sources is liable to French tax.

You will acquire a French 'fiscal domicile' in any one of the following circumstances:

(A) Your home (*foyer*) or principal place of residence is in France. You will generally be treated as having your principal place of residence in France if you spend more than 183 days in that country in any relevant tax year. You will be treated as having your home in France, even if you are more or less permanently out of the country, if your wife and children live in France.

(B) You carry on in France any occupation, whether salaried or on your own account, unless you can prove that that occupation is ancillary or subordinate to your main occupation.

(C) Your centre of economic interests is in France. This will catch people whose main source of income is, for example, rents from French property, and royalties from patents or copyrights which are situated in France.

Subject to the effect of any Double Tax Convention between your country and France, in any of the cases mentioned above, you will be liable to tax in France on the whole of your income, wherever it arises. You will certainly need advice on the effect of Double Tax Conventions, the basic object of which is to ensure that you do not pay tax twice in full on the same income in your country and in France. France has such conventions with many countries but not, it should be noted, with the Channel Islands (except in respect of very limited types of income) or many of the tax havens, which are regarded with grave suspicion.

INCOME TAX

Normally, a husband's tax return will include the income of his wife and children. However, a wife living separate from her husband and not married in community of property may be separately assessed and a wife's income from 1st January in any year to the date of her marriage in that year is separately assessed. It is also possible to arrange for the separate assessment of children's income, if it stems from sources individual to them, e.g. their own earnings or income from an inheritance.

There are a number of special tax *régimes* which can apply in certain cases and which are briefly referred to later. The straightforward method of assessment of income tax is based on the following system.

Certain allowances are available which are set out in Appendix H.

Each taxpayer is entitled to divide his taxable income (which is arrived at after including all appropriate items of income and deducting all available allowances) by a number which indicates whether he is single, married or married with children. A single person without children divides his income by one so that there is no reduction. A married couple without children divide their income by two and a married couple with one child divide their income by 2.5. This figure (*quotient familial*) increases according to the number of children to a current 5.0 for families with five children and thereafter, 0.5 is added to this figure for each further child. There are special arrangements for one parent families, widows and widowers and divorced persons who have dependent children, which include illegitimate and adopted children and those generally living with the taxpayer. For these purposes, children are counted only up to the age of eighteen but if they are (i) unmarried and under twenty-one or (ii) under twenty-five and pursuing full time study or (iii) of any age and doing their military service, they can be counted as part of the family and give rise to a somewhat reduced *quotient familial*. Since the end of 1981 certain financial limits to the effect of this system have been introduced, but more recently, the Government, faced with a declining birth rate, has given parents of large families special tax benefits.

Rates of tax are on a slice basis and are shortly explained in Appendix H. Notwithstanding serious attempts at simplifying tax returns, they are not all that simple to complete and the language is somewhat technical. This is particularly the case if your income comes partly from outside France (for example, from non-French property, where current legislation imposes a somewhat harsh basis for the taxation of its income) or is of a special nature or if you are allowed special deductions. Local tax offices are very helpful and will certainly assist you in completing your returns. If your non-French income is at all substantial, you would be well advised to use the services of one of the larger firms of international accountants.

The French tax year runs from 1st January. Tax is payable in three instalments in the year following that in which it arises. Two instalments of a third each are due on 15th February and 15th May, based on your assessment of your preceding year's tax. A final payment is due at the end of the year, adjusted if necessary, when the inspector has finally agreed your assessment.

In certain limited circumstances, such as where you have failed to send in a tax return after a formal reminder, or where there is a marked difference between the taxable income you have disclosed and your standard of living (*train de vie*) and you have not remedied the situation to the satisfaction of the tax authorities, income tax is levied on the *régime d'imposi- tion forfaitaire* basis. This means that your tax will be assessed according to certain norms, to some extent irrespective of what it really is. The rules relating to this system are circum- scribed and are rarely invoked (about two hundred cases a

A view of the town of Lannion, Côtes du Nord

Pyramide du Louvre, Paris

The cobbled square at Ardres, Pas de Calais

year). These rules are clearly intended to prevent you having
an income of millions of francs while paying tax on only a
few thousand. The method of calculating your tax is to give
your assets certain 'income' values such as five times the
cadastral value of all properties you own, three-quarters of
the value of a new car with an allowance for depreciation, a
minimum of 7,500 francs for the first three tons of every boat
you own with something extra for each additional ton, 450
francs per horsepower of your aircraft, 9,000 francs for each
horse after the first and a minimum of 30,000 francs for each
servant under sixty excluding the first. On the whole, it seems
clear that this method of extracting tax can be applicable to
only a limited group of taxpayers. If you are involved in
certain types of business, such as property dealing, certain
types of property lettings, agriculture (which includes the
ownership of a vineyard) and the profits of your venture are
comparatively low, the Revenue may also tax you on a
forfaitaire basis i.e. on an assumed figure to avoid the need
for you to prepare full accounts and for them to peruse them.

In very general terms, it is unlikely that the average non-
French owner of a holiday home in France will be involved
with the French tax authorities. Technically, rents received
from lettings of these holiday homes are subject to French tax
but in many cases the amounts will not be large enough to
merit any imposition. There is no tax levied on interest arising
from deposit accounts with banks in France belonging to
non-residents. Any tax paid in France by persons who are
resident in another country may well fall to be dealt with
under the appropriate Double Tax Convention and advice
should be sought.

Care must be taken about tax due from French companies,
if only because in many cases, the *société* involved is not a
company at all in the Anglo-Saxon legal sense but is more
like a partnership. In these cases, as indeed in certain cases of
the 'family' *société á responsabilité limitée* which is the French
equivalent of the UK private company, tax is paid not by the
société but by the individual partners or shareholders. Where
property is owned by a company, whether it is non-French or

French, when it will usually be in the form of a *société civile immobiliére* or SCI, the free occupation of the property by a shareholder or partner or a director or *gérant* is apparently not treated as a benefit liable to be taxed. Of course, if the property is let to strangers at a rent, a liability to tax in theory arises. You ought to take careful advice on the tax position which can arise if you become a *gérant majoritaire* of a *société* that is to say a director owning 50% or more of the shares.

CAPITAL GAINS TAX

The basic rule is that non-residents pay Capital Gains Tax at the rate of 33⅓% in respect of houses and flats and at the rate of 50% on sales of all other French property such as securities. If you are resident in France for tax purposes, different rules apply.

However, as the result of a recent change in the law, it is probable that very few non-resident house or flat-owners will be liable to this tax. Those who benefit from exemption are all EEC citizens and also citizens of all countries which have Double Tax Treaties with France which provide for the exchange of fiscal information. Included among such countries are Australia, Canada, Finland, Israel, New Zealand, Norway, Sweden and the US. The exemption applies to all such owners, provided that the property in question is in their occupation (i.e. not let) at the time of the sale. It applies to a series of properties but only to one property at a time. It will also in many cases apply to properties owned by companies, the only shareholders of which are persons who would themselves be exempt if they were the direct owners of the property in question – but this is a point which will need advice in each individual case.

The important thing to remember is that what is involved is not a blanket relief from French CGT but an exemption in suitable cases. Therefore, the warning on page 78 to read what is written in this chapter about this tax is still extremely important. The procedure outlined below *must* be followed in each case, or you may have considerable cause for regret.

On the sale of any property of any kind, the French Revenue

has four years in which to re-open any CGT claim to alter either upwards or downwards the tax paid on the sale, or to claim tax where, since none seemed to be due at the time of the sale, none was in fact paid. Where there is an evident liability on a sale, it is the duty of the *notaire* to deduct it from the proceeds of sale and pay it over. For its protection in the case of non-residents, the French Revenue may require all such sellers to appoint an *agent accredité* for a period of four years. This agent is usually a French bank which will charge a fee and in some cases retain a part of the proceeds of sale as security. The only way to avoid this is to apply *before* completion of your sale for a *dispense* from the appointment of such an agent. Few 'foreign' sellers know this. Fewer still are told of it by the *notaire* acting, whom the seller may never meet if he is foolish enough to have appointed the *notaire*'s clerk as his Attorney, or whom he is at best likely to meet for the first time at completion if he attends himself. It is absolutely essential to ensure that the *dispense* is obtained before the sale is completed because, if it is not, even if the Revenue is 100% in agreement that there is no CGT to pay, it cannot then relieve a seller from the need to appoint his fiscal representative in France. Do not, therefore, believe friends who tell you that you can now 'forget' CGT in France. You 'forget' it at your peril (though you may well have nothing to pay). This is just another of the many situations where a local adviser will look after your interests and see to it that your *dispense* is obtained.

In case, for one reason or another, you are not exempt from CGT in France, it is worthwhile having an idea of how a taxable gain is calculated. To the purchase price, you may add 10% for the costs of acquisition. To the resultant figure, you apply an inflation factor which varies according to the year of purchase. You then deduct the result from your sale price and the difference is your taxable gain. You may also reduce that gain by the cost of any restoration work, improvements or the like which you have carried out, but not the cost of pure decoration or, as the French, say, *embellisement*. Remember, however, that receipted bills showing TVA paid must be produced if their cost is to be used to reduce a CGT claim and that workmen paid in cash with no TVA added do not give receipts. Incidentally, bearing in mind what is said in Chapter 22, do not fall for the standard ploy of paying in cash free of TVA for work done to a house or flat. It is, as you will appreciate, very difficult to sue for bad workmanship when you cannot even prove to a Judge that you had the work done.

Remember also that if you sell part of the garden of your *résidence secondaire* to a developer or if you yourself have built a second house on your land with a view to a profitable scale, such a sale is not exempt from CGT though whether there is any tax payable will depend on the individual circumstances.

Whether it is worth indulging in schemes to avoid a possible CGT liability must depend on all the relevant circumstances. All that can be said is that schemes of this kind require special advice from experts and never from friends. They should also be considered before and never after buying what you have in mind to buy.

For persons who are fiscally domiciled in France and therefore subject to French tax, the rules about CGT are, despite all attempts at simplification on the part of the French Revenue, just as complex as in any other country and advice is needed. As in many other countries, one's principal private residence is normally free of tax. In certain circumstances, tax can also be avoided on secondary residences if, for example, you are not the owner but only the lessee of your principal residence, but this is hedged around with conditions and needs careful advice. Certain sales of agricultural land are exempt and the reliefs available on all CGT claims mean that in the case of sales of property owned for a least twenty-two years there is a nil liability.

On sales of antiques, jewellery and objets d'art generally, there is a 6% tax on the sale price reduced to 4% in the case of auction sales with certain reliefs. The seller may in certain circumstances opt to pay CGT on the ordinary basis which may prove to be advantageous.

WEALTH TAX

This tax, brought in in 1981 by the then Socialist government and abolished by the next, Conservative, government has been reinstated by the current left-wing government with apparently the support of some of the right-wing opposition.

DEATH DUTIES

The French system is unusual to some in that it applies rates of duty payable on death which vary according to the relationship of the beneficiary to the person who has died and the variations are startling. This philosophy stems from the French reverence for the *patrimoine*. If the family fortune is going to pass outside the immediate family, it pays more duty. It is for this reason also that duty is payable, not by the estate as a whole, but by each individual beneficiary. The rates and methods of application of this tax are to be found in Appendix H.

It must be remembered that in the case of a person who is not 'fiscally domiciled' in France, duty in France is payable on all his assets in that country. For example, a person, who is not 'fiscally domiciled' in France, will pay duty at the appropriate rate on his house or flat in France or on any cash in the bank, if the figures are sufficiently large. He may also be liable for death duties on that property in his own country. If he is and a Double Tax Convention exists between France and that country, he will usually be given an allowance in his country for the duty paid in France. The estate of a person who is 'fiscally domiciled' in France is liable for duty on all his assets, whether they are in France or out of France and whether they have produced income on which he has paid French tax or not: this is a point which must be borne in mind when Wills are being made.

Interest on death duties, the rate of which varies from time to time, is payable after a delay of one year in respect of a death out of France and six months if the death took place in France. As for all tax liabilities, the Revenue has four years in which to review a file and seek extra tax or duty. It is unlikely that the beneficiaries of a non-French deceased person will be chased for additional duty but at the end of every year, a good deal of reviewing does go on for the French and a good deal of explaining has to be done – or extra duty paid.

To avoid making it too easy to cheat, in every estate in which death duties are payable in France, an amount of 10% of the net estate is taken as the value of household goods and personal effects unless a formal valuation (usually by a Notary) is provided. Hence, the family of anyone dying outside France, owning a fairly valuable house with very little valuable furniture in it or where the furniture belonged to someone else will find the dutiable assets perforce increased by 10% of their value unless they care to produce an independent valuation. It is worth also remembering that the cost of funerals, which as has been said in Chapter 10 is high in France, is not allowed in full as a deduction for death duty purposes. Currently the allowance is the ludicrous figure of 3,000 francs.

GIFTS TAX
This tax follows more or less the same rules and rates as death duties. There are, however, certain exemptions and mitigating features, such as those available on gifts made on the occasion of marriage.

In addition, to some extent the reductions in this tax which used to be enjoyed some years ago have been re-established and if the maker of the gift is less than sixty-five years old, the tax is reduced by 25%, whilst the reduction is 15% for ages sixty-five to seventy-five but nil over that age.

COMMUNAL TAX
Taxe d'habitation covers primarily services provided by the local *commune* but includes a contribution for departmental and regional expenses. In cases of a principal residence, there are total exemptions for the elderly and sick and reductions for elderly relatives and the like, information about which is given on the back of the demand. You may find that you have mysteriously been given all the reductions to which you are

entitled, without having asked for them. This happens because the local authority is often quite happy to rely on information given to them about your family by your *Concierge* (who can usually be trusted only to impart information to your advantage to the authorities) but if you think you can claim more than you have been given, go to the local *mairie* and explain. This tax is payable by the occupier of a dwelling (furnished and habitable, even if not lived in) who was in possession on 1st January in any year. If you move in on 2nd January, you may well get a tax-free year. Do not worry, the unfortunate person who spent one day in the flat or house will pay (it is much easier to find people in France than in the UK) but he will not pay in that year in his new home. The tax is payable in one sum. The demand seems to arrive in autumn, but this varies from place to place and if payment is not made by a stated date, the amount is increased by 10%.

LAND TAX
Taxe foncière is payable by the owner of property. It is calculated on the estimated local letting value of the property. This tax tends to be in quite a small amount. No tax is charged on the first two years after completion of a new building or the restoration of a building and, as with *taxe d'habitation*, it is due from the owner on 1st January (see also Chapter 5).

TVA
This tax, only too well known in Common Market countries, is *taxe sur la valeur ajoutée*. The intention is that ultimately there will be only one rate prevailing in all the countries in the Common Market; Denmark alone has only one rate and Italy has seven, so the intention may take some years to realize. There are currently three rates in France (see Appendix H), which includes a luxury rate which applies to such interesting items as cars, jewellery, furs, caviar, radios and pornographic films. The tax is charged on food but at a reduced rate. Expensive hotels used to benefit from a reduced rate in respect of part of the services they rendered but now do not:

hence you may find that your favourite hotel has shed a star without noticeably reducing its quality in order to stay within the reduced rate of tax.

Apart from the irritation of the existence of this tax, in Chapter 5 you will have found a reference to TVA in connection with the sale of flats or houses. In the case of the sale of flats or houses, either prior to their completion (*en état futur d'achièvement*) or if the sale is the first one to occur within five years of completion of the building, TVA is chargeable on the sale price. Hence the reduced rate of 'stamp duty' during that period. The TVA is included in the price, and when you buy from a developer, you will notice that this tax has been charged and paid over to the fiscal authorities. However, if you sell within that period of five years from completion of the block in which your flat is, you will also be liable for TVA, and again it will be included in the price (i.e. you cannot increase the market price to cover the TVA). The result is not as serious as it sounds, for the tax for which you are liable is not the current rate on the sale price but that amount less the TVA which was paid on the sale to you. The calculation is not an easy one to make, but, as an example, a flat bought for 415,000 francs on which TVA was paid and sold for 475,000 francs within the five-year period will cost the seller about 12,000 francs in TVA on the sale. On the other hand, the seller must remember that, on the purchase by him, his 'stamp duties' were about 2,500 francs instead of over 20,000 francs. Again, remember that the five-year period runs from completion of the building and not from the date on which you completed the purchase, if you bought 'on plan'.

There are complicated rules about how you can recover in certain cases the equivalent of TVA paid in one country if you have to pay TVA on an item when it arrives in France or avoid payment of the tax in one country provided it is paid in France. French Customs or a Customs Clearing Agent can explain these to you and it is wise to ask in advance.

Finally, a word about the implications of buying property in France in the name of a non-French company. This used to be a very effective way of avoiding French tax but over the years, French governments have considerably hedged this type of operation around with restrictions. As the law stands today, any property in France belonging to a company registered in any tax haven country is subject to an annual tax of 3% on its market value. Tax haven countries include such obvious places as Panama, Liberia and the Dutch Antilles and also include such less obvious places as Liechtenstein, the Isle of Man and the Channel Islands. Switzerland gives rise to a special problem because the French tax authorities consider that Swiss companies are not exempt, but there are at least two judgments of French Courts holding that such companies are exempt because of the terms of the Franco-Swiss Double Tax Treaty. The criterion is whether the country in question has a Tax Convention with France which includes provisions for mutual assistance in the fight against what the French call 'fiscal fraud'. Property in the name of a company incorporated in a country which is smiled on by the French is subject to no such tax at all provided that it discloses every year to the French tax authorities certain details of its French property and its value and the identity and shareholdings of the shareholders of the company. Failure to do this will involve the tax of 3%, which is, in effect, a tax on capital. There can, however, be advantages in certain circumstances in owning property in France through the medium of a company but the most careful advice must be taken from the right source conversant both with the law in France and in your country and also in the country where the company is formed, which may well not be your own country.

CHAPTER 15

Insurance

The ingenuity of French insurance companies is no less than that of insurance companies in other countries. However, as one would expect, not only is French insurance law different but the language in which policies are written is also different from what you have been used to. What you might not so easily expect is the effect that the French mentality has on French policies, both in their terms and in the way that claims under them are dealt with. For example, if the wall of your garden is damaged by a passing lorry, you may find it very difficult to make a successful claim under the impact cover in your comprehensive policy unless you can produce the registration number of the lorry concerned. Why? Because your company will assume that you have deliberately done the damage yourself, if you cannot prove that you did not. Of course, you may be able to get special cover, but the point is that French insurance companies tend to treat their clients as rogues until proved otherwise, which is an attitude some may find unreasonable if not downright rude.

There is continuous talk of 1992, the year when all frontiers will disappear and, among other things, to oversimplify, there will be freedom for insurance companies in one EEC country to carry on business in another EEC country as though it were in its own home country. The most recent EEC Directive on this subject, apart from being couched in alarmingly complex terms, has failed to achieve this laudable goal because certain countries whose systems are perhaps less sophisticated than others have felt it necessary to protect their own insurance industries from those who could perform better. That being so, for the ordinary individual, it will be years before there is trans-frontier insurance in France and it continues to be of great importance to consider the peculiarities of the French insurance policy.

Quite apart from the overall need to be adequately insured, the risks against which you should cover depend on the type of property you own. The average non-Frenchman will need insurance in two spheres. He will need to insure his car, if it is registered in France and he will need to insure his home and its contents, whether it is his permanent home or a holiday home, whether he has bought it or leased it and whether it is a house or a flat. If he is a permanent resident in France, he may also need all-risks cover for special items such as jewellery, cameras etc and also for any items lodged with banks most of whom will cover items in safe deposit boxes only up to a maximum of (say) 100,000 francs. It is essential to ask what this maximum is when depositing anything at the bank. In addition, for the permanent resident with children at school in France, the law requires that you effect public liability cover against any damage they may do to third parties. This cover may well be included in your householders' comprehensive policy but it is as well to check. For quite a small sum, cover can also be effected for any accident a child may suffer at, or on the way to or from, school. Children in France suffer annually at least a thousand deaths and something like forty thousand injuries going to and from school, to say nothing of accidents at school itself. You would be well advised to use the proposal form for this kind of insurance which your child will bring back from school at the beginning of every scholastic year.

AS HOME OWNER

Your obligation to insure is to yourself only. In such cases, the Householders Comprehensive policy or '*police multirisque habitation*' is clearly what is required. Such a policy will, subject to exceptions and exclusions, cover the house against fire, lightning, explosion, storm, flood, burst pipes, riot, catastrophic risks and the like, and will cover the contents against much the same risks plus theft, accidental damage to glass and other risks. In addition, it will give you public liability cover (*responsibilité civile*) and cover against liabilities you have towards members of your family, your servants, your guests and the like (*responsibilité civile vie privée*). You have total freedom to insure with (but, as you will see, not necessarily to cease to be insured by) any company which is prepared to underwrite the risks against which you wish to cover at a premium you are willing to pay.

AS COPROPRIETAIRE

If you are a *copropriétaire* (see Chapter 8) your insurance problem is different. The block containing the flat you occupy is divided into common and private parts. Whilst damage caused to your flat by yourself or by persons foreign to the *copropriété* is a matter for insurance cover effected by you, damage caused to your flat by the building itself (e.g. a leaking roof or overflowing gutters) is the liability of the *copropriété*. If you damage your neighbour's flat by letting your bath overflow, the liability is yours and finally the common parts of the building must themselves be covered against the sort of risks covered by a householder's comprehensive policy. All this is dealt with in the *règlement de copropriété* which sets out what the *syndic* is to cover and what you are to cover. It is desirable to know just what the *syndic* has in fact covered since sometimes his policy covers flats as well as common parts. If this is so, you are not necessarily saving anything, since the premium which is shared out among all flat-owners as part of the Service Charges will be higher than if he covers only the common parts but if your flat is covered by his overall policy, you need not cover the risks he has covered. You would be left with the need only to cover the contents and your *responsibilité civile vie privée*. On the whole, the *syndic* covers the common areas only but it remains to add that it is rare that any *syndic* offers this information and it usually must be sought. In fact, not only do you need this information for the purposes of your own insurance but to ensure that the *syndic* has done his own job properly. To the extent that you need to insure as *copropriétaire*, your choice of insurance company is normally limited by a requirement that you cover with a company 'of repute' or as the French have it, which is *'notoirement solvable'*.

AS TENANT
You will be required as a tenant in general terms to cover (a) your contents (b) your liabilities towards neighbours and third parties, e.g. against damage to the downstairs flat due to a defect in your washing machine (*'recours des voisins et des tiers'*) and (c) your liabilities towards your landlord (*'risques locatifs'*) e.g. if your frying pan catches alight and fire damage is caused to the kitchen. Whether your lease is a Loi Quillot or a Loi Méhaignerie lease, you are by law required to effect these covers and produce evidence that you have on the grant of the lease and annually. Your choice of insurance company is unhampered; indeed, as has been said, it is unlawful for a landlord to provide otherwise. The difference between the two laws is that failure to insure under a Loi Méhaignerie lease is a ground for automatic determination by the landlord whereas under the earlier law it was one of the grounds available for non-renewal of a lease.

It follows therefore that in whatever capacity you wish to insure, it is unlikely that any interested party will or indeed can object to your choice of company. There are in these circumstances, good grounds for suggesting that you consider effecting cover through an insurance company in your own country and if this is the UK, through Lloyds rather than through a French company or a non-French company carrying on business in France.

In the case of the UK, it seems that none of the tariff companies give (or possibly can give) cover on French property except under policies written under French law and it seems as though, as has been said, notwithstanding the good intentions of 1992, it will be many years before this situation alters, if at all. Lloyds, on the other hand, will in many cases cover all the necessary risks under English policies and deal with claims *à l'anglaise*. It must be remembered that in addition to Lloyds' brokers in the UK, there are a number of firms in France who have been, to use the Lloyds' expression, 'tribunalized' or approved and are able to deal with the issue of Lloyds policies and deal with claims under them.

Care must also be taken to realize that if one in fact effects cover through such of the UK tariff companies as are represented in France, one gets French cover under French law with a French policy notwithstanding that the company giving the cover has an English name and cover was effected in the UK.

However, there may be circumstances when there is no choice but to resort to a French insurance company or a non-French company operating under French rules. Should this be the case, it is essential that you use the services of a broker or *courtier*, or the agent of a company who even if he is not familiar with insurance practice in your home country at least knows sufficient to warn you of the peculiarities of French insurance and of the meaning of some basic French insurance terms. At very worst, insist that you get explanations on the basic elements of any policy you take out and do not sign a policy until you have understood its terms. To do otherwise is to court disappointment on some occasion in the future.

One of the most important rules is that in normal circumstances non-life policies in France do not lapse on the non-payment of a renewal premium. Your policy will state how long is the period before the date of renewal of the notice you must give to cancel (*résilier*) it. The minimum period will certainly be one month but many companies require three months notice. It is in fact lawful for a company to insist on much longer notice (three years, or three years plus three years and thereafter annual) and although this is not common, the greatest care must be taken in *reading* the clause in the policy before signing it. Note particularly that if notice of cancellation arrives at your insurance company out of date, the company is under no duty so to inform you and almost certainly will not do so. If you do not give proper notice (*avis de résiliation*), your policy will continue in force and you will be chased for the premium. Finally, if you are more than ten days late with the payment of a premium, cover will be suspended thirty days after notice to that effect is given to you by the company but you will remain liable for the premium. An exception to the rule allows cancellation at short notice if you change jobs or are made redundant, if you get married or divorced or if you are being charged a loaded premium, and the company wil not reduce the loading if the circumstances which caused the loading cease to exist.

A special rule applies on the sale of property. Under French law, the seller's policy remains in force automatically for the benefit of the buyer. This means that the time limits in the policy now apply to the buyer who unless he is wary may find that he is too late to cancel a policy he does not want. As to the seller, if the buyer fails to pay a premium under such a policy, he may remain liable to the company for its payment. The solution to this problem is to ensure that the *acte de vente* deals with this problem and ensure that the seller cancels his policy as from completion and the buyer starts afresh.

It is not part of the *notaire*'s task to deal with questions of insurance after completion of the purchase or sale of your house or flat as would your Solicitor in the UK. This is up to you and your local adviser will, of course, deal with this for you if you wish. Indeed, this may well be essential for there seems in France to be no or no readily discoverable equivalent of a phone call to a company or a broker which will ensure immediate cover with details to be sorted out later.

A particular problem is, of course, the holiday home where it is inevitable that long periods of non-occupancy will render the policy void if not disclosed and give rise to a high premium if disclosed. The non-occupancy period is usually more than ninety days in any one year. It is possible at a cost to contract out of the problem but this also can be expensive with French companies and will almost certainly require the installation of security systems. Some companies, indeed, will not issue policies at all for holiday homes in certain 'burglar prone' parts of the country. The usual booty for thieves consists of jeweller, pictures, hi-fi equipment and arms. It is worthwhile informing the local police or *gendarmerie* of your comings and goings. Although there are expert thieves about, many burglaries in the south are committed by the hungry young on holiday whose funds have run out. They are looking for food and cash or items easy to turn into cash. A good front door lock whose keys cannot be cut in France and if necessary window fasteners all acquired 'at home' and installed by a locksmith you can trust is a cheap way of foiling this type of loss. Beware the locksmith who happens to turn up just after you have moved into your flat saying that he is 'locksmith to the block'. Doubtless he is, in the sense that he has special aptitude to open his own locks with a set of your keys that he has retained.

Without special explanations, insurers tend to cover contents on a room basis, i.e. a studio has contents worth so much and a four-roomed flat so much. Two distinct problems arise here. In the first place, unless a special policy is effected, replacement of such of the contents stolen as are 'precious objects' will be limited usually to 30% of the total cover. Clearly, it is desirable to effect separate cover for such items if the essential careful study of your comprehensive policy which will define what are 'precious objects' shows that otherwise you would be undercovered. The second problem is that before you give values to items of any significance, you must remember that prices of such things as curtain material, bed linen, china (but not glass) and clothing can be more expensive in France than at home and a careful survey of the local shop is desirable. To replace a carpet of the quality you bought from the UK or certain other countries will cost at least double what you paid for it, if indeed, you can find that quality in France.

You may have some practical problems about the valuation in France of jewellery and items of value which are not French. French insurance companies will, of course, require valuations to be French since the value of certain non-French items can differ considerably, both upwards and downwards, from that in certain other countries. Silver is a particular problem for if it is not French silver, little expertise seems to be available except possibly in Paris, which seems to have virtually the monopoly of knowledge of antiques and objets d'art. It is sheer lack of knowledge that is liable to give no premium, for example, to English early Georgian silver as compared to late Victorian pieces. Good Sheffield plate which is highly thought of in many parts of the world is often considered by the French to be a thin layer of substandard silver slapped on to copper and valued accordingly as *metal argenté*. Nine and fourteen carat gold are not considered as gold in France – only eighteen carat and above is accepted as such. The same problem arises with non-French antique furniture, which is, of course, very difficult to replace in France but which when it is and is sold by a knowledgable seller can command a fabulous price. Curiously, the French like their mahogany a dark plum colour (almost black) and such non-French pieces as one can find in that wood require stripping and repolishing to their proper colour. The price of jewellery is very high in France and any valuation for all-risks purposes should be made by a really first-class jeweller (preferably Parisian) whose fees are comparatively low.

MOTOR INSURANCE

You should not assume that French motor insurance and the law governing it is the same or even similar to that of your own country. Some cover offered in France is better than elsewhere, some a lot worse. There are also certain circumstances where, unless you have a special contract covering such an event you will not be able to claim anything except third-party. For instance, in most *départements* of France no matter how long you have been driving you cannot give a driving lesson to someone unless you are properly insured to do so and most insurance companies do not cover this possibility (see Chapter 11). If you skid, knock down a telegraph pole etc you will not be able to claim unless you have specifically asked for cover and this does not necessarily mean an ordinary comprehensive cover. Luckily most insurance companies, but not the *mutuelles*, have changed over to the totally comprehensive policy *tous accidents* so that this problem under the old type policy *dommages-collision* is on the way out. Either of these policies will cover you for damage to your car (but not the people inside) due to a terrorist act (*attentat*) which the ordinary obligatory insurance will not. Even when the car is driven without your knowledge by a thief, a friend or even a member of your family it is covered though only for third party. Cars parked illegally, e.g. on a double yellow line or causing an obstruction lose their comprehensive cover.

Foreigners are often unpleasantly surprised by what is *not* covered by a French '*tous accidents*' policy. For instance, the driver causing the accident is not covered and can claim nothing for himself. For that he needs a special, and separate, policy '*assurance conducteur*'. This will cover him, often again only to a certain extent, for medical treatment as well as payment of expenses. He should have complementary medical insurance in any event and this will be taken into account by the company insuring the car and its driver.

If someone else is proved responsible for the accident then his company will pay – eventually. These things take a long time in France and two to three years is far from unusual.

Accessories are rarely insured in France and if they are you will pay an enormous premium. Windscreen breakage can be covered and this will often include the rear and side windows and sometimes even headlamps and fog lights.

You cannot insure braking or reversing lights or indicators. As to stealing items such as a radio, tape recorder, luggage, etc., from the car you need a specific mention of these in your policy and if you have a franchise to pay you will pay the first 500 or 1000 francs or more of each and every loss. Therefore, in fact, you are at best only partially covered for theft from the car.

The good news is that once you have a car insurance which is '*tous accidents*' you are insured against terrorist attacks (in an airport car park for instance as well as in your own garage or on the street) and against Acts of God such as earthquake, flood, etc.

If you have a car worth in excess of 100,000 francs it must have a properly installed and approved alarm system plus the car number engraved on all the windows. If it is not properly garaged at night you will pay an extra premium and for this purpose open underground car parks in blocks of flats count as a garage.

Insurance companies cannot be forced to give cover to a particular individual but a driver *must* be insured. A driver who has been found guilty of dangerous or drunken driving will find his future premiums heavily loaded against him. Moreover, companies who have to pay out on accidents due to drunken driving are allowed to have recourse against the drunken driver though this seldom happens.

In France there are limits as to how much can be recovered by an injured party. These are 5,000,000 francs per person victim of an accident and 3,000,000 for a vehicle or damage to property. French law requires not only the taking out of obligatory third-party insurance but the showing of the insurance *vignette* (receipt) on the windscreen in accordance with Common Market rules and also the carrying of a Green Card or *Attestation d'Assurance* in the car at all times.

The current rule about the cancellation of motor cover by the insurance company is as follows. Third-party cover cannot be cancelled by the insurer unless either i) the driver involved in the accident was drunk or ii) the accident was caused by a breach of the French Highway Code which results in the suspension of the driving licence for at least one month. Of course, an insurer can refuse to give further cover at the end of the period during which the cover was in force but he must give two months prior notice of his intention. If a driver has difficulty in obtaining cover he can apply to the *Bureau Central de Tarification* who can require the company of your choice to provide you with cover at a premium fixed by the Bureau.

The insured driver must, of course, give whatever notice is laid down in the policy when wishing to determine cover. An *attestation d'assurance* will give cover for all Common Market countries, but you will need a Green Card (*Carte Verte*) for European (and other) countries not in the Common Market. Some companies charge for this; others do not. However, it is wise to remember that buying two or three weeks' insurance in a foreign country will be considerably more expensive than obtaining a Green Card on your own policy. The standard Certificate of Insurance issued in the UK will cover you for all Common Market countries but you will, as most other nationalities do, need a Green Card for other European countries. It is best to consult your own insurance company as to what cover you have when abroad before embarking on a journey.

French motor policies allow for a no-claims bonus. To those versed in simple Latin, the opposite of bonus is malus and whilst you can earn a bonus you can also acquire a malus – and more quickly! The malus is not an ordinary loading of premium, done on a one-off basis. There are precise rules about it and in view of the conduct of the average French driver it is as well to know something of these. For every year which is accident free you are entitled to a bonus with a maximum of 50% in the thirteenth year. Do not question the mathematics when these rules are applied to you. They are complex but logical. For every accident your premium is increased by 25% or a multiplying co-efficient of 1.25 with a maximum of 250% which is achieved after six consecutive accidents. Again, the mathematics are complex but logical. An example will suffice. Your first year's premium was FF1,000. You have two accidents in the first year. Your next year's premium will be increased by $1.25 \times 1.25 = 1.56$ and the result is the premium of FF1,560. Next year you have no accidents and your premium is reduced by $5\% - 1.56 \times .95 =$ FF1,480. This assumes that the basic premium does not increase from year to year which is most unlikely.

For accidents for which you are totally blameless, no malus is charged. If you are only partly to blame for an accident, then even if your share of responsibility is less than half, your malus is reduced by half. In cases where the driver is wholly to blame and causes injury to third parties or to himself or the car, the full malus is suffered. No malus is suffered if damage is caused to your parked car by an identified third party who is wholly to blame provided you can prove this to the company. However, damage by an unidentified third party can have an affect on your bonus/malus rating though in the first instance this is rare. You do not acquire a malus under the cover for theft, fire or breakage of glass; by the same token, you acquire no bonus in that year. Incidentally, your car cannot be considered officially stolen until thirty days have elapsed since you reported its disappearance. Moreover, those insuring with *mutuelles* should remember that a car is not considered stolen if found after the thirty days have elapsed but it shows no signs of forcible entry and although the premiums charged may be lower, for this reason alone, *mutuelles* are not recommended.

The bonus/malus calculations are based on what is called the *prime de référence* – that is the basic premium asked, having regard to the usual loadings for new drivers (less than three years since passing the driving test), certain accidents which have resulted in very severe penalties, the area in which the car is to be used etc. There are reductions for advanced drivers, for no accidents over a long period and for the obtaining of the maximum bonus as an incentive to keep you adequately motivated in the future!

Your bonus/malus position is transferable to a new or second car provided that the conditions remain the same and continues if you change insurance companies. If you have benefited from a bonus in your own country and wish to make use of this in France, bring with you a certificate from your old insurance company stating how many accident free years you have had and the percentage bonus you last enjoyed. This will be given due regard by the French companies.

In general terms, basic motor premiums in France are high and in such places as Paris, Nice or Lyon, are very high. Hence to start off with and to keep a no claims bonus in France is a highly desirable thing. Premiums may be paid yearly, half-yearly, quarterly or monthly with of course a weighting if paid by instalments.

If you are an EEC citizen or the car is registered in an EEC country, you will often find that the cover given abroad is not as comprehensive as in your own country and a Green Card will be needed to ensure comprehensive cover. Also, going from one EEC country to another often involves crossing a non-EEC country, e.g. Switzerland or Austria, where a Green Card is obligatory in any event if you want more than third-party cover.

If you are involved in an accident, you may well be asked by the driver of the other car to complete a *constat amiable*, setting out the details of the accident which is then given to each of the insurance companies involved. There is no obligation on your part to do this – certainly not to admit liability, however much in the wrong you may be – and in the most general terms, it is frequently better to decline politely to fill in the *constat*. However, since this form is now standard in EEC countries, it is a very good idea to keep one in your own language in the car so that if you are asked to complete one, you will at least understand the questions you are answering. Unless you are well-nigh word perfect in French, give your answers in English for it is very easy to make a literal translation into French with unintended results.

If, alas, you do have a claim, you will come into contact with the insurance company's *expert* who will inspect the damage and agree the cost of repair. Sometimes a company will agree to your using an *expert* who is not on their list and to proceed this way round usually saves time. Some companies will allow you to have small repairs done without an *expertise*. At least in the South of France where temperature and temperament play their part (except, it must be admitted, in the case of the very resistant strong characters of northern French extraction!) agreeing claims can take quite a long time and you will not be long in the country before you are amazed at the number of cars with dents, damaged bumpers and other minor and not so minor knocks, most leading to eventual rusting of the car, whose owners prefer not to make any claim on their own company. The leaving of a visiting card when you inadvertently damage a car whose owner is absent is a courtesy unknown in France. Whether you believe in the adage 'When in Rome . . . ' and act accordingly is up to you.

CHAPTER 16

Health and Pensions

If you are a citizen of a Common Market country, there are three circumstances in which you can become involved with the French National Health Service (*Sécurité Sociale*). You may be in France on holiday and need medical attention; you may be living or working in France and be under the statutory retirement age in your 'home' country or you may be over that age and in receipt of a state retirement pension. If you are not from a Common Market country, you may still become involved in the *Sécurité Sociale* but this is most likely to be because you are working in France or have voluntarily joined.

Sécurité Sociale, unlike National Health Services in certain other countries, is not a system under which either you benefit totally or you do not benefit at all. Certain hospitals, doctors and paramedical services can be used free of all cost. You can, if you wish, opt for wholly private medicine, which is likely to be very expensive and for which *Sécurité Sociale* pays nothing. In between, lies a wide range of hospitals and clinics together with doctors and ancillary services for which the French State will pay a proportion of the cost according to prior arrangements made and publicized.

For example, every large town has at least one *hôpital conventioné* for which one pays nothing and also a supply of doctors and other medical services which is free. Very often but by no means always, the services available are somewhat limited. *Hôpitaux conventionés* have no wholly private rooms. There are also hospitals and clinics which are not State-supported where *Sécurité Sociale* will reimburse you to an extent depending on what has been agreed between them and *Sécurité Sociale* and then each clinic will tell you the maximum amount so reimbursable. The way in which the French cope with the difference is to use the *mutuelle* or private health insurance, which in the case of many occupations it is obligatory to join. Almost every profession and trade has its own *mutuelle* which usually covers not only the difference between what you can recover from the Health Service and what your illness or medicines cost you but also 'tops up' your retirement pension. There are *mutuelles* which will pay for wholly private medicine and there are also Private Health Insurance policies issued by insurance companies.

If you are a Common Market citizen coming to France on holiday, you should obtain before leaving a form E111 which remains valid for three months and which entitles you to free treatment (or sometimes total reimbursement) provided you limit yourself to the use of *hôpitaux conventionés* and doctors wholly within the scheme. If you are unexpectedly out of your country for more than three months, the E111 can normally be renewed from a distance and if you are hospitalized, the Almoner can arrange for form E111 to be changed into a form E112 which is an undertaking by the issuing country to bear the full cost of hospital treatment. In the event, almost everyone nowadays takes out private travel insurance or Europassistance or the like and on the whole this is more satisfactory and simpler than relying on a form E111. Provided that the travel policy is sufficiently widely drawn (it pays to read them very carefully), it will procure better medical services than a form E111 and often will enable the insured to be repatriated free, which the majority of National Health Services (including the British) will not pay for. Most non-Common Market citizens must, of course, rely on private travel insurance.

If you are working in France, you will be required to join *Sécurité Sociale*, you paying part of your contributions and your employer paying the other part. If you are self-employed, you will pay a percentage of your taxable income as contribution and this itself is an allowable deduction for income tax purposes. If you are resident in France but do not work, you may voluntarily join the scheme when your contributions will be assessed according to your income for which purpose you will be required to produce a copy of your tax return. In the former case, you will almost certainly be required to join a *mutuelle*; in the latter, you may do so if you wish.

If you are retired, in the sense that you are entitled to a State Retirement Pension from 'home,' and 'home' is a Common Market country, you and your spouse are automatically entitled to the health benefits provided by *Sécurité Sociale* free of all contributions. This, of course, applies whether you arrive in France after you have reached retirement age or (assuming that you have not previously joined the scheme so that you would get these benefits anyway – but at a cost) you reach that age after having lived in France for some time. All that is needed is to produce to the appropriate office of *Sécurité Sociale* the form E121, which proves your entitlement to your pension. If you attain retirement age after leaving your home country, the form will be sent to you automatically; if you had reached that age before arriving in France, ask for the form before you leave home. Getting into the French system may not be quite as simple as it sounds for it entails initially a visit to the *Relations Internationales* Department of *Sécurité Sociale* and then probably more than one visit to another office to register but eventually it can be achieved. If your spouse is also claiming registration, remember to have available a marriage certificate obtained not more than three months previously plus a translation either by the Consul or an official translator. This is the rule. If you come properly armed, you will be told that it was not necessary but if you come with an old certificate and no translation you will be sent away to repair the omission.

Reimbursement by *Sécurité Sociale* is made on the basis of a *feuille de soins* which must be lodged with your local *Caisse Primaire*. A *feuille de soins* is a brown and white form which acts as a receipt for a payment made by you for any medical or paramedical treatment, e.g. surgery, consultation, medicines, blood-tests, physiotherapy, X-rays. The form shows the event which gives rise to reimbursement and is usually completed by the doctor or hospital or chemist. It defines the event, which is called an *acte*, by the use of a series of letters, such as C for a visit to a General Practitioner, Kc for Surgery, Z for X-rays and AMM for physiotherapy. Every *acte* is given a basic value. Thus, all operations (Kc) have a basic value of X francs and each type of operation is valued by reference to that basic value. To have your appendix removed is worth (say) 50 but to remove your tonsils is worth only (say) 25. If during the year – for the value of all *actes* can vary from year to year – Kc is worth 15 francs, to get rid of your appendix gives rise to a basic charge of 750 francs but if only your tonsils have disappeared, the basic charge is 375 francs. Of each basic charge, *Sécurité Sociale* repays a proportion and the rest which is called the *ticket moderateur* must be borne by you or your *mutuelle*.

Over and above this arrangement, *Sécurité Sociale* will repay 100% of the cost of certain serious illnesses of which there are thirty or so, such as heart diseases, cancer, certain diseases of the chest etc. However, what must be remembered is that 100% repayment means 100% repayment of the *Sécurité Sociale* rate and not necessarily of what your treatment has cost you. You must make the necessary enquiries in advance and also ascertain whether you are expected to pay in advance and claim reimbursement or whether the clinic will look to you only for a proportion of its charges and go direct to *Sécurité Sociale* for the balance.

The level of reimbursement of the cost of medicines is generally 70%. Certain medicines, which are treated as life saving are reimbursed at 100% and there is also a category (*à vignette bleue*) which are only 40% reimbursable. Reimbursement can vary from reasonably fast to very slow.

The above is not intended to be an exhaustive explanation of how *Sécurité Sociale* works. The system is extremely complex and it is reasonable to ask if its application is fully understood by the French. For the foreigner, there are two golden rules. First of all, try to find out in advance what the system will cover you for. If there is no urgency about your stay in hospital, make certain that you have understood what the final cost to you will be at the clinic of your first choice because in all probability, equally good service can be provided at other clinics and the irrecoverable proportion not refunded by *Sécurité Sociale* may well vary from clinic to clinic. Certainly, in cases of urgency when medical attention rather than its cost is for the moment paramount, there are going to be problems. Your doctor should know the answer but often does not and you must rely on husbands, wives or friends. On occasions there can be just a little more than a hint that certainty of payment of its bill is uppermost in the clinic's mind when you are delivered on its doorstep by ambulance in an emergency. The second rule is to keep a photocopy of all *feuilles de soins* which you send (all the French do this), and if you do not take them personally to *Sécurité Sociale*, to send them by registered AR post. It remains to add that there seems to be no logic in the order in which reimbursement cheques arrive and it is essential to check these against your photocopy *feuilles de soins*.

A question which is often asked is whether the non-French person living permanently in France should join *Sécurité Sociale* on a voluntary basis. In general terms, the answer is almost certainly 'no'. Your contributions may well be high and unless you are chronically ill, your annual medical expenses are likely to be less. Contributions are based on your previous year's income as computed for tax but without the benefit of certain tax allowances. By way of example, in the year June 1989/90, those whose income was in the bracket FF62,640–125,280, paid contributions amounting to 15.25% of their income. It is true that these contributions are allowed as deductions for income tax purposes and provide benefits in addition to mere health benefits but this may not be of much value to many non-French residents in France. Moreover, it must be remembered that the calculation of contributions requires the filing of a copy of your tax returns; otherwise, you will be assessed to the maximum contribution, currently just short of FF80,000. It seems preferable to take out private medical insurance in your own country or if you already have one, make sure that it covers you abroad on a permanent basis. The cost of doing this will almost certainly be less than your French *Sécurité Sociale* contributions and the medical benefits are almost certainly going to be greater. It is true that many (but not all) such policies will not pay for your general practitioner's fees in France nor for your medication except in hospital but they will ensure that you have hospital treatment in France in hospitals and private clinics for which *Sécurité Sociale* will at best only partially pay.

Common Market countries have rules about state retirement pensions and no difficulty arises about the receipt of such pensions paid by one country in another country. A stream of leaflets written with varying degrees of clarity and aimed at those living abroad on this type of benefit is readily available from the appropriate ministry in each country. There is, of course, no reason why a pension should not be paid in the country in which it arises, which is another excellent reason for keeping one's bank account there open. It is very useful to allow pension payments to roll up so that there is less need to indulge in one of the most expensive of all transactions – money changing – on paying visits to the family.

CHAPTER 17

Gardens and Balconies

Visitors to France are impressed with the lush green vegetation of the countryside but many, the British in particular, are of the opinion that the French do not make the most of what they have. Good at public gardens – yes, and superb at planting in pots, but Le Nôtre lived a long time ago, and they have had no one of his calibre since and so on and so on. There is some truth in this attitude but also a lot of prejudice. The French on the other hand have a high regard for the *'vrai amateur anglais'* and are unreserved admirers of the English garden in all its forms.

Gardening climates in the north, east and part of the west of France are much the same as in Great Britain, that is to say, temperate, except that the winters can be slightly more severe and the summers hotter and drier. Snow in the Mediterranean region, although unusual is nothing like as rare as the locals would have you believe. In the last ten years there has been snow in four winters in Nice and in early 1985 it stayed for several days. In the *arrière pays* you should count on having frost every winter for at least a few days in January and/or February above 300 metres. Higher than this you should think in terms of gardening for an almost continental climate. It is worth remembering though that even if a plant is struck down to the ground it is not necessarily dead and many shrubs behave in a somewhat herbaceous fashion putting out new shoots each spring. Once you can see this has happened all you need do is cut out the dead wood.

In the south and south-west of France (i.e. the Alpes-Maritimes, part of Alpes de Haute Provence, most of the Var, part of the Gard, part of Bouches du Rhône, part of Vaucluse,

Gardening climates of France

Unshaded areas can be treated as similar to the UK whilst allowing for exigencies of coastal areas. An area stretching from the north-east border of France and encompassing the *départements* of Meuse, Hte. Marne, Côte d'Or, Saône-et-Loire, Rhône, Ain, and part of Drôme can be said to enjoy a type of continental climate; the cold is never very intense but summers are long, hot and very dry.

Mediterranean type: vegetation in these areas is on average 40 days ahead of Paris. In the Alpes-Maritimes and the Pyrénées Orientales it is 60. Inland areas can be short of water from June onwards and winds are often a problem.

Mountain type: growth can be as much as a month behind Paris but normally only about a fortnight. Danger of night frosts sometimes until mid-June. Thus vegetation in Haute-Savoie can be a whole three months behind that of the Alpes-Maritimes.

part of Hérault, part of Aude and part of both the Gironde and the Pyrénées Orientales – see the shaded area on the map) things are very different. A lot of this area is the home of the olive and the citrus. In the south-west the soil is often acid, and rhododendrons, ericas and blue hydrangea hedges abound. In the real south the soil is more or less calcareous with odd outcrops of clay and granite. Do not go by the old adage that the presence of vines indicates limy soil. It does not; quite a lot of wine is grown in soil without benefit of a lime content. Any gardener worth his salt will note what is generally grown in the area surrounding his property and, if this is exclusively given over to vines, will test his soil for its pH content. Local wildflowers are also a good indication of soil type. If there is only asphodel and valerian, then beware, for you may well need to purchase a great amount of topsoil to get a garden going.

Growing a lawn in these regions is a problem unless you have access to an automatic watering system, and even then it is folly to expect Cumberland turf. Coarse grasses stand up better to the inevitable weed invasion as well as to the long periods of baking sunshine. At sea level, Bermuda grass *(Cynodon dactylon)* or *Dichondra* are best for where there is a chronic shortage of water. Clover is excellent.

The joy for the newcomer to the south and south-west of France is the novelty of growing with ease all manner of plants which normally require a heated greenhouse. Almonds, cherries, peaches, apricots, figs, plums, pears, oranges, lemons, grapefruit, avocado pears, melons, outdoor cucumbers, aubergines, peppers, sweetcorn, tomatoes and globe artichokes are all grown easily. Trees and shrubs such as mimosa, jacaranda, oleander, stephanotis and palms, to say nothing of huge bush cacti, are all easy garden subjects.

For those limited to a balcony there are the ubiquitous geraniums (pelargoniums), which need dividing and pruning each year (no wintering-over under the greenhouse staging any more), hydrangea, camellia and azalea (planted in pots in peat and watered with rainwater if in doubt about the pH value of your local water supply), fuchsia, medium-sized floribunda roses, veronica, cineraria and a vast variety of bulbs in spring. People even plant box (*buxus*) or *Lonicera nitida* and germander (*teucrium*) in pots to form balcony hedges or to put on roof gardens. For flat-dwellers care must be taken not to have anything by way of a container hanging over the balcony that the *copropriété* could object to, and great care must be exercised when watering. Most balconies of flats built since the War have drainage holes. Climbing plants should not be trained against the walls of the block without prior consent of the *syndic* of the *copropriété* – particularly when it is something very permanent like ivy, wistaria or Virginia creeper. When dead-heading or cleaning up the balcony, nothing should be thrown over the side. In many blocks balconies often form the fire escape of the building, and in such cases owners and tenants will have to curb their exuberance to make their balcony a jungle of vegetation or a riot of colour!

POT PLANTING

Starting on a warning note, those lovely olive-oil pots with which all newcomers fall in love become very heavy indeed when filled with earth and constitute a permanent planting since no two normal men can move them, and no removal man will even try. Also the bottom third of the pot should be filled with broken crocks for drainage purposes, and a fairly light compost should be used. Even with care these pots sometimes break open due to the compost swelling and/or the plant's rampant growth in such perfect conditions or unexpected frost.

Pots for balconies (*bacs* in French) are fairly expensive in France but cheaper than in the United Kingdom. The best bargains are to be had in Italy, and for those living on the Côte d'Azur a visit to one of the several manufacturers on the main road from Ventimiglia to San Remo (the via Aurelia – SS1 – *not* the *autoroute*) would be worthwhile.

Self-watering pots are much used in the Mediterranean area and vary from about 30 francs in the LeClerc Supermarket to 130 francs for the same size by the firm Riviera, though the latter is of infinitely better quality, in certain garden centres. If you go away a lot, geraniums stand up best to long periods of neglect and little or no watering, and often with judicious pruning and a good dose of water and a little liquid manure they can be coaxed into life again.

A point to remember is that rain usually does not come on to the balcony, and so one cannot rely on that source of water.

PLANTS SUITABLE FOR POTS
Azalea (in peat), begonia – all sorts, camellia japonica, Japanese chrysanthemum, cineraria, coleus, cyclamen (all sorts except the type which are used for naturalizing), dracaena, cordyline, fuchsia – providing they are not too vigorous – geranium (pelargonium), hydrangea in peat and often with added Sequestrene if blue flowers are required, impatiens, petunia, primula (all sorts), spirea, streptocarpus, rose HT and small to medium floribundas. Virtually all bulbs except the taller lilies do well in pots. Agapanthus grow so vigorously in the south that they will soon break any pot but the largest and large tubs are best.

CLIMBING PLANTS
Bougainvillaea (Fr. *Bougainvillée* f.) This is nearly always sold in the *B. glabra* variety rather than the *spectabilis*, and its often somewhat harsh magenta colouring can be softened by growing it in conjunction with plumbago. Semi-evergreen. NB. Many of the Bougainvillaea family have thorns. Not for balconies as they are too vigorous.
Clematis (Fr. *clématite* – f.) Large-flowered varieties must be planted facing north, particularly in the south and south-west of France, otherwise the colour will fade almost immediately. The pinker the flower, the less well it will stand up to the sun. This applies particularly to Ville de Lyon, Nelly Moser and Bee's Jubilee. The clematis species are better in these areas if you want to plant on a south or west wall. Remember that the maxim of cool roots applies even more strongly in the south for obvious reasons. Large-flowered varieties suitable for balconies are Bee's Jubilee, Comtesse de Bouchaud, Hagley

Hybrid, Mrs Cholmondeley, Nelly Moser, Perle d'Azur, The President and Vyvyan Pennell.

Clematis montana and its family can make really spectacular growth here in France and can all too easily become invasive. Growing clematis through shrubs or into trees is little known in France and always greatly admired when seen.
Ivy (Fr. *lierre* – f.) Contrary to general belief, ivy does no damage to sound walls though will, of course, worsen any mortar fault already there by entering any cracks. Make sure the wall is sound before you train ivy against it. *Hedera hibernica, H. canariensis* and a beautiful gold variety called Oro di Bogliasco are all excellent and easy ivies. The variegated ivies are ideal for covering ugly wire mesh fencing since they are not too rampant.
Roses Although the Empress Joséphine's rose garden at Malmaison was famous, the old-fashioned roses such as Chapeau de Napoléon, Maître d'Ecole, Alberic Barbier and damask roses are virtually unobtainable in their homeland except from the specialist growers Vizier, André Eve, Léon Beck and La Vallée Blonde. Blanc Double de Coubert, though, is fairly common and is excellent for hedging in all parts of France.

The French seem to prefer large, showy hybrid teas – the newer and more unusual in colour the better. Note that 'Peace' is known in France as 'Madame A. Meilland'. If there are certain roses you want in France, write to the breeder in the United Kingdom, Germany or America or wherever it hails from and ask for the name and address of the licence-holder in France. Alternatively, if you are a member of the Royal National Rose Society in St Albans, they will help you find a supplier in France. At the end of this chapter are the names of several rose-growers in France.
Wistaria (Fr. *glycine* f. *de Chine*, *de Japon* etc.) Wistaria is much sought after in France as it grows exceedingly well in any part of the country. If you must grow it on the wall of your house, do have a support for it which is independent of the building itself. It can pull a house down in the end and in any event makes painting difficult, if not impossible. Better by far to train it as a tree and use it as a lawn specimen (very

common in France), though you will have to do this yourself as it cannot be purchased from a nursery thus, or train it onto a wrought-iron boundary fence or a specially constructed support. The white variety looks lovely in the north and east but somehow once south looks rather washed out in the bright sunshine. The mauve and purple varieties are best in the most southern areas.

Russian Vine (Fr. *renouée de Turkestan* f.) This is strongly advised against because in the Mediterranean region after two years it is virtually impossible to control and should only be grown where you actually want the building to disappear without trace.

For those who live between Cannes and the Italian frontier, a visit to the Hanbury Gardens (telephone (184) 3.95.06) at Mortola in Italy (just before Ventimiglia when crossing the border at Garavan above Menton) is strongly recommended. Over 4,500 species of plants are grown there, and it is ideal for anyone interested in gardening and/or botany. It is open most weekdays, but it is as well to telephone in advance. It is *always* closed for lunch between twelve and three. Certain days, out of the spring and summer seasons, are kept as working days, *giorni di lavoro*, when no visiting is allowed.

WIND

The *mistral* and the *tramontane* in the south are deadly to plant life. Their drying effect is a prime factor of the terrible forest fires which periodically sweep across the dry regions of France.

If your garden is likely to be visited by one of these winds (always assuming that you have had the luck to hear in advance) for more than a couple of hours, do try to protect your more precious plants with cloches, home-made screens of plastic, canes, hessian etc. If possible, take in balcony plants. If this is impracticable, try to protect with plastic bags, plastic sheetings etc., well anchored to the balcony railings if all else fails. Keep an eye on the water content of both soil and plants and act accordingly. Finally, never throw lighted cigarette ends into your own or anyone else's garden or into any open space. Jettisoned glass and plastic bottles (such as Evian, Vittel, Contrexéville etc.) can cause fire some months later from the heat generated from the sun shining on them. Anyone who has seen or been through the full horror of a forest fire will tell you it is an experience to be avoided at all costs. The ravages of past forest fires are to be seen all over the southern region of France. You should constantly ensure that you or your children are not the cause, even unwittingly, of such a disaster. For good reason the French ask for your '*Pitié pour la forêt*'. It is the source of *all* life on this earth.

There are notable exceptions, of course, but the average French garden, by Anglo-American standards, seems neglected, particularly the flower garden. It is amazing to see the result of traditional British gardening. It could be said that gardening in France is even more rewarding than in Great Britain.

It is strictly forbidden to import trees, shrubs, and plants into France without a phyto-sanitary licence issued in the plant's country of origin. Licences can be obtained in certain special circumstances and certain UK firms will do this – at a price.

There is no embargo on importing seeds and most bulbs in France. One of the foremost British nurseries, Hillier and Sons, export their plants to France, the majority bare-roots in late winter and spring, but also in containers all the year round, to la Vallée Blonde at Lisieux. The prices compare well with those charged by other French nurseries and the choice of stock is undoubtedly greater than any other nursery in France, if not the world. Certain plants are not allowed to be brought into France – particularly those subject to fire-blight (*feu bacterien*) – the *prunus* varieties and all the pyra-canthas for example, and if you intend to bring in plants (with the appropriate Ministry of Agriculture sanitary certificate) it is as well to check before you import.

However, Thompson and Morgan seeds are available at many French garden centres. Well-known French seedsmen are: Vilmorin (the biggest), Curti, Ricci, Ets. Clause, and

Ets. Blain-Herba, 13210 St Rémy-de-Provence, for herbs and Provençal flowers.

Rosegrowers:
Ets. Clause, 91220 Brétigny sur Orge (Paris Region)
Gaujard 69320 Feyzin (Rhône – Lyon region)
Ets. Rivoire, 69372 Lyon
Ets. A. Eve, 45300 Pithiviers (Central France)
Vizier (Old Roses) – 77160 Provins (Seine et Marne – Paris
    Region)
Ets. Meilland-Richardier, 69160 Tassin la Demi-Lune, and
    gardens (no orders taken) at Boulevard F. Meilland, 06160
    Cap d'Antibes
Hilliers – la Vallée Blonde, RN 13, l'Hotellerie, 14100 Lisieux

Geraniums:
Ets. Clause – as above
Ets. Rivoire – as above (bedding geraniums)

Rare and unusual geraniums:
Marcel Bureau, 49170 St Georges s/Loire

General garden plants etc:
Ets. Clause – as above
Les Soeurs Schneider, 76 Avenue Mar. Juin, 06400 Cannes
Ets. Navello, route de Grenoble, St Laurent du Var 06 (Côte
    d'Azur region)
Pepinières Croux, 92290 Châtenay – Malabry
Ets. Delaunay, 49000 Angers (West)
Jacques Briant (mail order only) 49480 St Sylvain d'Anjou
Georges Delbard, quai de la Messagerie, 75000 Paris.
Pepinières Kerdalo, 22220 Trédarzec. Excellent also for Medi-
    terranean plants
Jardins de Provence, 13120 St Rémy de Provence
Pepinières du Littoral, 83600 St Aygulf, Fréjus
Hilliers – la Vallée Blonde (see above)
E. Lepage – 49000 Angers – Herbaceous Plants
Claude Thoby – 44470 Carquefou – Camellias

ENGLISH	LATIN	FRENCH
Ageratum	*Ageratum*	*Agératum* m.
Anemone	*Anemone*	*Anémone* f.
Arum lily	*Zantedeschia Ethiopica*	*Arum* m.
Balsam, Busy Lizzie	*Impatiens*	*Impatience* f.
Canary creeper	*Tropaeolum canariensis*	*Capucine de Canaris* f.
Canary ivy	*Hedera canariensis*	*Lierre de Canaris* f.
Carnation	*Dianthus*	*Oeillet* m.
Ceanothus	*Ceanothus*	*Céanothe*
Cherry, Cherry tree	*Prunus avium*	*Cerise, cerisier*
Clematis	*Clematis*	*Clématite* f.
Cornflower	*Centaurea*	*Bleuet* m.
Cotton lavender	*Santolina*	*Santoline* f.
Crocus	*Crocus*	*Crocus* m.
Cypress	*Cupressus*	*Cyprès* m.
Daffodil	*Narcissus*	*Narcisse (sauvage)* f,
Daisy (in general)	*Bellis*	*Marguerite* f,
Dill	*Anethum graveolens*	*Aneth*
Fennel	*Foeniculum vulgare*	*Fenouil* m.
Firethorn	*Pyracantha*	*Buisson ardent*
Fuchsia	*Fuchsia*	*Fuchsia* m.
Geranium	*Pelargonium*	*Géranium* m.
Germander (hedge)	*Teucrium*	*Teucrium* m.
Gladioli	*Gladiolus*	*Glaïeul* m.
Grapefruit	*Citrus grandis*	*Pamplemousse* m. or f.
Hawthorn	*Crataegus monogyna*	*Aubépine* f.
Heather	*Erica*	*Bruyère, Brande* f.
Honeysuckle	*Lonicera*	*Chèvrefeuille* f.
Hop (Japanese)	*Humulus japonicus*	*Houblon de Japon* m.
Hydrangea	*Hydrangea macrophylla*	*Hortensia* f.
Ivy	*Hedera*	*Lierre* f.
Hyacinth	*Hyacinthus*	*Jacinte* f.
Jasmine	*Jasminium officinale*	*Jasmin* m.
Jews Mallow	*Kerria Japonica*	*Kerria* m.
Judas tree	*Cercis*	*Arbre de Judée* m.
Lavender	*Lavendula*	*Lavande* f.
Lemon, lemon tree	*Citrus limonia*	*Citron, citronnier*
Lily of the valley	*Convallaria*	*Muguet* m.
Love in the mist	*Nigella*	*Nigelle* f.
Marigold – African	*Tagetes*	*Oeillet d'Inde* m.
Marigold – French	*Tagetes signata*	*Marguérite dorée* f.
Mandevilla	*Mandevilla*	*Jasmin de Chili* m.
Marjoram	*Origanum*	*Marjolaine* f.
Morning Glory	*Ipomea*	*Ipomée* f.
Narcissus	*Narcissus*	*Narcisse* f. (*Poetaz* etc)
Nasturtium	*Tropaeolum*	*Capucine* f.

ENGLISH	LATIN	FRENCH
Oleander	*Nerium*	*Rose-laurier* m. or *Laurier-rose* m.
Orange, bitter or Seville	*Citrus Bigaradia* (syn. *vulgaris*)	*Bigaradier* m.
Orange, sweet (many varieties – with various names)	*Citrus nobilis*	*Oranger* m.
Passionflower	*Passiflora edulis*	*Passiflore* f.
Pink	*Dianthus*	*Oeillet mignardise* f.
Plumbago	*Plumbago capensis*	*Plumbago du Cap* m.
Polyanthus	*Polyanthus*	*Primavère* f.
Poppy	*Papaver*	*Coquelicot* m.
Potato plant	*Solanum*	*Solanum* m.
Rhododendron	*Rhododendron*	*Rhododendron* m.
Rose	*Rosa*	*Rose* f.
Rose bush		*Rosier* m.
Rose, climbing		*Rosier grimpant* m.
Rose, standard		*Rosier à tige*
Rosemary	*Rosmarinus officinalis*	*Romarin* m.
Russian vine	*Polygonum Baldschaunicum*	*Renouée de Turkestan* f.
St John's Wort	*Hypericum*	*Millepertuis* m.
Sage	*Salvia officinalis*	*Sauge sauvage* f.
Snapdragon	*Antirrhinum*	*Gueule-de-loup* f. *Muflier* m.
Stephanotis	*Stephanotis floribunda*	*Jasmin de Madagascar* m.
Sweet peas	*Lathyrus odoratus*	*Pois de Senteur* m.
Thyme	*Thymus vulgaris*	*Thym (sauvage)* m.
Tulip	*Tulipa*	*Tulipe* f. (cottage *fleur de-lys,* parrot etc)
Veronica	*Hebe speciosa etc*	*Véronique* f.
Virginia creeper	*Parthenocissus quinquefolia* or *Ampelopsis veitchii* or even *Vitis muralis*	Vigne vièrge f.
Wistaria	*Wistaria sinensis* or *Wistaria japonica*	*Glycine de Chine* f. *Glycine de Japon* f.
Yew	*Taxus*	*If* m.

LIST OF THE MORE COMMON GARDEN PESTS FOUND IN FRANCE & FERTILIZERS ETC.

ENGLISH	FRENCH
slugs	*limaces* f. (always used in plural for obvious reasons)
snails	*escargots* m. (ditto)
blackfly	*puceron noir* m.
aphis; greenfly	*puceron vert* m.
whitefly	*cocinelle* f.
earwig	*perce-oreille* f.
rose chafer	*cétoine dorée* f.
red spider	*araignée rouge* f. Occurs in the open in the south of France.
mouse	*souris* f.: field mice *mulots* m.
maybug	*hanneton* m.
thrips	*thrips* m. pronounced 'treeps'.
rose rust	*rouille* f.
black spot	*la marsonia* f. *la maladie des tâches noires* f. or even '*le black spot*' will elicit sympathy.
chlorosis	*chlorose* f.
chelated iron with sequestrene	*chélate de fer avec séquestrène (reverdissant en granules)* m.
fertilizer	*engrais* m.
annual mulch	*pailli annuel* m.
potting compost	*terreau* m. (John Innes is unknown, and it can be quite difficult to get special composts – better to make and sterilize your own)
manure	*fumier* m. *(de cheval* etc) (This can be bought in dried condensed form in bags of five kilograms which equal approximately 1 cwt of fresh)
peat	*tourbe* f.

CHAPTER 18

The Telephone and Postal Systems

TELEPHONE

If you want a telephone in a new flat or house, there may be delays, varying from a few days up to about a year. Business lines and telephones for professional purposes usually incur no delay, and a medical certificate will give priority to those persons for whom a telephone is essential as on occasion, it must be admitted, will a letter from 'a friend at court'.

You should apply for a telephone, as soon as you have your new address, to the local *Agence Commerciale* armed with proof of ownership of your house or flat such as a notarial *attestation d'acquisition* or your lease. The address is to be found in the turquoise-edged pages of 'Yellow Pages'. Costs for installation vary of course from very little in a block of flats where the PTT already has a network to a considerable sum for a house in the deep, deep countryside where there are no other telephones for several kilometres. When your installation notice comes in and you see that you have a *'ligne mixte'*, you do not have a shared line but one that gives calls in and out. If you take over an existing telephone, there is a charge made for the change of subscriber. You may go ex-directory on request for a small monthly fee.

Each *département* has its own telephone directory (*Annuaire*) and Yellow Pages (*Professions*). The Yellow Pages directory contains in its initial pages edged in turquoise, green and pink, a great deal of very useful telephone and administrative information, which used to be (more reasonably) in the ordinary directory. Do not, therefore, content yourself with taking only that directory, the white pages of which now only list telephone subscribers under towns and *communes*.

So much progress has been made with Minitel since it first became generally available in France that it now deserves a 'write-up' of its own. Originally conceived as a computerized phone directory, it has now become an indispensable part of the thinking Frenchman's life. It will, indeed, produce phone, telex and fax numbers and addresses all over France, either by reference to a name or to a profession or trade and when used to its full for this purpose can track down the most inaccessible people. The problem is that it does need some skill to get the best out of Minitel and it also needs quite a knowledge not only of French (when tracking down by *rubrique*) but also of the mind of the programmer which is sometimes given to flights of fancy, for, contrary to what one is taught in the schoolroom, the French are no more logical than anyone else. However, since Minitel may be used free of charge for three minutes for this purpose, it is worthwhile getting the hang of it. If it proves stubborn or you are being less intelligent than Minitel, close down and start again for a further three minutes rather than persisting so that you start paying for time spent.

The alternative use of 12 (Directory Enquiries) to find numbers is expensive (currently about 4 francs) and not always very successful. Minitel has one serious disadvantage. It does not seem to be updated often enough so that new numbers take a long time to appear. This means that an appeal to 12 for a number not found on Minitel is going to be unproductive since 12 uses Minitel. Once you have found the number you want, if you press the right button it will dial that number for you but NOT if you are dialling to the Paris/ Ile de France area from an outside region or vice versa. It cannot cope with the necessary 16 prefix (see page 204).

Minitel will do many other things. It will give you postal codes and the current postal tariff. It will give you news in a number of languages, stock exchange prices and foreign exchange information, the weather, motorway conditions and an untold amount of other information. You can use it to book seats on trains or aircraft and at the theatre or to order goods from mail order catalogues.

The basic number to dial to use Minitel is 11. This gives you the directory enquiry service and a number of other basic services such as how to make a phone call, the price of calls, post-codes and generally how to make the best of 11. The code for telex and fax numbers is 3614 SCRIP. Apart from these services, Minitel works on a series of basic numbers and codes. The numbers are 3614 to 3617 and are being added to continuously. To find out the code of the information service you require, you dial 3614 and when the screen asks for the code, you type MGS. This will give you in one form or another all the numbers available on Minitel and their codes and you proceed accordingly. To make full use of this does require some practice.

The higher the number, the more expensive the call, though this is sometimes paid for by the source of information. At the most expensive end are the 'games' and soft porn entertainment and experience has shown that this is not a cheap way of obtaining amusement. Of course, there are Minitel locks to keep those who do not pay your bills, such as children and guests or tenants, from spending your money in 'undesirable' ways and they should be ruthlessly clapped on.

Minitel can be used as a telex machine by joining the Minitelex service. It must be admitted that typing a telex on a Minitel screen can be very irritating, but it can be linked to a personal computer (PC) and take telexes prepared there. It can also itself be used as a personal computer and a print-out can be linked to it either to record information thrown up on the screen or when used as a PC. All in all, a valuable machine. It comes in a number of types from the most basic to the most complicated and hence from the free of cost to that which has a rental of about 200 francs a month. Most people can do very well with one which is either free or has a rental of about 70 francs a month.

A word of warning. Minitel comes from you local *Agence Commercial*. The appropriate counter seems to be staffed by young girls who have little or no knowledge of the Minitel. It is really quite difficult to get any serious technical advice to enable you to choose which mark you need and you must insist on getting an engineer who will (but only in technical French) explain what you can have and what you need. This is likely to put you off Minitel for ever or immeasurably increase your knowledge of a somewhat specialized vocabulary.

All telephone numbers in France are composed of eight numbers in four groups of two figures each. When giving a number, it should be given in that form or it will be totally misunderstood. Generally when dialling from one number to another, all that is required is the eight numbers, the area code being the first two numbers. However, there are special rules for phoning to and from a number in Paris or the Paris region. In this case, from outside Paris, you dial 16, wait for the further dialling tone, then dial 1 and the eight figure number. When dialling from Paris or the Paris region to a number elsewhere, you dial 16, wait for the further dialling tone and then dial the eight figure number you want. Although this method came into force in 1985, there are still people who will give you numbers in the old form. This is particularly so outside Paris where the six-figure number is often found (but then so is the old franc despite its disappearance many years ago). There is also the curious expression '*par le . . .* ' so you may be told that the number is 12.34.56 '*par le 90*' meaning that the six figures must be preceded by 90 and the number is in the Vaucluse. It is, alas, no longer possible to be certain (though it is usually the case) that the first two figures of an eight figure number indicate the *département* in which that number is. The list on p. 21 shows the numbers which appear on car registration plates and as part of postcodes but not of telephone numbers.

The telephone system in France is fully automatic but there is no operator, who will generally be helpful as in many other countries. Unless the information you require falls within certain categories, it can be very difficult to solve telephone problems in France. In general terms, apart from dialling 12 for Directory Enquiries (if you have no Minitel) or 13 to report that your phone is out of order, there is not much help you can get. In fact, there are local engineers but their numbers seem to be kept a close secret and it takes quite a lot of endeavour to get these from 13. Certainly, France Télécom is not as user-friendly as it could be but, as with the Post Offices, this may be due as much to the caller as to the lack of interest by the system. The *Agences Commerciales* are strictly what they say they are and are unable to deal with technical problems.

The following are some important numbers which are standard throughout the country.

Police and ambulance: 17
Fire (and ambulance): 18
Directory Enquiries – inland: 12
Directory Enquiries – international: 19–33–12 and country code
Speaking clock: 36 99
International calls – automatic: 19 – country code – foreign area code (omitting the 0) – number.
International calls – through operator: 19 – 33 – country code – give number to operator.
Telegrams – inland: 36 55. (Also via Minitel on the same number).
Telegrams – overseas in English: (1) 42.33.21.11
in other languages: (1) 42.33.44.11

NB. (i) Some country codes are given in Appendix G. The full list is to be found in the 'turquoise' pages of the Yellow Pages (*Pages Jaunes*).

(ii) Some general information in English, Spanish, German and Italian is also given in the 'turquoise' pages.

There are special numbers available if you wish to contact someone in the USA, UK, Holland, Japan and Algeria on a reverse charge call or for the call to be charged to your phone number in that country if you have a national phone credit card. If you dial one of the following numbers, you will get an operator in the appropriate country who will deal with your call.

USA: 19 00 11
UK: 19 00 44
Holland: 19 00 31

This service will become available for further countries as time passes. There are corresponding numbers for calls made from the above five countries to France. Reverse charge calls to other countries should be made through the international operator.

Phone cards. These come in a variety of forms. The straightforward phone card or *télécarte* is for insertion into a phone in a call box. It can be bought from Post Offices, kiosks and tobacconists. The *carte pastel* is a credit card and calls made on it will be charged to your phone account in France. It can be either an international card so that you can use it both in France and abroad or a national card available for use only in France. You can also get a card which can be used only for up to 10 predetermined numbers in or out of France. These cards have a memory and can be used either in any phone which will accept a *télécarte* or (more expensively) by obtaining an operator by dialling 10.

Getting a non-French number from the international operators in France is not very easy, certainly not swift and is expensive. It is therefore useful to bring your home dialling code book (or a directory which lists them) for the towns in the foreign countries listed in the French Yellow Pages are limited in number and the reasons for their choice as obscure as for the choice of French towns in the Directories of other countries. Even if your home town phone directory is not up to date, it is worth having it on hand in France and, subject to weight problems, renewing it from time to time.

Since one cannot 'dial into' the directory enquiry service of another country from abroad, there are two ways of getting a non-French number which you do not know, both of which are more efficient and cheaper than using the French system. One is simply to ring a friend and ask him to ring you back with the number. The other is to know the number of your local telephone office at home, call them and beg for sympathy and they will often provide the information for you. It is a great pleasure to add that in the UK, almost every area telephone office will not only do this for you but frequently will phone you back to save you wasting money 'hanging on'. Write its number in your home dialling code book.

Telefax machines (*télécopieurs*) are, of course, available in France. On the whole, they are more expensive than those available in many other countries. It seems that most modern machines bought out of the country will function happily in France but there is a marked reluctance to repair machines of any kind which are not French. It seems sensible to pass on the advice that on the whole there is a risk that it may well be difficult to have a foreign machine serviced in France unless it is one whose make is so well-known worldwide that it would be shaming to deny knowledge of its existence. This is, of course, protectionism in a fairly subtle form and applies by no means only to telefax machines.

POST OFFICE

There are few countries whose citizens do not complain about their postal services. Even the Swiss, where the Post Office always had a reputation for impeccable politeness, cleanliness and swiftness, is nowadays the subject of complaints. Possibly Denmark has taken the place of Switzerland, since the British government seems to be using the services of the Danish Post Office for some of its mail. Be that as it may, the Post Office in France must rank among the least satisfactory in Western Europe.

However, if one realizes why this is, one can to a certain extent sidestep some of the problems. Whilst on the whole the personnel behind the counter tend to a grumpiness which can be very offputting, it is not unreasonable to say that the behaviour of the ordinary user of French Post Offices must in large measure contribute to this. It would be difficult to find a country where one hears continuously such stupid questions as one hears in a French Post Office. In general terms, the French public seems to know far less about the services available to it, their cost and extent than in many other countries.

It is only recently that some of the larger Post Offices have started selling stamps at most counters instead of limiting this to one or two out of a dozen counters. You will find that it is very rare to see letters being put into letter boxes after they have been stamped by the sender, since an enormous proportion of all letters are handed over the counter for stamping. One frequently sees someone waiting interminably in the queue to post one standard rate letter. Scales on which the public can weigh a letter are seldom seen, and where there is one, it is never used – nor indeed is its use encouraged since the Post Office would still have to check every letter posted in case it had been understamped.

Another problem is that the French are still wedded to the use of recorded delivery letters which must also be registered. This causes untold delay. The use of packages *valeur déclarée* or insured is also common. It is hardly worth paying a registration fee merely to cover the value of the contents of a package since the maximum cover obtainable is trivial. The use of AR registered letters is often a legal requirement since, as has been said elsewhere and cannot too often be repeated, it is the only method of ensuring that the person you write to receives your letter. The letter will arrive in any case but unless it is *avec avis de reception* if its arrival was unwelcome, its arrival will be denied. Even the honest French admit that this is a peculiarly French failing.

A further problem is that it frequently becomes necessary to visit the local Post Office to collect undelivered letters and packages. It would be dangerous to suppose that this is because these are usually registered and therefore require the postman to come to the front door for a signature whilst it is simpler to put a form in one of the letter-boxes on the ground floor. Suffice it to say that this is an irritation suffered by flat-dwellers more than by house-owners, although even they may find if they live in the country that regulations may require them to walk quite a distance to a group of letter-boxes serving a number of houses – and incidentally to have a box of regulation size. If one does have to go to fetch a letter from the Post Office, proof of identity will be asked for: a passport, *carte de séjour*, or driving licence will do. Many Post Offices will refuse to hand out to wives, letters addressed to husbands and vice versa ('they might be divorced or worse, they might not be') or to hand you, letters addressed to your guests care of you. There is actually a form of Power of Attorney for these circumstances! Services available and tariffs can be obtained from any Post Office or from Minitel (see page 202). Generally, a letter up to 20 grams costs the same to an address in France as to an address anywhere in the Common Market. There is a second-class post. Never use it. Do not insist that all letters in Western Europe go by air without the need to put on a sticker. They do but many counter clerks will not believe you. Nor in the case of letters or parcels to the UK can you persuade them that if the contents might be interesting to Customs, there is no need to put on a green label for letters but only for parcels.

In general terms, use French Post Offices as little as possible. Find out the tariffs and buy your stamps at the local tobacconist and post your letters yourself. If you must use a Post Office, be prepared for delay and irritation, unless you are using the local village Post Office where all is likely to be smiles and help with, perhaps, just a little less knowledge of geography than you might expect.

CHAPTER 19

Utilities

ELECTRICITY (Minitel 3616 code Intelec)
If you are buying a new house or flat, you will find that at some stage shortly before completion of the building you will be joined up to the main supply. *Electricité de France* will ask you for a deposit which obviously depends on the size of the flat or house. The deposit is refundable in two slices at the end of five and ten years, and after about six months you will receive two cheques in the appropriate amounts for encashment at the dates shown on each.

When the supply is connected, your meter will be installed, for which there is also a small charge, non-refundable, and sometimes they also ask for a deposit, refundable, against future electricity bills. This latter is fairly unusual. The supply in a new building cannot be connected until you produce a *certificat de conformité*. This must be given to you by the developer when the keys are handed over.

There are a variety of tariffs offered, and which you take will depend on the type of installation you have and your personal requirements. It is worth mentioning that French electricity is among the cheapest in Europe and that all modern houses and flats are built with such a degree of insulation that heating by electricity alone becomes a viable and indeed desirable method.

The current price of electricity for a normal household in France with a 6 kilowatt installation is approximately 62 centimes per kilowatt/hour with a standing charge of about 32 francs a month. If you opt for the tariff which provides cheap electricity during off-peak hours (*tarif avec heures creuses)*, the cost would be about 52 centimes during normal hours, 29 centimes during off-peak hours with a monthly standing charge of 65 francs. These figures are inclusive of TVA but not of a local tax, which varies according to your *département* from nil to 12% and is charged on 80% of your bill ex-TVA. Frequently it will be found that developers have not supplied enough power points (particularly in the kitchen), and in order to overcome this lack the house purchaser will have to run another phase in. *Electricité de France* will carry this work out within a few days and for a very reasonable price. Far too few French sockets are earthed, and the French tend to run many machines without benefit of an earth. They do, however, earth their washing-machines, dryers and dishwashers, and a special socket is supplied for cookers, hobs and ovens. Older earth trips are often 'timed', so once having tripped the earth you may find that after replacing a fuse you will have to wait some time before you get the supply back. Wait at least two hours before calling in an electrician. Most modern installations in France use the earth trip system (*disjoncteur*), which is obligatory in certain countries (it is only encouraged in France) but not yet in the UK. It is worth remembering that many microwave ovens bought in the UK and made specially for the UK market do not have the 'slow start system', which is not necessary in that country. Without this, the current surge when the oven is switched on will trip the *disjoncteur* and go on doing this every time. If you are buying a microwave oven in the UK for use in France, make certain that it is a model which is suitable for use in, for example, Germany or Italy, where the earth trip system is obligatory. Chandeliers and hanging light-fittings need professional fixing since they tend not to have wooden joists in French ceilings but reinforced concrete, and getting a 'fix' in such circumstances is well nigh impossible. Often you will have to change the 'hook' of your chandelier for a French one. EDF is capable of checking wiring if it knows that a building is old. It seems to be necessary, at least in some parts of France, to remind electricians that it is undesirable to instal equipment without testing the state of the wiring of the equipment itself if it is old, and of the circuit generally if it is not modern. What answer can one give to an electrician who has installed light fittings today and who one has had to call in on the next day for all his handiwork has 'blown'? 'But, Sir, we never check wiring unless specifically told to do so. Our customers would never pay the charges for that simple precaution if in fact we had found all was in order'. A wall socket is *une prise*, and a plug is *une fiche*. A fuse is *une fusible*. An adaptor is *une triplice*. Even in new buildings, the standard of the electrical work is frequently poor and many wall sockets are (quite literally) held on by rubber bands.

The current in France is 50 cycles/220 volts throughout the country. It is said that current surges have been eliminated but for those who use personal computers, it is desirable to use a Power Filter. They are said to be unobtainable in France because they are not needed but if they are really not to be found in France, they can be bought elsewhere for a few pounds. The French wiring code (which regrettably is not always adhered to) is earth – green and yellow, neutral – blue and live – brown or red or black. It is also possible to discover wires of other colours (grey, white and orange) used for two-way switches and the like.

GAS AND WATER (Gas – Minitel as for Electricity)
In France gas comes either through the town pipes or in containers. Great use is made of bottled gas. The reason may be that the electricity supply, cheap though it may be, is liable to failure from time to time. You are strongly advised to have a spare gas hob on your cooker or a camping-gas burner against an EDF strike.

In out-of-town centres, few properties have gas supplied. Most town blocks offer gas and electricity combined for cooking. As with electricity you can choose the tariff most convenient to your needs. Cubic metres of gas burnt are for the purposes of invoicing converted into kilowatt hours. In some cases of blocks of flats, where gas is used only for cooking, the cost is a standard charge, paid by the *copropriété* and included in your service charge.

Contracts to burn a minimum amount of bottled gas can be arranged at very advantageous prices, but this type of fuel is always more expensive than town gas.

If you think you have a leak (*une fuite de gaz*), you will find that the emergency service *Dépannage d'Urgence* figures in the white pages of your telephone directory under 'Gaz de France'. It is useful to write on page 1 of your Yellow Pages. In real emergencies call the fire brigade.

Water is not charged for by the local authority but by a local *Cie des Eaux de* . . . (name of town) on the basis of the amount actually consumed as shown on your meter. Special rates apply for swimming-pools, etc.

BILLS

Telephone bills are rendered every two months. Reminders follow fairly soon thereafter and, if not complied with, result in your phone being cut off. Callers will be greeted with the announcement in the standard Télécom France icy voice that 'service is interrupted'. Finally, a letter will announce intended cancellation of your contract. Recounting this sad and swift progress of events is not intended to imply that readers have suffered from it but as a reminder that uninhabited holiday homes have unopened letter boxes in which unopened telephone bills can moulder. It can take quite a few days to be reconnected if one's phone is cut off and few things can be less welcoming on arrival than a dead phone. A word of encouragement – TVA on phone bills is at a reduced rate.

On the whole, it is preferable not to pay phone bills through the post. It can take at least a week for a cheque received to be credited and it would be undesirable in any event to send payment by post except by registered AR post. Payment at a Post Office can be made and this produces immediate proof of payment. Less convenient but safest of these methods is payment at an *Agence Commerciale*. The best method for those not permanently in France is to make use of the *prélèvement* system. In this way, your phone bills will be sent to your French bank which will pay them for you during your absence. You will be sent a copy of the bill. Please note that it is a *copy* for information only and do not pay again. Certainly, it may happen that on occasion your bank will pay a bill which you do not agree. Ask therefore for regular itemized accounts (*facturation détaillée*) to be sent to you at a small additional cost: this will show every call made from your number, the date, time and cost. If you dispute a call, you can then take it up with France Télécom. This service is available to you only if you are on a modern electronic exchange. France Télécom is quite prepared to deal with complaints of over-charging on calls, whether thrown up on a detailed bill or simply because your account seems overlarge. A payment of what you think correct to an *Agence Commerciale* will satisfy and result in an enquiry being made into your complaint. At least, unless you are a permanent resident in France, or pay by *prélèvement*, have telephone bills (and those for other utilities) sent to your non-French home address.

If you let your home in France, the detailed account will, of course, let you know what your tenant has been doing but depending on when he comes and leaves, you may have to wait days or weeks before this information is available. You can also by arrangement with your local *Agence Commerciale* organize that tenants can receive incoming calls but are restricted to the *département* for outgoing calls.

Electricity and gas bills also come every two months and can also be paid by *prélèvement*. Bills are alternatively estimated and 'real' and estimates can be surprising. Electricity and gas bills bear TVA at the standard rate. Electricity bills in addition bear a local tax for the benefit partly of the *commune* and partly of the *département* based on 80% of the ex-TVA bill at a varying but average over the country rate of 9%. It is also possible to pay personally on a monthly basis. On the whole, Electricité de France (which is also Gaz de France) is very much politer and easier to deal with than France Télécom and mistakes seem rarely to occur. It is also much quicker to get reconnected after an unpaid bill than it is with the telephone. If you have only a holiday home in France which you visit infrequently but usually at the same time every year, you can arrange for your gas and electricity meters to be read at that time once a year only. This arrangement is available to those who pay by *prélèvement* or by monthly instalments.

CHAPTER 20

Education

The French have a great respect for education. It can start at three years old in an *école maternelle* and continue for another twenty-five years up to one of the *grandes écoles*. A permanent love affair with erudition, one could say. However, for the ordinary man in the street education begins at around five or so in an *école maternelle* (kindergarten). The first formal class is the twelfth, *douzième*, and the last is *terminale*, fourteen years later. After *école maternelle*, comes *école primaire*, then on to a *collège d'enseignement secondaire* or CES for short (secondary school) which finishes at the third form – *troisième*. Then comes the crunch. A child who is relatively bright will go on to a state *lycée* to do a *baccalauréat* in one of several disciplines. *Lycées* start at the second form, i.e. *seconde*, and take a child up to university entrance. What is known as 're-doubling' is allowed once or at the most twice. Attendance at a French university is the road to a better career – one hopes – and is required for all the professions and higher echelons of the civil service etc. Post-graduate studies are undertaken at one of the *grandes écoles*, and attendance at one of these is normally a passport to success.

In between leaving school and going to university comes military service for all young men who are fit and over eighteen. This can be deferred until after University studies are completed. Those with the right educational qualifications can become officers; otherwise it is a question of mucking in with everyone else from the rest of France. Military service has been retained by the current government but slightly changed in its concept. It is unlikely that the participants will be aware of any difference or improvements.

For those less academically gifted, leaving *troisième* in the

CES is usually followed by attendance at a technical college or an apprenticeship. Virtually every occupation has some form of recognized apprenticeship – even that of shop assistant or filing clerk, and a certificate of competence is issued.

It will be seen that, after the period of CES has been completed, the French educational system becomes highly competitive. Few second chances are given, except for strictly medical reasons. Someone who is lazy and does not bother to work will not be counselled or encouraged to do so. This holds good for the university period also. The motto is 'You're on your own.' If you work, the facilities are there, and if you do not, '*Tant pis pour vous.*'

Education is free in France, but textbooks and stationery have to be purchased. Textbooks are often available second-hand if the requirements are known early enough before the mad rush. A good 1,500 francs per annum per pupil is not unusual. University tuition is free, but again books, stationery and keep have to be found by the parents. Grants and scholarships do exist for needy or bright pupils, but these are not common. The unfortunate French parent is obliged (by law, believe it or not) to keep his brilliant child at university until he is twenty. Thereafter, in his most difficult year, the student may well be obliged to get a job to continue his studies.

Unless a child has been in the French education system from about the age of eight, there will be a fight to integrate him into the state education system. If the child speaks fluent French, half the battle is over. If he does not, he will not only be unable to understand; there will be no one to help him over the many hurdles of the language. It takes approximately six months for a child under twelve or thirteen to learn to speak French fluently.

In the country, there are schools which will take foreign children, teach them French and integrate them into the system. In the towns, where the schools are full and the teachers over-worked, it is unlikely you will have the luck to find such an institution. The best solution to the problem is to put the child into a private, fee-paying school for a year and get him up to standard in spoken and written French. After that, once he can satisfy the powers that be that he is up to standard, he can enter a state school. Insisting on 'your rights' can lead to your child being placed into a class far below his age and mental capacity. It has been known for foreign children to be put into a class for the educationally subnormal, not because they were that but because there was nothing else to do with them. Running such risks is very unfair to any child.

The entire education system in France, both state and private, is run by twenty-six academies dotted over the country, each with at least one university attached to it. It is the academies who set the examinations. There is, no matter what subject is being read, a very strong emphasis on French civilization and literature, and this stress accounts for the fact that even the most modestly educated French seem to be better read and more articulate than their European and American counterparts.

The French State runs the most marvellous education counselling services for parents, who should avail themselves of such an excellent and free service as much as possible.

The *baccalauréat* is taken in two halves. During the year in *Première* the examination in French Language and Literature is taken and must be passed before any other examination can be taken. The second half of the *baccalauréat* is taken in *Terminale* and there are several groups ranging through the humanities, mathematics, science, agronomics, engineering, economics etc and virtually every subject which can be read at university is catered for.

Going back to schools, parents will find that these are run in a rather rigid fashion with all absences officially noted on a special form, certificates, medical or otherwise, being required for many minor items and a prodigious number of photographs being needed of the individual pupil. Truancy is a very serious offence in France and can result in expulsion, as can forging a parent's signature on something (who has not done that at some time in his school career?) and being found out.

'As previously mentioned, there are private schools in most large towns. A great number of these are run by religious institutions (there is no compulsory religious instruction in State schools), not only Roman Catholic but Protestant and Jewish also. Many boarding schools are run by the Catholics, but it is as well to remember that the State system also runs boarding schools. They, in common with the private institutions, usually send their pupils home or board them 'out' at weekends. It would not be unfair to say that by and large State education is better than private education in France. There are one or two notable exceptions, but these are very rare. If the school's name is 'College . . .', it tends to indicate that it is a private school. All lycées are state run.

There has been a relatively recent endeavour to abolish private (but State-aided) schools. The majority of these are religious foundations and many are to be found in the more Catholic parts of the country such as Brittany or the Savoy. Such an endeavour met with vociferous public opposition and for the moment the measure has been withdrawn. This quarrel certainly brought out all the old anti-clerical enmities as well as all the fears of the Church for France's religious future.

For those living temporarily in France but not educating their children in a boarding school in their home country, there are certain compensations to be had from putting their children into the French system. It is more or less free; it is, almost always, good, and usually on return home the child will often find himself approximately a year ahead in most subjects including maths and science but a lifetime ahead in French language and literature. Only your national history suffers, and that can be quickly remedied.

School holidays in France are as follows: – there are two very short periods at Christmas and Easter, often less than a fortnight long, and a very long period in the summer, sometimes lasting from mid-June until late September for the lucky children of *seconde* and *première*. Half-term comes at Carnival time in February, and there is another over All Saints at the beginning of November, two hangovers from the days when the Church controlled the schools. Strangely enough,

Good Friday is not a public holiday in France, and it is not uncommon in some years to go to school on that day. No one is going to complain at those who take the day off for religious reasons. The same applies to Jewish and Moslem holidays.

CHAPTER 21

Supermarkets and Shopping

It is fairly safe to say that most housewives go to the local market at least once or twice a week, and most working wives tend to use the supermarket rather more than local shops or markets.

The distribution of food in France is highly organized and very competitive. Hypermarkets, supermarkets, freezer-centres and shopping centres abound, and most medium-sized towns boast at least one of the bigger supermarket chains such as Auchan, Carrefour, Casino, Leclerc, Prisunic or Sodim. Many of these outlets provide superb parking arrangements to encourage the shopper to come by car and make purchases for up to a month in advance, they hope.

Which supermarket to choose depends so much on personal tastes, the town you are shopping in and the price you are prepared to pay. Companies like Leclerc and Prisunic seem primarily interested in being cheaper than their competitors. On the other hand local markets, which are usually a bit more expensive, sell local fruit and vegetables picked the night before, or even that morning, which have not suffered damage from the long supermarket distribution chain before reaching the customer.

Supermarkets, as elsewhere, are undoubtedly cheaper provided you are not an impulse shopper, but you do not, for instance, get the service from the meat department that you would get from your local butcher, who will do infinitely more for you than his average non-French counterpart. Meat carcasses are approached very differently (and more economically) in France, and a butcher will advise you what French cut you will need for the particular dish you have in mind. It is unlikely that you will find help of this kind in a supermarket. Offal, except for pig's liver, commands extremely high prices in France. This is because there is a long tradition of luxury dishes of calves' sweetbreads, veal kidneys, calves' liver (now well over 100 francs the kilo) and few French have any natural dislike of the idea of eating offal – quite the contrary. Tripe in France is nearly always in its uncooked state and unless it is served in a very good and expensive restaurant (where there are more exciting things to have!) it is not as good as it would be in the UK or Italy for instance. Indeed, it would be safe to say it's better to avoid tripe and its nearest relative chitterlings.

The French, after the Portuguese, are the largest fish-eaters in Europe, and about half the supermarkets carry a fresh-fish counter. The Mediterranean sea is, it must be admitted, a pretty poor fishing ground, but France has advantageous fishing agreements with Atlantic coast countries such as Senegal (to say nothing of fishing Cornish waters dry of lobster), so that there is a vast selection of fish to be had even in the smallest inland towns. Fish is expensive, but it is usually very fresh, and the tired frozen fillet of plaice and fish finger are not much used in France except for five-year-olds. Oysters are available at, to British thinking, ludicrously low prices, and there are dozens of uncommon shellfish which should be tried, first in a specialist restaurant and then at home with the right recipe book.

Most people are forced to re-assess their attitude to tinned vegetables when coming to France. Quite simply the French produce the best tinned and bottled vegetables in the world – particularly *petits-pois*. Except for spinach, their frozen vegetables are less spectacular.

French jam is rather ordinary except for some of the Lenzbourg (Swiss) which is produced in Lyon under licence, Bonne Maman, Fauchon and Hédiard. It is worth remembering that the French like Americans actually *prefer* jelly to jam.

Their orange marmalade is frankly awful, but luckily Cooper, Baxters, Roses, Keillers etc are all imported.

Coffee is cheaper and better in France than in most countries other than, possibly, Italy and very often supermarkets do their own mixtures, which are excellent. Only trial and error will find coffee to suit your personal taste. Foreigners are often flummoxed by the words Arabica and/or Robusta on the coffee packet. Arabica, provided it has not been over-roasted, is the milder sort with fuller flavour and is the closest relation to old-fashioned Mocha coffee. Robusta, which mostly comes from Africa or Brazil, takes to higher after-dinner type roasting. Skilful roasting methods can turn an ordinary Robusta coffee into something better than it really is. It is also the cheaper of the two types. Frequently you get a blend of the two – Arabica for flavour and Robusta for strength – the higher the Arabica content the more you pay. Pure Arabica is the most expensive and is best made by the drip, filter or jug method rather than by perculating or espresso. If you want the latter you should get the coffee from an *Italian* source who are the only people who know how to roast and grind Arabica coffee for espresso machines.

Tea is another matter altogether. It is expensive and ill understood in France. The British are always amused at the luxury status of Typhoo and the prices for Twining's have to be seen to be believed. If you cannot be parted from your cup of tea, it pays to stock up each time you or your friends come from your home country or pass through a country seriously dedicated to tea-drinking, particularly if you are wedded to something as recherché as Darjeeling Broken Orange Pekoe – Muscatel flavour. The French consider tea to be highly stimulating, and it is, therefore, strictly forbidden to children. Great believers in *tisanes* or infusions (which are usually infinitely more 'exciting' to the nervous system than any ordinary cup of tea), they consume vast quantities of camomile, lime, verveine and marshmallow which is no relation to the American marshmallow. Nothing is safe from being made into an infusion – even cherry stalks; these are much valued by old ladies against arthritis, and such is the belief in their efficacy that this particular *tisane* has been most successfully commercialized.

There are few foreigners who do not envy the French their rich assortment of cheeses and their vast range of wines to go with them.

Sad to say, the number of cheeses falls yearly, and whereas, between the wars, there were over 480 different cheeses, by 1960 there were a mere 280. A drop of two hundred over a period of thirty years does not augur well for the French table, and it would not be an exaggeration to say that at least ten cheeses a year disappear from the market. Today there are perhaps less than 125 cheeses on sale. The reasons are legion, but the prime causes are pasteurization, the demand for a standard product by the large supermarket chains and the changing taste of the public which has been conditioned by these supermarket chains. It is still possible to buy real farmhouse cheese in most large towns from a specialist *fromager*, and a few of the larger supermarkets run cheese counters which have the odd farmhouse cheese made from unpasteurized milk. The nearest corollary one can draw is that cheese in France is going the way of beer in Great Britain. Every new keg bitter is introduced on the grave of at least one if not two local breweries just as every pasteurized factory cheese spells the death of four or five farmhouse cheeses. The difference between an ordinary Camembert made in a factory and one made by hand on the farm from *lait cru* is overwhelming. With the listeria and salmonella scare in the UK, one of France's best cheese, Vacherin, is no longer imported. It is always made with *lait cru* and strangely enough there have been no accidents reported from eating it. That is not, however, to say that there have been no accidents. For an ominous month two years ago, in mid-Vacherin season, the cheese was taken off the market. It is now on sale again and there appear to have been no mishaps.

There is nothing wrong with Boursault, Boursin or Belle de Champs; they are at least more honest than the pale imitations of Brie, St Paulin and Port du Salut on sale all over the country. Boursin was the invention of a newly retired advertising account executive. He wanted 'something to do' and invested a little money and all his marketing expertise in launching Boursin. The rest is history.

One or two cheeses have scarcely changed at all. Among these is Roquefort, which dates from before Charlemagne. Some say Pliny mentioned it. The conditions required for ripening Roquefort cheese, involving as they do a local breeze called the *souffline*, cannot be remotely imitated by a factory, and so it is unlikely to change for some time to come. But the market for Roquefort is diminishing also, since it is considered by some to be rather salty for today's insipid palate. Few French now eat it 'as is' but mix it down with an equal amount of butter. Maroilles from the north does not lend itself to factory production, nor do many of the goat's milk cheeses. There still seems to be market for farmhouse Bries made from unpasteurized milk (never in packets), and most supermarkets who pride themselves on their cut-cheese counter will have at least a couple of *lait cru* Bries.

The French have adopted Gruyère and Emmenthal as their own with scarcely a mention of their native Switzerland. Beaufort is the nearest French equivalent to Gruyère, and there are those who consider it a better cheese, particularly for cooking since it does not prick the throat or go into such long strings. It is no relation to Beaumont as so many foreigners believe, which is, almost always, a factory-made cheese.

The French are great eaters of *fromage frais*, which is an acquired taste but once acquired stays for ever. If you find French thick cream 'off', then you will never like *fromage frais*. La Roche aux Fées make the nearest equivalent to British/American/Danish/Dutch double cream. This also appears under the guise of Casino's own double cream. The most 'French' of the thick creams is Isigny. For whipping, purchase a cream suitable for making '*crème à la Chantilly*' – ordinary double cream can easily separate – so it is important to keep everything extremely cold. The taste of French cream is due to a culture deliberately put into it, and it is nothing to do with lack of hygiene or poor refrigeration. The

French like their cream that way and, after a time, so do many foreigners.

Opposite is a list of a few of the main cheeses of France and the best wines to accompany them, as set out by Brillat-Savarin in the last century. These are counsels of perfection of course. As will be seen from the table, a fairly good rule is that the *vin du pays* usually goes very well with the *fromage du pays*. After that it is a case of trial and error, and the research can be a very pleasant undertaking.

Once resident in France, there comes a time, sooner or later, when the local *vin du pays*, no matter how good, begins to pall. Every town of any size has at least one *marchand de vin* or *caviste*. Like all French *commerçants*, he is out to make a profit, and his reputation is built on the satisfaction of his customers. He will be happy to be used, to give advice on setting up a small cellar etc. Of course he will be more expensive than your local supermarket, but usually he is selling a superior article. Remember, only if you are a grower can you think in terms of a cellar devoted to a single wine – usually a great wine with several generations of *vignerons* behind it.

Many supermarkets do special offers on wines, usually of local or nationally well-known wine. You are unlikely to get Meursault on special offer for instance. Some of these offers are excellent value – some are just awful and of wine that needs to be shifted quickly. Always taste a bottle before committing yourself to a dozen. The supermarket chain, Carrefour, does a number of wines under its own label which are excellent and their Nouveau Beaujolais and Nouveau Beaujolais-Villages are among the best – and incidentally the cheapest on the market.

A modest cellar can be started with about ten dozen good bottles and need not be the horrifically expensive undertaking it would be in the United Kingdom, Denmark or the United States. Of course, if you insist on confining yourself to the first-growth Bordeaux reds and the finest Burgundies, then you will end up paying even more than if you bought it through a London wine-merchant since the best Bordeaux

CHEESE	PROVENANCE AND TYPE	BEST WINE
BANON	Provence. Soft cheese – should be made of sheep's milk but now seldom is. Now a mixture of cow's and goat's milk.	Cassis, Gigondas
BEAUFORT	Savoy. Gruyère type.	
BEAUMONT	Savoy. Medium hard.	
BRIE de Meaux, Melun, or Coulommiers	Ile de France. Soft cheese.	Fleurie, Pomerol, Chinon, Médoc-Pauilliac. Bordeaux rouges
CAMARGUE	Provence. Sheep's milk if lucky. Usually a mixture.	Cassis, Mondeuse, Crépy
CAMEMBERT	Normandy. Soft cheese.	Beaune, Vougeot, Morgon
CANTAL	Auvergne. Hard cheese.	Chinon, Rully, St Pourçain,
CARRE DE L'EST	Lorraine and Champagne.	Bouzy and Pinot rouge d'Alsace
COMTE	Franche-Comté. Gruyère type.	Brouilly, Fleurie, Mâcon and Rosé d'Arbois
CREMET	Anjou. Soft and very creamy	Anjou sec, Vouvray, Muscadet
FONDU aux raisins	Savoy. Soft cheese with grape-pip crust.	Mondeuse, Vin d'Arbois
GEROME	Vosges. A Munster-like cheese, *q.v.*	Beaune, Pinot d'Alsace
LIVAROT	Normandy. Very rich, creamy and strong. Known by the three bands. Where there are five bands on it, known as '*le Colonel*'.	Morgon, Ermitage or Côte Rôtie
MÂCON	Burgundy. Not much found out of the immediate area. Made from goat's milk.	Viré, Fuissé and Chablis
MAROILLES or MAROLLES	Picardy. Also has cousin from the Nord and Lille even stronger known as *Puant macéré*, a name which tells all. Semi-hard.	Beaune, Côte Rôtie, Châteauneuf du Pape, Corton
MONSIEUR FROMAGE or FROMAGE DE MONSIEUR	Invented by a man actually called Mr Fromage – very rich and creamy.	Volnay, Mouton-Rothschild, Chénas
MORBIER	Semi-hard with familiar dark line in centre from soot from poplar or vine cutting.	Muscadet, Arbois, Loire, Sancerre or Roussette
MUNSTER	Alsace. Very strong and very rich and smelling of drains. Often accompanied or covered in caraway seeds when it is called *au cumin*.	Morgon, Côte Rôtie, Corton, Médoc and for Munster *au cumin* – Pinot d'Alsace
NEUFCHATEL	Normandy. Brie type cheese sold in logs, bricks or hearts and sometimes called Gournay.	Fleurie, Pomerol, Volnay, Ermitage

CHEESE	PROVENANCE AND TYPE	BEST WINE
POIVRE D'ANE	Provence. Goat's milk cheese with addition of the herb savory – hence the name.	Dry white Graves, Rosé de Provence, Cassis and white Châteauneuf du Pape (if you can get it)
PORT DU SALUT	Brittany. Takes its name from the Cistercian abbey. Now much copied by factories.	Bourgueil, Bouzy
PONT L'EVEQUE	Normandy. Semi-hard and now mostly found in its factory-made form.	Bourgueil, Pomerol, Fleurie, Volnay
REBLOCHON or ROBLOCHON	Savoy. Semi-hard cheese – very strong and smelly.	Crépy, Seyssel, Apremont
ROQUEFORT	Aveyron (Languedoc border). A sheep's milk cheese with blue veining.	Chambertin, Châteauneuf du Pape, Haut Brion, Provence Rouge *Fauqères*
ST. MARCELLIN	Dauphiné. Made from goat's milk but often factory made from mixture of cow's and goat's milk.	Mondeuse rosé, Condrieu, Bourgueil, Haut-Médoc
ST. NECTAIRE	Auvergne. Semi-hard to hard cheese. Much factory-made.	Chinon, Bouzy, Fleurie
ST. PAULIN	Made all over France and ninety-nine per cent of the time in a factory from pasteurized milk.	Beaujolais, Cabernet
TOMME DE SAVOIE	Savoy. Hard cheeses mostly but each area in the Savoy produces its own – often on the farm.	Arbois, Crépy, Apremont, Seyssel
VACHERIN D'ABONDANCE	Savoy. Semi-soft, very creamy.	Apremont, Roussette, Crépy
VACHERIN DE BEAUGES	Savoy. Similar to above.	As above and Pinot d'Alsace
VACHERIN DE JOUX	Franche-Comté.	Arbois, Beaujolais
VEZELAY	Burgundy. A famous goat's milk cheese.	Irancy, Chablis

and Burgundies, particularly the latter, command rather higher prices at home than abroad. Starting with half-dozens of six or seven whites from Alsace, Jura, Burgundy, Loire, Bordeaux and Provence, six light reds such as Bordeaux, Loire, Provence and Beaujolais, six heavier reds will encompass Burgundy, Languedoc, Côtes du Rhône and the more robust Bordeaux reds. Most French cellars have a few bottles of *vins doux*. These can be anything from the relatively inexpensive Baumes de Venise (Provence) to Château Yquem. This latter is something most British feel unnecessarily luxurious, but later they appear to change their mind.

The really serious amateur can content himself with the knowledge that a cellar of fifteen hundred bottles will fully represent the best wines of France. Most people content themselves with about a quarter of that number. The two golden rules are to drink what you like and not to get a reputation for your cellar or you will find yourself quickly drunk dry. Certain wines are meant to be drunk young and are fairly cheap such as the rosés of Provence, Beaujolais (which has become fashionable and therefore rather overpriced of late), Alsace, Chablis, Jura, Sancerre and the lovely red Gigondas of Provence. There is no point wasting money to put such wines 'down'. Incidentally, beware any other sort of Beaumes-de-Venise other than the Muscat. Red, rosé and white Beaumes-de-Venise are not up to their Muscat counterpart in quality. In fact, they are usually pretty disgusting.

Another time-honoured method of buying wine in France is *après une dégustation*. Make sure you are at least tasting in the areas of wine you think you will like. If you hate sweet wines, there is little point in tasting any of it, no matter how good it may be. Perhaps the safest method is to remember the vineyard-owner's name or his *negociant*'s name whose wine you have drunk and liked. Above all, forget shippers' names since once you are buying in France it is irrelevant to know the names of shippers to other countries. Once at a *dégustation*, take in the atmosphere very carefully. Do not be too put off by a commercial atmosphere since the *vigneron is* in business, but do be put off if the seller seems to be silent or almost unenthusiastic. Be suspicious too if you are offered nuts with your wine, since it will probably be a bit harsh on its own, and anything salty makes any glass of wine pleasurable. 'When in doubt, do nowt' is good advice. At the worst, just buy a couple of bottles and drink them in the peace and quiet of your dining-room.

It is not within the compass of this book to advise about wine. Suffice to say that following statistics speak volumes.

There are 1,170,000 hectares (2,890,000 acres) of vineyard in France producing 60 million hectolitres of wine. (A hectolitre is approximately 46 Imperial gallons (or 57.5 US gallons).

The *Appellations Contrôlées* wines account for some 16% of the total. *Vins de Qualité Superieure* account for a mere 5% of the total. Therefore almost 80% of France's wine production is unclassified.

The Midi (particularly the *département* of *l'Hérault*) accounts for 54% of the total wine production of the country, and the Champagne district a tiny 1.1%, but almost all that is AC. It goes without saying, therefore, that the majority of wine drunk by the French is plonk.

The restaurant is the best (and easiest) place to discover good wine. Again a few statistics:

> The average restaurant mark-up in France on wines is:
> 300% on *petits vins*, i.e. Bordeaux rouge, non-AC local wines etc.
> 200% on *grandes ordinaires* such as Beaujolais.
> 30–50% on *vins de crus* such as St Emilion, Chablis.
> 20% or less on *très grands vins* such as Château Latour, Gevrey-Chambertin.
> Moral: The plonk drinker subsidizes the Burgundy drinker.

A good wine which is expensive at its place of origin is hardly likely to be cheap in a restaurant. When reading the wine list, look for the place of origin, and the addition of 'bottled by the producer' is an added guarantee.

The *vin du patron* is one of two things, excellent or mediocre. Usually its provenance is secret for the simple reason that if it is so good, the restaurateur does not want his competition to get it, or if it is so bad, he does want the customer to know where it comes from. The *vin du patron* is a direct reflection of the quality of the restaurant.

Occasionally you will find the *vin du patron* described as something like *l'Anjou du Patron* or *le Rosé de Provence du Patron* – never will you find *Chambertin du Patron* or *Montrachet du Patron*!

The wine label should tell all and should correspond with the wine list. *Vins d'origine* never used to show the degrees of alcohol on the label. This information is the sign of *Vin ordinaire*. However, EEC regulations now require this to be shown on the label of every bottle.

Bread comes in all sorts of shapes and sizes. The most common are the *baguette* and the *restaurant* made of white flour and liable to go stale very quickly. It is baked at least twice if not three times a day. There is also *pain complet* which varies from a pale beige loaf of some four hundred grammes to a large dark-brown monster of about a kilo. *Pain au levain* is the nearest to English old-fashioned bread and the best for slicing and toasting for breakfast toast and marmalade. It, too, goes stale rather quickly. Turner now do a *Pain de mie à l'anglaise* which is quite close to English bread. However, it is very difficult to get in normal sizes and is usually produced in minature slices, as is their *pain special pour huitres* which is quite close to the old-fashioned close-textured Hovis. Both these breads toast well, but not in a toaster since they are too small to get out easily. *La Vie Claire*, a health-food organization with shops throughout France, produces a stoneground wholemeal bread which is greatly sought after by back-to-nature types. *Pain au son* is a bran bread – how much bran depends on where you buy it. *Pain de mie* is sandwich bread very suitable for toasting, but it has added sugar and tastes more like American than British bread, and it does not go so well with marmalade. *Pain de seigle* is rye bread and much used for eating with shellfish. Again how much rye is in the bread depends on the individual baker, but colour is a good guide. The darker the bread is, the higher the rye content. Scandinavians and Dutch are among those who complain the most about French bread, and rightly so.

Certain bakeries also sell *croissants* and *brioches* and even *pâtisserie*, just as certain *pâtissiers* sell bread, but usually the two are kept apart. Unless for health reasons you cannot eat butter, it is most important to specify that your *croissants* etc should be made with butter, otherwise you will be sold a product made with oils specially formulated for *pâtisserie*. These leave the mouth with a greasy coating for about two or three hours, and it is better not to consider what they do to the stomach. It must be stated that hungry children do not seem to notice the difference, particularly if the *croissants* are served warm.

As with bread so with *pâtisserie*. It can vary from the commonplace to food for the gods. Old-fashioned *pâtissiers* with a pride in their calling still exist in goodly numbers throughout France. Trial and error is the best way to find them.

Most household products are more expensive in France than in any other country in the world – though special supermarkets for *droguerie* exist – and it pays to buy detergents etc in the bulk sizes. Bleach is sold either already diluted as in the United Kingdom or in small plastic packets for dilution at home from forty-eight degrees down to the twelve degrees normal with the addition of a litre of water. Never use this forty-eight degree *eau de Javel* neat since it quickly burns a hole in anything, including porcelain. Due perhaps to a long tradition of somewhat dubious plumbing, there are spectacularly powerful drain-unblocking products available in France. It is relatively rare to have to call in a plumber to unblock drains, though if all else fails, he will take just as long and be just as unreliable about his time of arrival as his foreign counterpart.

There is not in fact a widespread tradition of antique-collecting among the French, and therefore furniture- and silver-polish are neither as cheap nor as efficient as elsewhere. Anyone with a lot of silver or plate to polish should bear in mind that Silvo is available in a few places (made in Holland),

and Goddards products scarcely at all. The French products are all universally awful and to be avoided.

Particularly in the south and south-west most of the floors are made of tiles or marble. This last is a very fragile material, contrary to expectations, and should never, never be washed in anything but *savon noir* (preferably *à l'huile d'olive*). Products such as Ajax, Flash, Vigor etc. will quickly break down the surface and cause irreparable damage. Any products with soda or ammonia are death to marble. Also marble should not be polished with anything at all unless it is very old and beyond redemption. There are specialist firms who can 're-fill' marble floors and bring them back to something approaching their original shine, and the cost is around 45–50 francs a square metre, minimum.

As in most countries, there are stringent regulations intended to protect the consumer. On the whole these are followed by the majority of shops. For example, if you happen to pick up an item from a supermarket after its 'sell by' date, there will normally be no difficulty in exchanging it provided you produce your *ticket* for the purchase. This is a general rule in all shops and those who are used to screwing up those long rolls of paper on which their purchases are recorded are strongly advised not to do this until they have checked the contents of their bags. Unless you are well known at a shop, complaints unaccompanied by a cash till receipt are treated with a measure of disbelief ranging from the polite through the very firm to the extremely rude. There is a certain lack of the free and easy assumption to be found in other countries that the shopper does not cheat.

Since shops in France are as liable to hold sales as shops anywhere else, it may be of interest to know the precise rules which govern these. French shops are limited to two sales per year each of not more than two months duration. Bearing in mind that most shops are shut either for the whole month of August, or for at least another month in the year, this leaves them with the possibility of only seven month's normal trading in the year. The 'posher' shops call their sales '*fins de serie*', ordinary shops have *soldes*. Presumably for tax reasons,

French shops seem to go in for refurbishing on frequent occasions and before closing for the work to be done they usually hold sales *avant travaux*. In all cases, shops must show two prices on all items in a sale – the lowest price (struck through) at which the item was on sale during the month before the sale and the sale price. Failure to comply with this rule entitles you to complain to the local Consumer Protection Office – address from your nearest Préfecture.

The consumer protection laws are strict, as also are the general rules about buying and selling. On the other hand, the enforcement of one's rights in the Courts in France can be a tedious business; unless the amount involved really makes it worthwhile, it is best to avoid 'going to law'. Generally speaking, not only is legal procedure in France slow but the Courts' and the lawyers' attitude to the citizen's difficulties may seem, and often is, very different from that which you are used to. You would, for example, be surprised to know that in many civil cases, the parties need not be and often are not present and their evidence is assumed to be prejudiced. Even their witnesses often give their evidence only in the form of statements.

However, if you do feel that you have a serious consumer problem, ask your local adviser or, if you have not got one, the local Consul for the name of a good French *avocat* (preferably one who speaks your language) and let him get on with it. You will get nowhere if you try to solve your own problem.

There is a magazine for the benefit of consumers and there are local offices but they are not likely to take up cudgels for you themselves. Nor is the advice given by such an office in one town in France, that a letter from the local Consul will work miracles, good advice because that kind of assistance falls wholly outside the scope of a Consul's activities.

CHAPTER 22

The Media

France compared with Great Britain reads considerably fewer daily newspapers, and often these are local and not Paris-based. Local newspapers appear to be even more parochial than their British counterparts and frequently ignore world-shattering events in order to headline some local event. The magazine readership in France, however, is very similar to that of the United Kingdom at 550 readers per thousand inhabitants compared with 650 in the United Kingdom.

The following is a list of the better-known and most widely read French publications.

L'Aurore. Daily. Right wing and under the same management as *Le Figaro.* A paper much read by the *piednoirs* from France's former possessions in North Africa. It is also considered to be pro-Jewish/Israel.

Le Canard Enchaîné. Weekly. Left wing. Somewhat of a scandal sheet and considered by some to be the cause of many a politician's downfall. (The Press is free in France but this has not stopped *Le Canard Enchaîné* from being 'seized' from time to time.) Their revelations are always backed by documentary proof.

La Croix. Daily. No politics. This has a circulation in the region of 130,000 and is owned by the Bayard Press which is probably the largest Roman Catholic publisher in the world.

Le Figaro. Daily. Right wing though not militant. Probably its nearest equivalent in Great Britain is the *Daily Telegraph.* Births, deaths and marriages are usually announced in *Le Monde* and *Le Figaro* at the same time. It has an excellent weekly magazine (but not during August) and a bi-monthly *Madame Figaro.*

France-Soir. Daily. No politics as such since it tends to concentrate on gossip, scandal and supposition. Has the largest sale of any French newspaper, which perhaps says a lot about the French.
France-Dimanche. Weekly on Sundays. As above but more so.
L'Humanité. *The* Communist daily paper in France.
Ici-Paris. Weekly. Another scandal sheet; it is produced by serious journalists but with somewhat less documentary proof than *Le Canard Enchainé.*
Le Matin. Daily. Socialist. Economic supplement each Tuesday.
Minute. Weekly. Right wing. This magazine appears on the same day as *Le Canard Enchainé* with which it is in direct opposition. If you must read scandal, you should read these two magazines in tandem.
Le Monde. Daily. France's most serious daily and more or less the equivalent of *The Times.* Ostensibly it is above politics. *Le Monde*'s literary supplement appears each Friday, and they publish an economic review each Tuesday. Once a month there is *Le Monde Diplomatique* and *Le Monde – Musique* which are digests of the diplomatic and musical articles which have appeared in the paper during the previous four weeks.
Les Echos. The financial and Stock Exchange journal and published daily except Saturday and Sunday.
The Guardian. Produced in English in Marseilles and therefore on the news-stand before any other English paper.
New York Herald Tribune. Produced in Paris in English. US viewpoint on world news.

There are hundreds of weekly and monthly magazines covering every subject under the sun. Some of the most famous are *Paris-Match, Jours de France, Vogue, Marie-Claire, Marie-France, Elle, Maison et Jardin, Femmes d'Aujourd'hui.* Only a country as republican as France could produce a weekly magazine devoted entirely to the monarchs (both reigning and dispossessed) of Europe and *la haute société.* For those interested it is called *Vue et Images du Monde.*

Two of the most popular French 'penny-dreadful' magazines, '*Intimité*' and '*Nous Deux*', are nearly always purchased 'for a friend, not for me'.

It is interesting to note that the Press in France is virtually controlled by a mere handful of Press groups among which Hachette is undoubtedly the most important. Founded in 1826, it has successfully fought off government (and others') endeavours to curb its share of the market. Before the war it had the Press distribution monopoly. This was taken from them at the Liberation, but the nationalized enterprise which replaced them rapidly failed, and Hachette were back in harness. Hachette now control nearly 40% of the export of French publications and have offices in twenty-nine countries. They own a considerable number of publishing houses including Stock, Fayard and Livre du Poche, several newspapers including *France Dimanche* and magazines such as *Elle* and *Télé-7 Jours*.

Other important groups are Prouvost which owns *Cosmopolitan*, *Marie-Claire* and *Parents* and Hersant, which among many other publications controls *L'Aurore* and *Le Figaro*.

Television has made great inroads into Press readership, and many people now merely 'watch' the news rather than read a newspaper. There are three French television channels, two of which are more or less state controlled. The staff change according to the government in power. Late in 1984, an additional channel, 'Canal Plus' was inaugurated. This requires a special aerial/decoder and an additional fee is charged. This channel provides mostly old films, some new, but is on twenty-four hours a day. Two other channels are available in parts of France.

French television leaves a great deal to be desired from a purely technique point of view, and most of the channels rely heavily on old US films, dubbed into French, for evening entertainment. The documentaries are rarely of the quality of BBC, ITV or American productions, but there have been recent notable exceptions. Newscasting is excellent, and the erudition of some of the newscasters is obvious. News editing, though, is poor, and the choice of position for news items is to say the least capricious. Football seems to be more important than peace in the Middle East. Every now and again there are excellent plays, and occasionally (about once a month) there are undubbed Shakespeare plays from Stratford. (These films are about 15 years old.) In the south of the country viewers have the dubious benefit of one more channel, Télé-Monte-Carlo. They too have a film every evening, usually dubbed into French.

There is a large choice of radio stations in France.

France-Culture: From about 9 a.m. to 8 p.m. Rather like the BBC Third Programme but little or no music, which is dealt with on

France-Musique: from 9 a.m. to 8.30 p.m. Virtually non-stop music – mostly classical but some modern items and classical jazz also.

France-Inter: This differs from region to region. News at very frequent intervals early in the morning from about 6.30 a.m. Much listened to by commuters.

Europe 1, RTL and *Radio-Bleu* are all very similar (though they would hate to hear that opinion). Pop and/or light music and the odd chat show/interview. Punctuated fairly frequently by advertisements.

Radio-Monte-Carlo covers the Côte d'Azur and has the following different services:

RMC Light music, chat shows, interviews, news fairly frequently and advertisements.

RMC – Côte d'Azur: Non-stop music from 7 a.m. until midnight together with coverage and news of local events. No advertisements.

RMC Classique: Non-stop classical music from 7 a.m. until midnight.

RMC Rock: Non-stop rock music from 7 a.m. until midnight.

There are plenty of other local radio stations, pirate or otherwise, which come and go overnight. Radio Luxembourg can also be heard loud and clear on short-wave and for those who are on the south coast, there is an English station broadcasting from just over the border in Italy, which can be heard round the clock all along the coast. British newspapers are available all over France within twenty-four hours of their publication and sometimes even less. They are expensive particularly when compared with their French counterparts' price abroad. This is because air-freight costs are not subsidized by the British government as the French subsidize theirs. Seldom, if ever, will you get the weekly magazine which goes with your favourite Sunday newspaper. Prices are set by the *British* and not by the French. The New York Herald Tribune, published in Paris, is available all over France and the Wall Street Journal in the capital and large provincial towns. Dutch newspapers are fairly common; Scandinavian, less so. Usually the best place to find foreign newspapers is either an airport or a railway station after about midday.

French books are expensive because the readership is smaller – only France and their former overseas possessions – and cannot approach the size of the market presented by the UK, USA, Australia, South Africa, Canada, New Zealand etc, to say nothing of half the world wanting to learn English as its second language. French may be a very beautiful language, but it is way down the list of world languages. Books in English on sale in France are even more expensive than French and take into account freight charges, stocking charges and higher VAT. If you are buying more than the odd paperback, it often pays to buy books in Britain. This is one item, within reason, where the French do not charge VAT provided it is marked as a 'gift'. There are English bookshops in several of France's cities. There is a W. H. Smith branch in Paris; in Nice, there is The Cat's Whiskers, 26, rue Lamartine (93.80.02.66); and in Cannes The English Bookshop, 11, rue Bivouac Napoléon (93.99.40.08). Where there is an English church, there will usually be an English library to join as well. You do not have to be Church of England to join the library. Americans frequently run libraries in the larger towns also.

It is unlikely you will not be contacted to pay your TV licence either due to the declaration at the Customs that you are importing a TV set or when you purchase or hire one in France. The current cost is 331 francs per annum for black and white and 502 francs for colour. Retired persons over sixty living alone or with their spouse whose income is too small to be subject to income tax do not need to pay this *redevance* (licence fee).

Details of overseas radio services can be found in Appendix D.

CHAPTER 23

Building and Restoring Houses

How desirable it may be to seek fields (perhaps literally) in parts of France which, presumably for very good reasons, have for many years remained unsought by the non-French is a matter for debate. Inspired perhaps by the dream of a quick 'nip' down the Channel Tunnel on Friday nights and an equally quick 'nip' back on Sunday, the British seem to have discovered areas in the north of France which the French had never hoped to offload onto the foreigner. Much property on the market in these areas is in need of restoration. Some is land sold as available for building and some are existing houses. In both cases, the prices are noticeably lower than they are in those parts of the country in which the foreigner has traditionally bought or built.

Buying property in the country in France can be a hazardous pursuit, but then building property anywhere in the world is always hazardous unless one stands over the builder and architect with a whip. This chapter is a short résumé of the problems involved in buying country property with a view to its restoration or to the building one's own house. Clearly, few will be able to find, let alone be inclined to buy, land in a town and most of the properties available for restoration are rural. Some of the general problems to be encountered in buying property in France are dealt with in Chapter 5. This chapter relates rather more specifically to country properties.

All that has been said about the Notary in Chapter 5 applies in the country – but more so. One of the problems is that the country Notary is treated by his clients with a mixture of reverence and fear that is more or less absent in the case of the town Notary. Another is that, in all conscience, the standard of the country Notary may not be as high as that of the Notary in the town or city. There is a tendency for country transactions to have been incestuous over a period of many years since seller and buyer will probably have used the same Notary over and over again. This does not make for independent enquiries or investigation of title. A third problem is that the French Land Registry is far less accurate than the English Land Registry when it comes to recording things like rights of way, water and drainage rights and party walls. There is a tendency for these easements to be copied in successive documents without as much enquiry as would take place in England.

There is another problem peculiar to the country – the payment of the seller's agent's commission. The basic rule is that the seller pays the commission; though it is true that there are regional variations, more frequently in country areas rather than in towns or developed areas since it is there that the Estate Agent has come into his own. In France as a whole, it is said that only about 40% of sales are arranged through Estate Agents; but since this includes vast areas where the non-French would not normally buy, the proportion of sales negotiated by Estate Agents where there is a non-French buyer is considerably higher.

If a sale is organized by a Notary, his commission, which is about half of what an Estate Agent will expect to receive, is considered to be part of the *frais d'acte* or *frais de notaire* which (as has been said in Chapter 5) is paid by the buyer. It has been said, perhaps a little unkindly, that the reason the buyer pays the seller's commission is that the French countryman cannot understand why he should pay for the buyer having the privilege of buying land from him. Whatever the reason may be, it is absolutely essential to determine at the very outset what expenses you as a buyer will be liable to pay – and not be satisfied with a round figure. Notaries do not normally share their fees with anyone, so care must also be taken to ensure that you are not being asked to pay both a fee for someone having found a property and a fee for having bought it.

There may well be special problems which you cannot reasonably be expected to handle yourself. You may, for example, be buying land which is partly let for agricultural purposes and special and traditional rules may apply. You may be involved with SAFER or local Agricultural Committees. You may find you have a listed building on your hands. And so on. Just remember that it is better to be safe than sorry, and get advice in advance.

It goes without saying that disaster looms where one Notary sells to you as the seller's agent, and also acts for both of you on the sale itself. Do not be misled by being told that this is the way it has been done for years. You should put a stop to this practice in the case of your property. *If there was ever a need for advice from the very outset from a competent local adviser, it is in the case of country property of every kind – whether built, to be built or to be restored.* Ideally, you will need a Surveyor, but British Surveyors are far and few between, and the French architect, the *geomètre* or the *expert foncier* do not quite provide the same service. Your local adviser will do what he can to find you what you need.

Planning is an obvious problem. Initially, the best step is to pay a visit to the local *mairie* to find out what the situation is, but you really need to have an expert with you. Do not rely on photocopy planning documents shown to you by the seller or his agent. The contract should include the clauses needed to protect you if the planning situation is not what it is said to be. Searches are made *after* contracts are signed.

For those who think they can cope with these problems themselves, the following information may help.

The local planning unit is the *commune* and most have published a *plan d'occupation des sols* (POS). This is the local planning map and shows what land is available for building and for what purposes. When a search is made of the *commune*, it is answered by a *certificat d'urbanisme* which details the effect of the POS on the property sold and gives such information as whether the land is *constructible* (available for building), what the density regulations are, whether compulsory purchase orders are in force, what road-widening schemes are planned, etc.

Apart from the creation of fairly small swimming pools, not much work to an existing building and none for a new building can be carried out without a *permit de construire* or planning consent. When the building works have been completed, a *certificat de conformité* should be obtained to prove that the requirements of the *permit de construire* (but not of any other planning regulation) have been complied with. There are certain time limits involved, but it is never safe to start work on an implied *permit de construire* i.e. one which is deemed to have been granted because it has not been refused within the official time limit. Three years after the grant of a *certificat de conformité*, you are safe from its revocation if it is found that in fact you have not complied with the terms of the *permit de construire*.

Take the greatest care in the choice of your architect if you yourself are building or restoring. Never use the architect recommended by the builder you are using, or by the seller, without an independent recommendation. Never employ an architect without a written contract and never sign such a contract without independent advice.

Apart from the purchase of a house or flat on plan or *en état d'achèvement* (see Chapter 5), you can either get a professional builder to do a 'one off' job of building or restoring, or you can turn the whole problem over to the architect of your choice and let him find a builder and supervise the building work. Architects' fees increase the cost of work by about 12%. You would be ill-advised to employ local labour and try to control them yourself, with or without the help of an architect. Every building contract needs professional vetting and you should try to avoid any provision in a building contract which provides for price increases. If you agree otherwise, the builder will know that he will not suffer from delay on his part. In any event, insert a ferocious penalty clause on which you will be fought tooth and nail.

Some figures are interesting. Builders, other than the recognized top ten firms in France, who will provide a 'one-off' house, go bankrupt in about 13% of all cases, are guilty of delay in completing works in nearly 35% of their contracts, ask for price revisions in nearly 20% of building jobs and about one in every four of their contracts need subsequent alteration. Recourse by the owner to the Courts is necessary in about 10% of all these cases. Curiously, local boys on the job have a slightly better record – 7% bankruptcies, 26% delayed completions, 10% price revisions and get taken to Court on one in every five contracts. But remember that these figures taken from the French equivalent of *Which* apply to French and not foreign owners for whom it is certain that the disaster rate is higher.

Despite all that has been said, building a new house for oneself or restoring an old house is by no means always going to be a failure and obviously there are builders who have just that 'feel' which is needed. The art is to find them and have sufficient control over them, thus ensuring that however beautifully they may do the work, they do it your way – for all builders are contemptuous of your ideas – and complete more or less when they promised they would. Time becomes of less and less importance (to builders) the further south you go. Remember also that France is a very large country and there are very considerable regional variations of style. You do not deserve to own anything anywhere if you are not prepared to slot in with the local traditional style!

There are a number of special points which you must watch out for since building traditions and requirements in France are not necessarily those of elsewhere. Many is the wife with a permanently ruined back who failed to insist that the builder set all working surfaces at 'home' height: in France they tend to be lower by at least 5 cms than in the UK.

French electricity can be strange and wiring can fail to follow the proper colour code. You will find plenty of plugs scattered all over rooms, but many appear in the wrong place.

Many plugs are unearthed and their quality can be poor. Remember that if you are in the South that you will need outside plugs.

In theory, the French are good at insulating houses. Insist on insulation (for cold in winter and heat in summer), but do insist on *seeing* it installed.

If you are going to have a garden and your house is in the south, try to have a large tank of water for dry periods. It is often unsafe to rely on your own supplies, particularly in the country when if you are the only person seen to be flush with water from your own spring in summer, you may well find the odd pipe appearing across your land where previously there was none and your precious source of water diminished.

The best thing to do is to make a comprehensive list after you have wholly captured the 'feel' of the area and not rely on what a builder or architect will provide for you on the basis that you are content to accept local standards.

APPENDIX A

Embassies and Consulates and Information on Births and Marriages

Note:
1. The information contained in this Appendix on births and marriages has been supplied by the Consulates of various countries and it must be emphasized that it is only of a very general nature. It is essential that elaboration should be sought of the appropriate Consulate, not only because there are always special cases but because of possible changes in the law of any country.
2. Marriages, valid according to the laws of France, will be recognized as valid in any of the countries mentioned in this Appendix but marriage to a citizen of one nationality by a citizen of another nationality by no means always confers the nationality of the first.
3. In some cases, a child born to a citizen of one of the undermentioned countries will acquire by birth the citizenship of his parents but this is not always so and each case requires checking with the Consulate.
4. If a French document which must be in the form of an *acte notarié* (e.g. a Power of Attorney) is signed before a French Consul, care must be taken that the Consular Official is not merely a Consular Agent, who does not have powers equivalent to a French *Notaire*.

AUSTRALIA

The Australian Embassy and Consulate,   Tel: (1) 45.75.62.00
4, rue Jean Rey,
75724 Paris. Cedex 15
French Embassy,   Tel: Canberra 95 1000
6, Darwin Avenue,
Yarralumla,
Canberra.

There are French Consulates General in Sydney and Melbourne.

1. Consuls are empowered subject to certain conditions to perform marriages where both parties are Australian citizens.

2. Marriage to an Australian citizen does not confer automatic Australian citizenship. Application must be made to the Department of Immigration and the various requirements fulfilled.

3. A child, born out of Australia, to an Australian citizen by descent, acquires Australian citizenship by registration and application to an Australian Consulate but this must be done before the child is eighteen. A child who acquires such citizenship by descent cannot pass on this citizenship unless he has lived in Australia for at least two years.

CANADA
Embassy and Consulate of Canada,   Tel:(1) 47.23.01.01
35/37, avenue Montaigne,
75008 Paris.

Consulates

33080 Bordeaux	Tel: 56.96.15.61
13000 Marseille	Tel: 91.37.19.37
67000 Strasbourg	Tel: 88.32.65.96
69003 Lyon	Tel: 73.61.15.25

French Embassy,   Tel: (613) 232 − 1795
42, Promenade Sussex,
Ottawa.
Ont. KIM 2C9

There are French Consulates at Calgary and Edmonton (Alberta) and an Honorary Consul in Chicoutimi (Quebec)

1. Consuls are not empowered to perform marriages.

2. A non-Canadian citizen does not automatically obtain Canadian citizenship on marriage to a Canadian citizen. A formal request must be made and medical and security clearance obtained. The applicant must be admitted to Canada as a landed immigrant and live in Canada for at least three years before such an application will be granted.

3. A child born out of Canada, one at least of whose parents is a Canadian citizen has automatic Canadian citizenship. Registration of the birth is not necessary but to obtain a Certificate of Canadian Citizenship, it is necessary to apply to a Consulate in the country of birth.

DENMARK

Royal Danish Embassy and Consulate, 77, avenue Marceau, 75116 Paris.	Tel: (1) 47.20.32.66

Consulate General

13000 Marseille	Tel: 91.90.80.23

Consulates

There are many Danish Consulates in France of which the following are in the more important towns.

14000 Caen	Tel: 31.82.33.13
62100 Calais	Tel: 21.34.44.00
50100 Cherbourg	Tel: 33.44.00.22
76200 Dieppe	Tel: 35.82.53.50
59140 Dunkerque	Tel: 28.65.99.44
17000 La Rochelle	Tel: 46.41.43.76
59370 Lille	Tel: 20.04.30.58
76600 Le Havre	Tel: 35.21.11.22
69008 Lyon	Tel: 78.72.55.38
34000 Montpellier	Tel: 67.75.13.10
06000 Nice	Tel: 93.85.35.49
66000 Perpignan	Tel: 68.34.61.57
76000 Rouen	Tel: 35.98.77.77
34200 Sète	Tel: 96.94.01.08
35400 St. Malo	Tel: 99.56.07.21
44600 St. Nazaire	Tel: 40.22.30.00
67000 Strasbourg	Tel: 88.84.20.11
31000 Toulouse	Tel: 61.52.87.65

French Embassy, 4, Kongens Nytorv, 1050 Copenhagen K.	Tel: (1) 15.51.22

There are Honorary French Consulates in a number of towns in Denmark including Aarhus, Odense and Esbjerg.

1. Consuls are not empowered to perform marriages.
2. Marriage to a Danish citizen gives automatic Danish citizenship.
3. The child of a Danish citizen acquires automatic Danish citizenship. No registration at a Consulate is necessary.

EIRE

Irish Embassy and Consulate, Tel: (1) 45.00.20.87
12, avenue Foch,
75116 Paris.

Consulate
06660 Antibes   Tel: 93.61.50.63

French Embassy and Consulate, Tel: 694.777
36, Ailesbury Road,
Dublin 4.

1. Consuls cannot perform marriages.
2. Marriage to an Irish citizen does not automatically confer Irish citizenship. A woman may acquire Irish citizenship on marriage to an Irish citizen after making a declaration of post-nuptial citizenship.
3. Children of Irish-born citizens are automatically Irish citizens from birth and registration is not necessary.

THE NETHERLANDS

Embassy and Consulate,   Tel: (1) 43.06.61.88
7–8, rue Eblé,
75007 Paris.

Consulates
20176 Ajaccio   Tel: 95.21.00.58
33000 Bordeaux   Tel: 56.52.16.75
29268 Brest   Tel: 98.80.32.70
62106 Calais   Tel: 21.95.55.03
21000 Dijon   Tel: 80.30.10.66
59377 Dunkerque   Tel: 28.66.74.00
38100 Grenoble   Tel: 76.23.14.90
64700 Hendaye   Tel: 59.26.65.66
76067 Le Havre   Tel: 35.22.57.25
59000 Lille   Tel: 20.54.07.04
69002 Lyon   Tel: 78.37.45.97
13008 Marseille   Tel: 91.71.47.84
44002 Nantes   Tel: 40.73.27.60
06000 Nice   Tel: 93.87.52.94
66000 Perpignan   Tel: 68.34.28.72
51054 Reims   Tel: 26.07.39.34
17009 La Rochelle   Tel: 46.34.98.66
76000 Rouen   Tel: 35.89.81.81
Rijssel (see Lille)

35400 St. Malo	Tel: 99.56.03.22
34203 Sète	Tel: 67.48.63.16
67300 Strasbourg	Tel: 88.62.24.69
31000 Toulouse	Tel: 61.52.64.92
37000 Tours	Tel: 47.61.30.49

French Embassy,   Tel: (70) 46.94.71
Smidsplein,
B.P.683,
Den Haag.

There are French Consulates in Amsterdam and Rotterdam.

1. Dutch Consuls cannot celebrate marriages in France.
2. Marriage to a Dutch citizen does not confer automatic Dutch citizenship. The non-Dutch party to the marriage must have been married for three years.
3. A child, one or both of whose parents are Dutch, has Dutch nationality by birth. It is desirable to register the birth abroad of such a child at a Consulate.

NEW ZEALAND

Embassy and Consulate,   Tel: (1) 45.00.24.11
7 ter, rue Léonard de Vinci,
75116 Paris.

French Embassy,   Tel: (4) 720.200/1
14th Floor,
Robert Jones House,
1–3, Willeston Street,
Wellington.

1. Consuls are not empowered to perform marriages.
2. Marriage to a New Zealand citizen does not give automatic New Zealand citizenship. The non-New Zealand spouse must have lived in New Zealand for three years immediately before applying for New Zealand citizenship and must have some 'ties' with the country, so that each application is dealt with on its own individual merits.
3. A child born out of New Zealand of either a mother or a father who is a New Zealand citizen by birth automatically acquires New Zealand citizenship. This birth must be registered either with the

New Zealand Embassy in the country of birth or with the D.I.F. in Wellington before the child is twenty-two or the right to citizenship will lapse.

SWEDEN

Embassy and Consulate of Sweden,   Tel: (1) 45.55.92.15
17, rue Barbet de Jouy,   -
75007 Paris.

Consulates

20000 Ajaccio	Tel: 95.21.00.13
80000 Amiens	Tel: 22.91.62.41
33075 Bordeaux	Tel: 56.39.33.33
29283 Brest	Tel: 98.44.49.95
62105 Calais	Tel: 21.34.77.34
50100 Cherbourg	Tel: 33.53.31.08
59377 Dunkerque	Tel: 28.66.74.00
17009 La Rochelle	Tel: 46.42.13.44
76051 Le Havre	Tel: 35.42.23.54
59800 Lille	Tel: 20.54.27.80
69100 Lyon	Tel: 78.93.11.77
13008 Marseille	Tel: 91.76.30.14
44029 Nantes	Tel: 40.73.85.59
06000 Nice	Tel: 93.87.79.44
66000 Perpignan	Tel: 68.61.07.44
51100 Reims	Tel: 26.40.22.73
76000 Rouen	Tel: 35.71.96.97
34201 Sète	Tel: 67.48.63.16
67400 Strasbourg	Tel: 88.39.43.91
31000 Toulouse	Tel: 61.52.66.45

French Embassy,   Tel: (8) 630.02.70
28, Narvavagen,
115 23 Stockholm.

There are French Consulates in Goteborg and Malmo and Consular Agencies at Gavle, Helsingborg, Harnosand, Karlstad, Lulea, Norrkoping and Sundsvall.

1. The Swedish Ambassador in Paris is empowered to conduct marriage ceremonies when both parties are Swedish citizens. The Consuls have no such powers.

2. Swedish citizenship is not automatically acquired by marriage to a Swedish citizen of either sex.
3. Children of Swedish parents born in France are automatically Swedish citizens and no registration is required.

UNITED KINGDOM

Her Britannic Majesty's Embassy, 35, rue du Fauburg St. Honoré, 75008 Paris.	Tel: (1) 42.66.91.42
Her Britannic Majesty's Embassy, Consular Section, 109, rue du Fauburg St Honoré, 75008 Paris.	Tel: (1) 42.66.91.42

Consulates General
33001 Bordeaux	Tel: 56.52.28.35
59800 Lille	Tel: 20.52.87.90
69288 Lyon	Tel: 78.37.59.67
13006 Marseille	Tel: 91.53.43.32

British Honorary Consulates
62201 Boulogne-sur-mer	Tel: 21.30.25.15
62100 Calais	Tel: 21.34.45.48
59377 Dunkerque	Tel: 28.66.11.98
51200 Epérnay	Tel: 26.51.31.02
76600 Le Havre	Tel: 35.42.27.47
44009 Nantes	Tel: 40.48.57.47
06000 Nice	Tel: 93.82.32.04
66000 Perpignan	Tel: 68.34.56.99

French Embassy, 58, Knightsbridge, London SW1	Tel: 071.235.8080
French Consulate-General, 24, Rutland Gate, London SW7 (for notarizing documents etc)	Tel: 071.581.5292

29–31 Wrights Lane, Tel: 071.937.1202
London W8
(for visas and information)

There are Consulates-General also in Belfast, Cardiff, Edinburgh, Liverpool and St. Helier, Jersey. There are Consular Agents in Folkestone, Lowestoft, Newhaven, Plymouth and Southampton. Note that notarial documents, such as French Powers of Attorney, cannot be made before Consular Agents but only before Consuls who have the powers of a *notaire*.

1. Consuls do not perform marriages.
2. Marriage to a British citizen does not confer automatic British citizenship. The non-British spouse must reside for three years in the UK before making an application for British citizenship which, if accorded, will be of the same type as that of the British spouse.
3. In most cases, children born to British citizens are British. Registration at the Consulate is not required but strongly recommended.

UNITED STATES OF AMERICA

American Embassy, Tel: (1) 42.96.12.02
2, avenue Gabriel,
75008 Paris.

Consulates
33000 Bordeaux Tel: 56.52.65.95
69006 Lyon Tel: 78.24.68.49
13006 Marseille Tel: 91.54.92.00
06000 Nice Tel: 93.88.89.55
67000 Strasbourg Tel: 88.35.31.04

French Embassy, Tel: (202) 328.2600
2535, Belmont Road, N.W.
Washington D.C. 20008

There are French Consulates-General in Boston, Chicago, Detroit, Houston, Los Angeles, New Orleans, New York and San Francisco. These cover all the fifty States. Addresses and telephone numbers can be obtained from the French Embassy in Washington.

1. Consular Officers have no authority to perform marriages.
2. Marriage to a US citizen does not confer automatic US citizenship.

3. In most cases, a child born to parents, one or both of whom are US citizens, acquires US citizenship by birth. Registration of a birth at a Consulate is not required but advisable for future proof of citizenship.

APPENDIX B

Some Useful Organizations in France

SOS-Help

The Samaritans are an organization which was originally founded to help people in moments of deep distress. They still provide this wonderful service but because to find oneself alone in a foreign country without a knowledge of the language can well be or lead to a crisis, they also provide a considerable amount of basic information to anyone 'lost' in France. SOS-HELP is an English language crisis line in the Paris region. Its telephone number is (1) 47.23.80.80. and it operates from 3 p.m. to 11 p.m. throughout the week.

Local Consulates or places of worship can provide names and addresses of local organizations in addition to those listed below.

CANADA
Association France-Canada. 5 rue Constantine, 75007 Paris. Tel: (1) 45.55.83.65.
There are branches in forty other French towns details of which can be obtained from the Paris branch.

DENMARK
The Danish Church in Paris, 17 rue Lord Byron, 75008. Tel: (1) 42.56.12.84 will give a list of various Danish Associations throughout France. Scandinavian Club c/o Madame Sorne, la Rescampaldo, chemin St Paul, 06570 St Paul. Tel: 93.20.68.77.

EIRE

The Irish Export Board, 33 rue de Miromesnil, 75008 Paris.
Tel:(1) 42.65.98.05.
Comité France-Ireland, 1 rue Auguste Vacquerie, 75116 Paris.
The Irish Wild Geese Society, 13 rue Simon Dereure, 75018
Paris.

THE NETHERLANDS

Nederlaans Vereniging in Frankrijk, 19 rue Mayet, 75006
Paris.
ANEAS 22 Place du Général Catroux, 75017 Paris. Tel: (1)
47.66.04.96.
Institut Neérlandais, 121 rue de Lille, 75007 Paris, Tel: (1)
47.05.85.99.
Association France-Hollande, 79 av. des Champs Elysées,
75008, Paris. Tel: (1) 261.51.15.
Nederlaans-Frans Kamer van Koophandel, 109 Bd. Mals-
herbes, 75008 Paris. Tel: (1) 45.63.54.30.
Vereniging van Nederlaanders in Zuid Frankrijk: Cannes:
93.39.18.56. Ferney-Volatire 50.40.78.06. Toulouse-
Blagnac: 61.71.34.63.
There are branches in other towns details of which can be
obtained from the above telephone numbers.

NEW ZEALAND

Association France-Nouvelle Zélande, 8 rue St Louis, 78000
Versailles.

SWEDEN

Cercle Suedois, (Svenska Klubben), 242 rue de Rivoli, 75001
Paris. Tel: (1) 42.60.76.67.

UNITED KINGDOM

Franco-British Chamber of Commerce and Industry, 26 av.
Victor Hugo, 75116 Paris.
Tel: (1) 45.01.55.00. There are regional branches for
Southern, South Western and Northern France, Normandy
and Rhône-Alpes.
British Institute in Paris, 9 rue Constantine, 75007 Paris. Tel:
(1) 45.55.71.91.

British Council, 9 rue Constantine, 75007 Paris. Tel: (1) 45.55.54.99.

Royal British Legion, 8 rue Bourdreau, 75009 Paris. Tel: (1) 47.42.19.26. and 2 Boulevard de Cimiez, 06000 Nice. Tel: 93.85.12.74.

RNVR Association in Paris. Tel: (1) 45.75.62.00

RAF Association. 6 rue de Général Larminat, 75015 Paris. Tel: (1) 42.85.35.18.

Association France-Grande Bretagne, 17 rue Philibert Delorme, 75017 Paris. Tel: (1) 47.66.43.01 and 47 bis rue Barberis 06000 Nice. Tel: 93.89.09.55.

British Association of the Alpes-Maritimes, Nice. Tel: 93. 88.62.70.

There are other branches the telephone number of which can be obtained from Nice.

Hertford British Hospital, 48 rue de Villiers, 92300 Levallois-Perret. Tel: (1) 47.58.13.12.

Sunnybank Anglo-American Hospital, 133 av. Petit Jouas, 06400 Cannes. Tel: 93.68.26.96.

Mediterranean Property Owners' Association 93.87.57.09.

UNITED STATES

American Aid Society, c/o American Embassy, Paris.

American Centre, 261 boulevard Raspail, 75014 Paris. Tel: (1) 43.21.42.20.

American Chamber of Commerce in France, 21 avenue Georges V, 75008 Paris. Tel: (1) 47.23.80.26.

American Hospital in Paris, 63 boulevard Victor Hugo, 92200 Neuilly. Tel: (1) 47.47.53.00.

Sunnybank Anglo-American Hospital, 133 av. Petit Jouas, 06400 Cannes. Tel: 93.68.26.96.

American Jewish Committee, 4 rue de la Bienfaisance, 75008 Paris. Tel: (1) 45.22.92.43.

American Legion, 49 rue Pierre Charron, 75008 Paris. Tel: (1) 42.25.41.93 and 26 boulevard d'Italie, Monte Carlo. MC98000. Tel: 93.41.04.47.

American Library in Paris, 10 rue du Général Camou, 75007 Paris. Tel: (1) 45.51.46.82.

Ass. of American Residents Overseas, 49 rue Pierre Charron, 75008 Paris. Tel: (1) 42.56.10.22.

Ass. of American Wives of Europeans, 9 avenue F. D. Roosevelt, 75008 Paris. Tel: (1) 43.59.45.16 and c/o Mrs B. Thomas-Richard, 15, rue Guiglia, 06000 Nice. Tel: 93. 87.57.89 and c/o Madame D. Van De Waale, 90 La Croisette, 06400 Cannes. Tel: 93.43.06.24.

English Language Library for the Blind, 5 avenue Daniel Lesueur, 75007 Paris. Tel: (1) 47.34.56.10 (closed Mondays).

YWCA, 22 rue de Naples, 75008 Paris. Tel: (1) 45.22.72.70.

Women's Club of the Riviera, Hotel Aston, 12 avenue Félix Faure, 06000 Nice. Tel: 93.80.62.52.

APPENDIX C

Places of Worship

DENMARK
Paris: The Danish Church, 17 rue Lord Byron, 75008 Paris. Tel: (1) 256.12.84.
Aix en Provence: Skandinavisk Kirkekomite, 37 traverse Barlet. Tel: 42.21.20.09.
Nice: Dansk/Norsk Kirkekomite, 6 avenue Durante. Tel: 93.88.40.86.
Port de Bouc: Skandinavisk Kirkekomite. Tel: 42.06.64.12.

EIRE
St Joseph's Church, 50 avenue Hoche, 75008 Paris. Tel: (1) 563.20.61.

NETHERLANDS
Paris: Eglise Lutherienne de la Trinité, 172 boulevard Vincent Auriol. Tel: (1) 45.82.70.95.
Eglise Réformée, 41 avenue Balzac, 92410 Ville d'Avray. (Open July and August only).

SWEDEN
Svenska Kyrkan, 9 rue Médéric, 75017 Paris. Tel: (1) 47.63.70.33.
See also under Denmark.

UNITED KINGDOM
Church of England

Paris: St Michael's Church, 5 rue d'Aguesseau, 75008 Paris. Tel: (1) 47.42.70.88.

St George's Church, 7 rue Auguste Vacquerie, 75016 Paris. Tel: (1) 47.20.22.51.

Beaulieu sur Mer: St Michael's Church. Tel: 93.27.53.46.

Biarritz: St Joseph's Church, avenue Victor Hugo. Tel: 59.62.56.45.

Bordeaux: St Nicholas's Church, 10 cours Xavier Arnozan. Tel: 61.54.30.05.

Caen: at Chapelle de la Miséricorde, rue Elie de Braumont. Tel: 31.73.18.80.

Cannes: Holy Trinity Church, rue du Canada. Tel: 93.94.54.61.

Dunkerque: Missions to Seamen, 130 rue de l'Ecole Maternelle. Tel: 28.63.39.47.

Grenoble: at Centre St Marc, av. Malherbe. Tel: 76.23.23.97.

Lyon: at les Mains Ouvertes, la Part-Dieu. Tel: 78.59.67.06.

Maisons Lafitte: Holy Trinity Church, 15 avenue Carnot. Tel: 39.62.34.97.

Marseille: All Saints' Church, rue de Belloi. Tel: 42.22.48.71.

Menton: St John's Church, avenue Carnot. Tel: 93.57.20.25.

Nice: Holy Trinity Church, rue de la Buffa. Tel: 93.87.19.83.

Pau: St Andrew's Church, rue O'Quin. Tel: 59.62.56.45.

St Raphael: St John the Evangelist's Church, avenue Paul Boumer. Tel: 94.44.44.55.

Strasbourg: at l'Eglise des Pères Dominicains, rue de l'Université. Tel: 88.61.19.28.

Toulouse: at Chapelle de Sainte-Marie Réparatrice, place du Parlément. Tel: 61.54.30.05.

Versailles: at Ecole de Grandchamp, 22 rue Henri Regnier. Tel: 39.46.31.86.

There are a number of other places of worship and information can be obtained from the telephone numbers shown below.

Boulogne: 21.31.49.89.

Cahors: 65.35.08.18.

Calais: 21.36.65.48.
Cognac and Charente: 61.54.30.05.
Duras: 58.94.76.37.
Le Havre: (4) 457.37.22.
Lille: 20.44.08.30.
Ribérac: 61.54.30.05.
Rouen: 35.71.84.10.
Vence: 93.87.19.83.

Church of Scotland
Paris: 17, rue Bayard, 75008 Paris. Tel: 878.47.94.

Roman Catholic Church (English speaking)
Paris: St Joseph's Church. (See note under Eire)

UNITED STATES
American Church of Paris, 65 quai d'Orsay, 75007 Paris. Tel: (1) 47.05.07.99.
Episcopalians and all other Christian denominations are welcome at all Church of England services. Those wishing to attend other services should apply to the American Embassy in Paris for the Embassy's List of Churches.

SYNAGOGUES
There are a considerable number of synagogues in the Paris area, Ashkenazi, Sephardi and Reform; their addresses, times of services etc. can best be obtained from the Consistoire Israélite de Paris, telephone (1) 42.85.71.09, the Association Culturelle Sépharadite de Paris, telephone (1) 47.00.75.95 or the Liberal Jewish Union, telephone 47.04.37.27.

There are synagogues in over a hundred cities and towns in France outside Paris of which the following is a selection.
Aix en Provence: 3 rue de Jérusalem. Telephone 42.59.49.30.
Antibes: Villa la Monarda, chemin des Sables, Antibes. Telephone 93.61.59.34.
Avignon: 2 place de Jérusalem, Avignon. Telephone 90. 86.42.49.
Bordeaux: 8 rue Labirat, Bordeaux. Telephone 56.91.79.39.

Cannes: 19 boulevard d'Alsace, Cannes. Telephone 93. 38.16.54.

Dijon: 5 rue de la Synagogue, Dijon. Telephone 80.66.46.47.

Grasse: 6 bis rue Mougins-Roquefort, Grasse. Telephone 93. 36.01.56.

Grenoble: 11 rue André Maginot, Grenoble. Telephone 76. 87.02.80.

Libourne: 33 rue de la Mothe, Libourne. Telephone 56. 51.45.99.

Lille: 5 Auguste-Angellier, Lille. Telephone 20.52.41.59.

Lyon: For information apply Consistoire de Lyon, 13, quoi Tilsitt. Telephone 78.37.13.43. or Consistoire Israélite Sépharade de Lyon, 317 rue Duguesclin, Lyon. Telephone 78.38.18.74.

Mâcon: 7 rue St Jean, Mâcon. Telephone 85.38.27.75.

Marseille: 119 rue Bretile, Marseille 6. Telephone 91. 37.73.35.

For addresses of the many other synagogues in Marseille apply to the Conseil d'Administration, telephone 91.52.87.49.

Menton: 1 bis avenue Thiers, Menton. Telephone 93. 35.23.19.

Nantes: 5 impasse Copernic, Nantes. Telephone 40.73.48.92.

Nice: rue Gustave Deloye, Nice. Telephone 93.85.44.35.

Pau: 8 rue des Trois-Frères-Bernardac, Pau. Telephone 59. 62.37.85.

Toulon: 6 rue de la Visitation, Toulon. Telephone 94. 92.61.05.

Toulouse: 17 rue du Rampart, St Etienne, Toulouse. Telephone 61.21.69.56.

Versailles: 10 rue Albert-Joly, Versailles. Telephone (1) 951.05.35.

APPENDIX D

Overseas Broadcasting and TV Services

Most countries operate an overseas service for their own nationals and to listen to the news and other programmes is the easiest way of keeping in touch with 'home'. It is not necessary to invest in a very expensive or complicated radio but there are certain basic facts it is as well to know if you are to get the best out of your set. A small portable set is all that is required. It should show wavelengths in metres (m) or frequencies in kilohertz (kHz) or Megahertz (MHz). Your receiver should cover at least the 49 to 16 metre or 6 to 17 MHz range, since this should enable you to receive broadcasts from all the countries mentioned below. Choose a receiver which is easy to tune, with a broad tuning scale and, if possible, with a number of shortwave scales. Avoid one where the whole range mentioned above is packed into one scale only, a few inches long. Sets with these facilities are quite easy to come by. Portable transistor sets come with telescopic aerials and usually these are quite sufficient. You should, however, vary its length and position until best reception is received. It sometimes helps to place the set near a window, especially if you live in a block of flats which has a lot of steel in its construction. You can coil six or so turns of aerial wire on a paper or thin cardboard tube which you slide over the telescopic rod and hang the other end of the wire outside the building; this can help to increase reception. During the day, reception is best on higher frequencies (15 to 21 MHz). At night, lower frequencies (around 6 and 7 MHz) are best whilst at dusk and dawn the middle bands (9 to 11 MHz) are best. However, at the present time, the sun is going through a particularly active phase and the sunspots associated with this seriously disturb reception. The BBC announced in 1987 that we had passed through the worst and things were due to get better over the next five years! This is particularly noticeable in day time and a few hours experimenting will soon show which frequencies give the best reception. If you get fade-outs due to this, tune to a higher frequency but during the worst fade-out periods, you may hear nothing at all for short periods. In some places, reception is always bad simply because of your location e.g. high hills or mountains very close to you and then an outside aerial, raised as high as possible may well help. Not only does reception vary by day or by night but also in winter and in summer. For this reason, countries transmitting overseas services tend to change their frequencies once or twice a year. Application to any of the Overseas Broadcasting Authorities mentioned below will readily produce the current frequencies used by them and often programmes as well. Personal experience is that without much difficulty one becomes quite conversant with the best frequencies to use at any time of the day or night throughout the year.

A word of warning. It is not always safe to leave a set tuned to a frequency and expect to get the programme you want day after day and at any time of the day or night. Shortwave reception idiosyncrasies simply do not allow this.

Early in 1989, a private radio station just over the Italian border at Seborga (Elektra 108) began broadcasting on FM on 108 MHz the BBC Overseas Service twenty-four hours a day. This can be heard with total clarity westwards about as far down the coast as Théoule but geographical conditions cause certain gaps in reception areas and the station cannot be heard in Nice. The BBC says that more and more stations in Europe receive the programme by satellite and rebroadcast it locally on FM.

Greenwich Mean Time (GMT) and Co-ordinated Universal Time (UTC) represent the same time. Some countries (e.g. Australia, Canada) use UTC and other countries (e.g. the UK and the USA) use GMT. France is one hour ahead of UTC or GMT, except when it has Summer Time, when it is two hours ahead. All countries in the EEC (with the apparent exception of the UK) change to Summer Time and back again on the same dates.

AUSTRALIA
Programmes and frequency charts from Radio Australia, GPO box 428G, Melbourne 3001. Australia.

CANADA
Programmes and frequency charts from Radio Canada International, PO Box 6000, Montreal, Canada H3C 3A8.

DENMARK
Programmes and frequency charts can be obtained from Danmarks Radio, Kortboelgetjenesten, 1999 Copenhagen V. Denmark.

NETHERLANDS
Details can be obtained from Radio Nederland, Witte Kruislaan 55. Hilversum. Holland.

SWEDEN
Programmes and frequency charts from Radio Sweden International, S-105, 10 Stockholm, Sweden.

UNITED KINGDOM
The BBC World Service broadcasts on a very large number of frequencies throughout the whole of the twenty-four hour period. The times when best reception is received varies upon whether one is in the north, the south-west or the centre or south-east of the country. In addition, one can often receive programmes destined for the Near and Far East and for Africa.

Programmes and frequency charts from London Calling, PO Box 76, Bush House, London WC2B 4PH. Telephone 071.240.3406. In addition, you can subscribe to London Calling, a monthly magazine, which gives a lot of extra information, for the annual subscription of (currently) £10.00.

UNITED STATES
Programmes and frequency charts from Voice of America, 300, C Street SW, 20847 Washington DC. USA.

TV by satellite can be received all over France. The smaller dish will receive BBC and the larger dish a number of additional transmissions from the UK and many other countries. The BBC has appointed a number of Authorized Dealers/Distributors of the Direct to Home Decoder. In France, these are currently:

Paris area – David Evans. Phone (1) 42.35.38.38
Dordogne area – Michael Mitchell. Phone 53.91.81.57
Southern France (Var) – Oliver Babb. Phone 94.73.82.52
Southern France (Alpes-Maritimes). Phone 93.28.37.36
Monaco – Donald Wilson. Phone 93.41.85.71

Any of these Dealers will advise generally and where necessary install dish aerials. It is probably better to use their services or, if they are out of your area, someone recommended by them, than the local French shops. Beware of buying equipment in the UK without being absolutely certain that it is suitable for reception in your area. The BBC also runs a Video Library which, for a subscription of around £200 a year, will supply you at regular monthly intervals with tapes of a variety of up-to-date programmes.

It is advisable to check details both about satellite TV and the Video Library from the BBC TV Europe in London.

APPENDIX E

Medical Assistance

A number of French doctors speak English and other languages but unless one is reasonably fluent in French and has a moderate command of illnesses and medical terms in that language, quite serious problems can arise.

Most Consulates will have lists of doctors who speak the language of the Consulate's country but Consulates are open for comparatively short hours only and not usually after about 4 p.m. at the latest.

For English speakers, there is an organization called International Association for Medical Assistance to Travellers (IAMAT), one of whose objects is 'to provide world wide medical assistance . . . by the provision of locally licenced medical practitioners who have a command' of English. There are some thirty such doctors in France, who undertake to work for IAMAT and who charge fixed fees for their services. The Head Office is at 417 Center Street, Lewistone, New York, NY 14092, USA. There are several numbers in France which will provide information including 93.88.42.14.

SOS is a wonderfully useful service. It is an insurance organization which will provide for those using its services, medical aid and if necessary repatriation. Information is easily obtainable in Scandinavian countries and from PPP in the UK, but in an emergency in France can also be had from 93.08.66.10.

For those from the UK, the AA has set up AA St John Alert, which is an emergency service for travellers in urgent need of help. It runs a twenty-four hour emergency contact number and has a panel of practitioners and consultants in France (and indeed in most other countries) able to advise on any conceivable medical emergency. Information may be obtained from AA St John Alert, Fanum House, Basingstoke, Hants, RG21 2BR (Tel: 0256 24872).

It cannot be too highly stressed that whilst inter-EEC country arrangements provide for free or substantially free medical attention for nationals of one EEC country taken ill in another EEC country, not all countries provide for free repatriation. This can only be achieved by insurance or other arrangements made before you travel.

Appendix F

Costs Relating to Property in France

PURCHASES

1. A purchaser is liable for three payments (the fees of the *Notaire*, Stamp Duty and Land Registry fees) on completion in addition to the purchase price and the total of these payments must be in the hands of the *Notaire* on or before completion.

2. The fees of the *Notaire* (inclusive of TVA) for the preparation of the *acte de vente* are in accordance with the following scale:

Slice of Purchase Price	Percentage fee
Up to 20,000 francs	5%
20,000 to 40,000 francs	3.3%
40,000 to 110,000 francs	1.65%
Over 110,000 francs	0.825%

3. Stamp Duty (*Enregistrement*) is made up of a number of taxes, recovered by central and local government and its full rate is 16.6% in all but two regions of France, where it is slightly lower. This is because the Regions can set annually their own scale (not exceeding 1.6%) for this tax and there are slight variations. There are many exceptions to this very high duty. The state also makes a small charge for the privilege of collecting the duty.

4. The following are the most usual exceptions to the imposition of the full rate of stamp duty:

(a) On sales still within the scope of TVA (see Chapter 14 under the heading TVA). This duty in such cases is nil. Such sales are called 'new sales'.

(b) On sales outside the scope of TVA, when the purchaser

undertakes in the *acte de vente* to occupy the house or flat as a private residence only. The duty is then reduced to 5.4% plus the regional tax. For this purpose, a garage or parking lot counts as a residence. If the undertaking is broken, not only will the balance of the full duty become payable but there is a 6% penalty. Such sales are called 'old sales' or 'resales'.

(c) On land bought for building, whether for a private residence or not, no stamp duty at all is payable, if the purchaser undertakes to build within four years. This period can, with consent be extended. If no such building takes place within this period, the full stamp duty becomes payable plus a six per cent penalty. It is important to note that in the case of such a purchase, TVA is payable, currently at 13.2%, *by the purchaser* in addition to the price of the land and it is not included in the price and accounted for by the seller as in the case of a 'new sale' – see (a) above. If building is not completed within the time limit imposed and full duty is payable, the TVA payable on the original purchase price is refunded.

(d) Agricultural land, including agricultural buildings (e.g. farm buildings) bear a basic stamp duty of 16.6% plus regional tax. In certain circumstances this basic rate can be reduced to 8.6% and in the case of the purchase of such land by a person who (or whose spouse, ascendants or descendants) has been a tenant of the land for at least two years and who undertakes to work the land for a minimum of five years, the total stamp duty is reduced to 0.6%.

5. A fee is payable for the registration of the purchase at the local Land Registry.

As a rough and ready guide, notarial fees, stamp duties and similar disbursements in respect of flats and houses can be assumed to be about 2% of the purchase price for 'new sales' and about 10% of the purchase price for 'old sales'.

SALES

In most parts of France, the seller pays no notarial fees or disbursements but there are local customs which sometimes vary this practice. Normally, however, he will pay commission if he sells through an estate agent. Obligatory commission scales have recently been abolished and commission has settled down at around 5% TVA included. Negotiations may reduce this on large sales but on small sales, more may be asked for. Again, there are parts of France where commission is shared between seller and buyer. There are also parts of France where by tradition or by arrangement sales of property are handled by notaries and not by Estate Agents. In these cases, the sale commission is considered to be part of the *frais d'acte* or the cost of the transfer and as such is payable by *the buyer*.

MORTGAGES

1. Notarial and Land Registry fees are payable in connection with mortgages and the amounts do not differ depending on whether a mortgage is contemporaneous with a purchase or not.

2. On the repayment of a mortgage, if a formal release is registered, there are also notarial and Land Registry fees. The registration of every mortgage automatically lapses two years after its date for final repayment. The usual practice in France therefore is, on repayment of a loan not on a sale, not to go to the expense of registering the release of the mortgage but to allow it to remain on the Register until either it automatically lapses or if a subsequent sale before that date occurs, the cost of registering the release can be paid out of the proceeds of sale.

LETTINGS

Non-holiday lettings

1. In rare cases where a letting which is not a holiday letting takes place (see chapter 6 on Renting Property), a special scale applies and the agent involved should be asked to produce it.

2. For lettings over one year, the commission is 10% of the rent (excluding Service Charges) charged for the first year of

the letting plus 1% of the rent for each of the other years of the letting. If the rent exceeds 12,000 francs per annum, commission in respect of the rent in excess of 12,000 francs and up to 18,000 francs is 9%, in respect of the excess between 18,000 and 24,000 francs is 8% and is 7% on any balance.

3. Remember that only half of the Agent's commission, which is payable initially by the landlord, can be charged to the tenant.

4. If an *Etat des lieux* is prepared by a *huissier*, that cost can also be shared by landlord and tenant. If it is prepared on 'a friendly basis' by the agent, he may not charge anything in addition to his commission.

5. The figures given above are maximum figures and lower commission can be negotiated.

HOLIDAY LETTINGS

1. The scales of commission apply to true holiday lettings, not exceeding ninety days in length, during holiday periods. They do not apply, for example, to a short let to a businessman taking a *pied à terre*.

2. When the letting is a weekly letting for a period of less than four weeks, commission is 15% of the rent charged.

3. When the letting is not by the week or is by the week for a period for four or more weeks, commission is 12% of rent up to a rent of 3,000 francs, 10% on rent between 3,000 and 5,000 francs and 8% on any excess.

APPENDIX G

Selection of International Dialling Codes from France

Australia	61	Japan	81
Austria	43	Kuwait	965
Bahamas	1809	Lebanon	961
Bahrain	973	Liechtenstein	41
Belgium	32	Luxembourg	352
Canada	1	New Zealand	64
Channel Islands	44	Norway	47
Cyprus	357	Portugal	351
Denmark	45	Singapore	65
Egypt	20	South Africa	27
Gibraltar	350	Spain	34
Greece	30	Sweden	46
Holland	31	Switzerland	41
Hong Kong	852	UAE	971
Irish Republic	353	United Kingdom	44
Israel	972	USA	1
Italy	39		

APPENDIX H

Tax Information

1. The information in this Appendix is correct as at 1st January 1990. It is, of necessity, brief and should not be applied to individual cases without the benefit of expert advice.

2. The allowances available for setting off against tax include: –

a) certain amounts, depending on the family situation of the taxpayer, expended in connection with major repairs to property or the provision of energy-economizing systems.

b) (i) payments made to certain close members of the family in accordance with the requirement of French law that in cases of need there is an obligation to subsidize such persons. (ii) maintenance payments made after a divorce or separation (iii) gifts and subscriptions to charities and similar organizations generally up to 1% of total taxable income and 5% in the case of payments to *Fondation de France*, the French Red Cross and certain other public charitable institutions (iv) certain Life Assurance Premiums and contributions to *Sécurite Sociale*.

c) Certain interest payments.

d) A Dependant's Allowance is available in respect of children under four in the case of tax payers who are single, widows or widowers, divorced or separated.

3. The calculation of income tax actually payable by anyone liable to French tax is extremely complicated, not only because of the *quotient familial* system but because once one has been able to apply the rules, there are still a number of reductions and allowances which can apply. It is calculated on a slice

basis, so that for they year commencing 1 January 1990 for a married couple with no children, one should pay no tax if one's income does not exceed 56,303 francs but even this threshold can be higher with benefits from certain reductions such as old age relief. Persons liable to tax for the first time are well advised to get professional advice especially if some or all of their income is from non-French sources. Returns will come automatically in the second and subsequent years. For the mathematically-minded, books containing pages of calculations appear shortly after 1st January in every year and you can also get a tax calculation from Minitel by dialling the right number.

4. The rates of Death Duties are as follows:

a) In the case of that part of the Estate which passes to a surviving spouse or an ascendant or descendant in direct line there is an initial allowance of 275,000 francs per beneficiary.

b) thereafter, the share of each such beneficiary is liable to duty as follows: –

SURVIVING SPOUSE	RATE	ASCENDANTS/ DESCENDANTS
Under 50,000 francs	5%	Under 50,000 francs
50,000–100,000 francs	10%	50,000–75,000 francs
100,000–200,000 francs	15%	75,000–100,000 francs
200,000–3.4m. francs	20%	100,000–3.4m. francs
3.4–5.6m. francs	30%	3.4–5.6m. francs
5.6–11.2m. francs	35%	5.6–11.2m. francs
In excess of 11.2m. francs	40%	In excess of 11.2m. francs

c) In the case of brothers and sisters, there is an initial allowance per beneficiary of 100,000 francs if that relation has never married or is divorced, has attained the age of fifty or by reason of infirmity is incapable of earning a living and had lived with the deceased continuously for five years before his death. Subject to this, the rate is 35% up to 150,000 francs and 45% in excess of that amount.

d) In the case of uncles, aunts, nephews or nieces or cousins the rate is 55% on the whole benefit received.

e) In the case of beneficiaries related to the deceased beyond the fourth degree or in the case where there is no relationship at all the rate is uniformly 60%.

f) In cases where no other allowance is available, each beneficiary is entitled to an allowance of 10,000 francs.

g) There is a special allowance of 300,000 francs for any beneficiary who suffers from a physical or mental handicap such as makes it impossible for him to earn his living or lead a normal; life.

5. The rates of Wealth Tax are as follows:

Not exceeding 4,130,000 francs	Nil
4,130,000 to 6,710,000 francs	.5%
6,710,000 to 13,320,000 francs	.7%
13,320,000 to 20,660,000 francs	.9%
20,660,000 to 40,000,000 francs	1.2%
In excess of 40,000,000 francs	1.5%

6. The rates of TVA are as follows:

Reduced Rate: 5.5% which applies to most food and agricultural products, travel, hotels (other than luxury hotels), books, medicines, gas and electricity accounts but not telephone bills.

Standard Rate: 18.6% which applies to the majority of services and articles.

Luxury Rate: 28% which applies to precious stones, cars, furs, scent, TV sets, photographic material, caviar, tobacco and pornographic books and entertainments etc.

Appendix I

Specimen cheque and Paying-in slip

Paying Bank   Payee   Amount in words   Amount in figures   Place and date cheque drawn

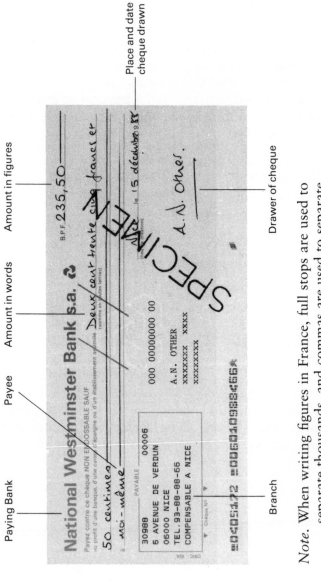

Branch   Drawer of cheque

Cheque drawn on local Bank

Cheque drawn on Bank elsewhere

Account holder's name

National Westminster Bank s.a.r.l.
Membre du Groupe National Westminster Bank

versement de chèques

Account holder's account number   Total paid in   Number of cheques paid in

Note. A different but similar form must be used for cash paid in.

Index